Passport to Assassination

Passport to Assassination

The Never-Before-Told Story of Lee Harvey Oswald by the KGB Colonel Who Knew Him

Oleg M. Nechiporenko

Translated from the Russian by Todd P. Bludeau

A BIRCH LANE PRESS BOOK
Published by Carol Publishing Group

A Birch Lane Press Book
Published by Carol Publishing Group
Birch Lane Press is a registered trademark of Carol
Communications, Inc.
Editorial Offices: 600 Madison Avenue, New York, N.Y. 10022
Sales and Distribution Offices: 120 Enterprise Avenue, Secaucus,
N.J. 07094
In Canada: Canadian Manda Group, P.O. Box 920, Station U, Toronto,
Ontario M8Z 5P9
Queries regarding rights and permissions should be addressed to
Carol Publishing Group, 600 Madison Avenue, New York, N.Y. 10022

Carol Publishing Group books are available at special discounts for
bulk purchases, for sales promotion, fund-raising, or educational
purposes. Special editions can be created to specifications. For
details, contact: Special Sales Department, Carol Publishing
Group, 120 Enterprise Avenue, Secaucus, N.J. 07094

Manufactured in the United States of America
10 9 8 7 6 5 4 3 2 1

Library of Congress Cataloging-in-Publication Data

Nechiporenko, Oleg M.
    Passport to assassination / Oleg M. Nechiporenko : translated from
the Russian by Todd P. Bludeau.
       p. cm.
    "A Birch Lane Press book."
    Includes bibliographical references and index.
    ISBN 1-55972-210-X
    1. Kennedy, John F. (John Fitzgerald), 1917–1963—Assassination.
2. Oswald, Lee Harvey. I. Title.
E842.9.N4 1993
364.1′524′092—dc20   93-35965
                                                      CIP

Contents

PART THREE: Fates

Preface

Among the questions that will undoubtedly be asked after this book's publication is, why did so many years elapse before it was written, and why did I decide to write it? Like a woman who carefully carries her future child, the work lived inside me for almost thirty years.

In 1964 I read the *Warren Commission Report,* which purportedly explained the purpose of Lee Harvey Oswald's visit to the Soviet embassy in Mexico. Subsequent years saw a constant flow of information, primarily from Western publications, that reexamined the enigma of Oswald's trip to Mexico and added mystery to the Kennedy assassination.

During the Cold War period the assassination was used for psychological advantage by both superpowers. The dark and murky aspects of the president's murder served to nourish recriminations on both sides. From time to time there would appear "reliable evidence" pointing to "genuine" instigators of the assassination. Oswald's "Mexican trail" is a prime example of dual interpretation: From our Soviet point of view, Oswald had been deliberately sent by American intelligence as an agent provocateur; to the Americans, Oswald had been directed by the KGB in Mexico to assassinate the president.

Because of this mutual mistrust, I, an experienced and, more important, active intelligence officer, could not divulge classified information kept in secret Russian files or offer my own opinions on this material while still in service.

I retired in May 1991, in the midst of the Soviet Union's dramatic transformation from a monolithic empire to a land of separate nations. In the fall of that year the KGB also ceased to exist, and I decided the time had finally come to set down my long-held thoughts in a book. My goals were to definitively document the KGB's role in Lee Harvey Oswald's life during his stay in the Soviet Union; to state accurately what happened during his meetings with Soviet intelligence in Mexico; and to recount the KGB's actions after the assassination. I also intended to offer my version of events at Dealey Plaza on that fateful November day.

I turned for help to the new leadership of the Russian Foreign Intelligence Service (FIS), the Russian Ministry of Security (MBRF), and the Belarus KGB. All three organizations were extremely supportive and directed me to the relevant archival materials.

The actual birth of the book, including research, took more than a year. The rapid pace of the work was motivated by a desire to complete it in time for the thirtieth anniversary of the assassination. I wanted to fill in the blanks connected with the Soviet trail of Lee Harvey Oswald from Moscow to Minsk to Mexico City. Finally, I sought to put to rest the controversy about Soviet defector Yuri Nosenko: Was he bona fide or a "plant"? The work is composed of three sections, and although each can be read on its own, the relationship between Oswald and the KGB connects all three.

I am deeply grateful for the help of many people. I wish to extend heartfelt thanks to the leadership of the Russian FIS, the Russian Ministry of Security, and the Belarus KGB for their invaluable assistance. I also wish to thank the people of the aforementioned organizations for their attention and time.

I would like to acknowledge all my friends and colleagues who shared their reminiscences of these distant years.

I am also grateful to the experts whose appraisals enabled me to understand the fragments and sundry elements of the entire problem.

Thanks, too, go to the authors whose works I used to prepare this book. The various conspiracy theories were extremely useful to me, because they enabled me to view the assassination from different, indeed contradictory, angles and thereby stimulated my thought process.

I owe a great many thanks to Joseph Ritchey, chief of CBS News, Moscow, and former CBS Moscow correspondent Anthony Mason, who, understanding my need for information, provided me with many difficult-to-find American books. This literature was no less valuable in my research than our own Moscow archives.

I would also like to thank the estimable Hillel Black, my editor, for patience and grace under pressure and for his ongoing support. I sincerely hope he found the effort rewarding. Kudos also to translator Todd P. Bludeau for turning out a respectable translation under difficult circumstances.

It would be fair to say that the book before you would not exist were it not for the direction, encouragement, and efforts of my business manager, adviser, and friend Brian Litman, president of Entertainment and Communications Holdings Organization. He spent many sleepless nights counseling me from his West Hollywood office and working closely with me on the English of the manuscript. Brian also manages the business interests of several other interesting and highly placed KGB veterans. In this regard he has managed to "penetrate" the KGB—not as an agent of the CIA, but rather of Hollywood—and with our full support. I am deeply indebted to him.

There are others who Brian has asked be recognized for their assistance in this project. Within Carol Publishing Group they are publisher Steven M. Schragis and president Bruce Bender, for their vision; Denise O'Sullivan, editorial assistant; Kent Holland, publicity manager; and Meryl Earl, subsidiary rights director. Elsewhere, important assistance was provided by Stephen Stim, legal counsel; Paula Litzky, Lynn Franklin, and Todd Siegel, literary agents; Ivan Kadulin, in Moscow; and James Lesar, of the Assassination Archives and Research Center.

And the last, and most important, thanks are for my dear wife and helper, Lydia, who freed me from household responsibilities so that I could write this book.

Passport to
Assassination

Who Is Doing What to Whom?

Long live the friendship and cooperation of the peoples of the Soviet Union and the United States of America in the interests of liquidating the "cold war" and strengthening peace around the world!

—From the "Appeals of the Central Committee of the Communist Party of the Soviet Union" on the 42d anniversary of the Great October Revolution.*
Pravda, October 4, 1959

Outside the train windows the small villages, groves, and cottage settlements of my native suburban Moscow flashed past in rapid succession. A delicate blanket of fresh powdered snow covered everything. Just two weeks before, when the train had traveled in the opposite direction, from Moscow to the West, we were still in the rather gloomy autumnal days of November 1959. My mood at

*All Soviet central newspapers, on the eve of the holidays commemorating May Day (May 1) and the anniversary of the October Revolution (November 7), published over the course of many decades the "Appeals of the Central Committee of the Communist Party of the Soviet Union," which reflected the foreign and domestic politics of the Party.

The texts of the Appeals were used in the festive decoration of the cities, adorned the banners carried by parade marchers, and were recited through loudspeakers during the mass celebrations held in Red Square in Moscow and in other cities.

the time matched the weather, though I tried not to let it show.

As a case officer of the KGB's Moscow regional directorate, I was part of a group of young graduate from Soviet higher-educational institutions traveling to Scotland under the auspices of the recently founded travel agency for young people called Sputnik. Under the guise of group leader, I was responsible for "taking care" of our tourists in the counterintelligence sense, as we referred to that sort of activity. That is, my job was to make sure no one defected or made contact with, or was contacted by, foreign—in this case, British—intelligence. In those days such "caretaking" gained popularity within our organization, and later, as group tourism expanded, it became standard routine for the Soviet state security organs. (Individual trips outside the borders of the USSR were virtually unknown.)

I already had the opportunity to acquire some valuable experience in counterintelligence activities while working a few months at the Soviet pavilion during the 1958 World's Fair in Brussels. At that time I was a member of a team of officers, working alongside older colleagues and in constant contact with our KGB *rezidentura,* or station, in Belgium. But now I had sole responsibility for each and every tourist and for any emergency situations that might befall our group. Moreover, I was separated from the Soviet embassy and our rezidentura in London while simultaneously closely scrutinized by British counterintelligence.

And we felt their eyes on us throughout our trip. Once, for example, we discovered by chance that our English guide just happened to have studied Russian while serving in specially designated units of the British army. Students of an intelligence school located somewhere on the outskirts of the city of Dundee, or near Aberdeen—I don't remember exactly which now—used every opportunity they had to "break in" their Russian-language skills with us. From our contact with them it was revealed that some of the teachers from this school were Soviet émigrés, while still others were so-called displaced persons, DPs, former Soviet citizens who had settled in the West after World War II. Apparently they felt the need to upgrade their language with freshly minted Russian and Soviet turns of phrase for use in the classroom. We were later able to ascertain that a few of these teachers were known to the KGB as Nazi collaborators during the war.

Curious episodes often took place whenever we registered at our hotels. One time we were put up in an old, typically English residence, the kind described in classic literature, with winding staircases and dark wood-paneled walls in a spacious drawing room. We were told that this house was at our complete disposal and that our group would be the only one staying there. That very same evening, we heard voices and other noises coming from one of the rooms along the hall on the first floor. One of the braver souls among us, who had heard that spirits dwell in many old English homes, decided to explore a bit and cracked open the door leading into the room. There, lounging and drinking beer, were several young lads, very much part of this world.

Both sides exchanged surprised glances, after which the "apparitions" quieted down and the din from behind the door ceased. Most likely this was yet another opportunity for someone to practice Russian—without having to come into direct contact with a native speaker.

On the final day of our stay in Great Britain, while the members of our group took in some last-minute sightseeing of London and bought souvenirs to take home, I had to spend half a day in the rezidentura there, reporting on everything seen and heard during the trip.

I was finally able to relax only when our train crossed back over the Soviet border in Brest and I was convinced that all heads were accounted for. At the station restaurant I ordered two skewers of shish kebab and a healthy portion of cognac and then turned in for the night with a light heart and a sense of accomplishment for bringing my assignment to a close without incident. Now all my charges were on their own, and if they wanted to run along the roofs of the cars or jump out of the windows of the train while it was moving, that was their business. My counterintelligence worries about them were over.

The following morning, as the train pulled into Moscow, my mood was upbeat. Soon I would be back with my wife, skiing season was just around the corner, and my mission as a "tourist" had ended on a successful note.

All these memories passed through my mind in the summer of 1992 while I sat turning the yellow pages of an old file for research on this book in the archives of the Russian Foreign Intelligence Service in Yasenevo.* I was especially fascinated by a top-secret document entitled "Report on the Stay of American Tourist Lee Harvey Oswald in Moscow," prepared by the Fifteenth Department of KGB foreign intelligence in November 1959. The word "tourist," and the coincidence of his stay in Moscow with my period abroad in Scotland, had evidently made the associations that led me back into my past. As I acquainted myself more fully with the contents of the document, my thoughts became more philosophical in nature.

It seemed to me very interesting that in that long-ago past, while I was vigorously exercising caution abroad to make sure that none of my young Soviet tourists would defect to the West, an equally youthful American tourist, a citizen of the bulwark of capitalism, would at the same time vigorously try to become a citizen of the bulwark of socialism.

How could I have ever possibly imagined back then that fate would bring us together under strange circumstances in a country that was neither his nor my own, and just two months before he became a riddle to both American and world history, still unsolved to this day?

I read the report and then read it again with greater attention. And then a new thought came to mind: After everything that had happened to this tourist, was it conceivable that I would someday not only be seriously looking into this riddle but even publicly daring to express my opinion on it?

Before delving into the story of this unusual visitor to the Soviet Union and his "Moscow trail," I would like to provide the reader with a picture of the Cold War climate in which the secret services operated in order to provide the essential background against which the events in Moscow, swirling around the book's main figure, Lee Harvey Oswald, will have greater clarity.

*A suburb of Moscow, where the headquarters of the Foreign Intelligence Service is located.

Let me make it clear from the outset that I am not a political analyst. My reflections are only those of a former professional counterintelligence and intelligence officer of the KGB. My views are based on several personal impressions of isolated events in which I participated.

The 1950s could be called a decade of temperature changes that occurred during the Cold War. International relations resembled the condition of someone sick with fever, when the temperature sharply spikes higher (Iran, 1953; Guatemala, 1954; Hungary, 1956; the Arab-Israeli War, 1956; and other localized crises), then just as suddenly reverts to normal (the cease-fire in Korea, 1953; the Geneva Accords on Indochina, 1954; and the first postwar meeting among the heads of the four great powers in Geneva, 1955). This meeting, involving the Soviet Union, the United States, England, and France, did not lead to any concrete results, but it did give rise to the "spirit of Geneva" and was characterized as "the first in a series of periods of détente in U.S.-Soviet relations."*

Here it should be explained that the "operative circumstances" of domestic politics are straightforward from an intelligence point of view, while international politics is a tangled pas de deux danced with the enemy. The more the opposing leaders hiss at and kiss each other, the more difficult the conditions become for the intelligence community. While the combative nations' leaders appear smiling at each other and making toasts and "peace-loving" declarations on the nightly news, the special services do not alter their course. Insofar as the functional responsibilities of the intelligence services do not principally change in relation to the political climate, the problems that are created during the confrontational period rarely go away during the "warming" trends. The dichotomy between the leaders' public statements and the special services' actions is so great that the slightest miscue can focus tremendous attention on the services and turn them into "whipping boys" or lightning rods for infuriated statesmen.

Through the long years of their existence, the special services have been able to develop their own professional strabismus, or

*Ray Cline, *The CIA: The Evolution of the Agency from Roosevelt to Reagan* (New York: Liberty House, 1989), p. 181.

"squint eye." It differs from the usual ailment in that it does not
exhibit the characteristic external symptoms. But what is specific
about it?

Imagine that you are watching a game of water polo from above.
Later that evening, the game is recapped on television, showing all
the highlights of thrashing and dunking captured by an underwater
camera. Now it is possible to see clearly where and how the contest
was decided. In similar fashion, employees of the intelligence services constantly see diametrically opposed political events on both
the international and domestic arena from two points of view. Such
"squint-eye" vision helps them "to survive" and to react flexibly to
changes in politics

Sometimes, in order to choose the best vantage point, the intelligence services have to undertake mind-boggling actions and literally go underground or underwater or ascend to the heavens. As
always, there is considerable risk attached, and the outcome is not
necessarily favorable.

Just such an intrigue occurred in the 1950s that subsequently
became one of the most striking Cold War episodes.

In the mid-1950s British and American intelligence devised and
put into play what they code-named "Operation Gold," but which
was later erroneously called "Operation Tunnel" by the mass
media. It was an ambitious and complex endeavor for those times.
An underground passage was dug from West Berlin into the territory of the former German Democratic Republic, specifically to the
site where subterranean communication lines for Soviet military
and other institutions lay buried. These lines were tapped into,
turning the tunnel into an informational gold mine for Western
intelligence.

The sense of euphoria from the results of this operation are
vividly described by Ray Cline, a former deputy director of the CIA
for informational work, in his memoirs:

In the beginning of the 1950s the CIA undertook a grandiose project, costing them millions of dollars and providing
reams of factual information reports (author's emphasis) on the
USSR. This was the Berlin tunnel project.

Careful clandestine operational techniques permitted this to be done without arousing the suspicions of the ubiquitous East German and Soviet guards. Access was gained to an unused building near the border, tools and equipment were spirited in at night, and a tunnel was dug through to emerge under the floor of another unused structure on the other side.

The combination of the talents of the spies, the communications specialists and the DDI (Directorate of Intelligence) scholars provided one of the best examples of what modern centralized intelligence in the CIA could accomplish.*

The authors of the project must be given their due and the operation can safely be listed as a sensational intelligence achievement. Both the concept and its technical embodiment were brilliant. Security measures guaranteed the secrecy of the work from the ubiquitous sentries and patrols of the enemy. But as so often happens in intelligence planning, you can never tell beforehand where you will find something and where you will lose it.

While the executors of the project burrowed at a mole's pace under the ground in strictest secrecy, a surface "mole" in the circle of the "initiated" had a shorter route for connecting with the East.

George Blake, who later became widely known as a Soviet mole in British intelligence but at the time was an employee of MI6 in West Berlin, also recalls Operation Tunnel in his memoirs, *No Other Choice:*

During the night of the 22nd of April, 1956, Soviet signals troops, carrying out urgent repairs on a cable which had shown signs of sagging, "stumbled" on a telephone tap. They discovered a tunnel leading in the direction of an American army store, just on the other side of the sector boundary . . .

In the Western press the tunnel operation was generally hailed as one of the most outstanding successes of the CIA in the Cold War. Although it was noted that most of the equipment found was of British manufacture, there was no suggestion by anybody that the British had in any way participated

*Ibid., pp. 184–85.

in or had known about the project. This was too much for Peter Lunn. As soon as the news broke in the press, he assembled the whole staff of the Berlin station, from the highest to the lowest, and told the whole story from its inception to its untimely end. He made it quite clear that this had been essentially an SIS [British Intelligence] idea and his own to boot. American participation had been limited to providing most of the money and facilities. They were, of course, also sharing in the product.

Up to then hardly anyone in the station had known about the existence of the tunnel. Apart from himself and his deputy, I had been the only officer who had been in the "know" and that only by virtue of my previous job in "Y." My former colleagues in that department, who were in Berlin working on the tunnel operation, lived completely isolated from the Berlin station and I had had no further contact with them. My information on developments affecting the project had come henceforth only from the Soviet side.

I, for my part, had naturally been watching these developments, which I knew were about to occur, with some anxiety, on the alert for any signs of suspicion on the part of SIS [British Intelligence] or the CIA that the Soviets might have been forewarned. So skillfully had the "discovery" of the tunnel been stage-managed, however, that a subsequent SIS/CIA enquiry into the circumstances surrounding the collapse of the operation produced the verdict that the cause had been purely technical and that there was no question of a leak. . . .

Only in 1961 did SIS discover, as a result of my arrest, that the full details of the tunnel operation had been known to the Soviet authorities before even the first spade had been put in the ground.

Thus, what Western operatives were joyously extracting from the ground as "reams of factual reports" was in turn being diluted by Soviet intelligence with a healthy dose of disinformation. Significant effort was required on the part of the KGB to conceal its knowledge of the source of the leak and thereby prevent the "illumination" of its invaluable source. Against its will, Operation Gold turned into a grandiose operation for the KGB, demanding great expenditures of labor and money.

Another story developed under the surface, this time in the sea, where crabs instead of moles played the critical role. This happened in Great Britain at practically the same time as Operation Gold was being "discovered."

On April 18, 1956, four days before Operation Gold was unearthed, Nikita S. Khrushchev, head of the Soviet Communist party, and Marshal Nikolai A. Bulganin, premier of the Soviet government, began a state visit at the highest level to England on board the cruiser *Ordzhonikidze.*

While the leaders of the two countries talked peaceably among themselves, the *Ordzhonikidze* and two accompanying Soviet destroyers "parked" at none other than Her Majesty's royal dock in Portsmouth. Downing Street, eager to avoid any kind of unpleasantness, issued a secret directive to its intelligence services to "leave the Soviet delegation alone" during its stay in England.

Despite the orders from their superiors, a couple of brave souls from MI6 could not resist the urge to take a closer look at the latest-model Soviet cruiser moored right under their noses. They "chartered" an experienced marine diver, retired commander Lionel Phillip Kenneth Crabb, to carry out a clandestine inspection of the *Ordzhonikidze*'s underside. Twice, on April 18 and 19, Crabb plunged below the surface.

On April 19, at a luncheon given by the British prime minister in honor of his Soviet guests, Khrushchev made several jokes that left his host befuddled as to their origin. Then, at a press conference toward the end of the visit, Khrushchev, commenting on the talks, said there had been "sharp moments" and they had met "certain underwater rocks." What the British leader did not know, but Khrushchev did, was that the diver had not returned from his second expedition. Later, when this story, but not Crabb, "floated" to the surface, it gave rise to numerous versions and speculation.

In one of the books devoted to this secret operation of British intelligence, the authors, two Irish journalists, describe the event:

> Crabb, who had a weak heart and suffered from alcoholism, made two dives under the ship. He did not return from the

second. The Russians, who discovered that their ship was being subjected to inspection, announced a sharp protest. Prime Minister Anthony Eden was furious and demanded an immediate explanation from whomever had sanctioned this act. It turned out that, even though several employees of the Ministry of Foreign Affairs were informed of the plan, it was not discussed at the corresponding level. As a result the director general of British intelligence, John Sinclair, was fired.*

On July 9, 1957, at a great distance from the former mooring site of the Soviet ships, a corpse, minus its head and hands and clad in a light diving suit, was fished from the waters. It was identified as Crabb's remains. The forensic conclusion was that his head and hands had been bitten off by crabs.

But there was another version which stated that the Russians had captured the diver and taken him back to the Soviet Union, where, under an assumed name, he began working for Soviet military intelligence. Photographs, supposedly depicting Crabb in a Soviet uniform, were even published that allegedly "confirmed" this version. In any event, the entire mysterious Crabb incident remains one that Cold War historians would like to get their claws into.

In the search for similar vantage points from which to view events, especially those taking place in enemy territory, operatives did not limit themselves to working only on the land, underground, and underwater. In the second half of the 1950s, the CIA resorted to the realization of a new, "lofty" project.

The top-secret U-2 intelligence-gathering flights over the territory of the USSR continued until May 1, 1960, when the spy plane was shot down outside Sverdlovsk and its pilot, Francis Gary Powers, was captured and sentenced at an open trial in Moscow to ten years in prison. Everyone in the American government blamed the embarrassing incident on the CIA, even though, as the politicians admitted later, both President Eisenhower and Vice President Nixon not only knew about but sanctioned the operation.

In all the instances described thus far, Western intelligence ser-

*Jonathan Blotch, and Patrick Fitzgerald, *The Secret Operations of British Intelligence* (Moscow: Politizdat, 1987). In Russian.

vices took the offensive, causing the KGB to counterattack. But the KGB also searched for suitable points of access on enemy territory in order to observe events at close range.

On June 21, 1957, a meek photographer by the name of Martin Collins, a.k.a. Kayutis, a.k.a. Goldfuss, a.k.a. Col. Rudolf Ivanovich Abel, was arrested in New York. In fact, his birth name was William Fisher, and he was operating in the United States as a KGB illegal assigned the code name the Mark.

In August 1957, while working as a translator at the Congress of the International Federation for Democratic Youth in Kiev, I looked at some American newspapers that were roughly one month old and read for the first time about Abel's arrest. The photograph that accompanied the item showed a person in handcuffs sitting in a vehicle. I remember being struck by the piercing look in his eyes, like that of a rapacious bird that has suddenly fallen into a trap.

Rudolf Abel's downfall was the result of betrayal by another Soviet illegal, code-named Vick, who was sent to help him. For the first time in its history, American authorities had factual evidence that professional KGB officers were directing illegal Soviet rezidenturas on U.S. soil.

Abel's trial in the autumn of 1957 in New York created as much stir as did Powers's Moscow trial in the Hall of Columns in the House of Soviets. True, three years later, American justice was less merciful to Abel than the Soviets to Powers—Abel was handed a thirty-year prison term.

On February 10, 1962, Colonel Abel was exchanged for Powers on Gliniker Bridge, connecting East and West Berlin. This exchange established a precedent for "gentlemanly cooperation" between the hostile intelligence services and led to a series of exchanges of "burned" spies from both sides during the following decades.

Sometime in the beginning of the 1970s, after I had returned from an assignment in Mexico, I was on my lunch break in the KGB cafeteria in the Lubyanka. I approached a table at which an elderly man sat hunched over his food. Wishing him bon appetit, I asked if I could join him. He raised his head, and I saw those same eyes which had struck me with their expression in a newspaper photograph in 1957. The gaze of Colonel Abel—and it was he—was as penetrating as before, but at the same time I could see a kind of hidden sorrow. Nodding his head yes to my request, he again bent over his lunch. Seeing that he was absorbed in his thoughts, I did not dare engage him in banal conversation and also lit into my food. When he had finished, Abel wished me bon appetit in return, carried away his empty tray, and, hunched over, made for the exit.

This was my first, last, and only contact with a live "exhibit," as Abel had recently taken to referring to himself to close friends. Several months later, on November 15, 1971, Colonel Abel died, a symbol of the classic Soviet illegal/spy.

Meanwhile, Francis Gary Powers, for whom Abel had been exchanged on the German bridge, lived for six years more before dying in a helicopter crash near Los Angeles on August 2, 1977.

During the 1950s two concepts reverberated in the mass media and in political speeches: the "Cold War" and the "Iron Curtain." The first defined the harsh conflict between two camps, both on the brink of employing military force, including nuclear weapons, while the second defined the closed Soviet society and the isolationist policies of its leaders. But precisely at that historical juncture the second concept began to change, which to a certain degree reflected changes in the first.

In 1953, Soviet society suffered a shock. Joseph Stalin, the Great Leader, died. Three years later, the new political leader and Stalin's close associate, Nikita S. Khrushchev, unmasked the cult of the "genius of all mankind" and presented him as a tyrant who had carried out genocide in his own state. This was an even greater shock. The era of "de-Stalinization" and, at the same time, the gradual lifting of the Iron Curtain had begun.

In 1957, Moscow played host to the First International Festival of Youth and Students. Tens of thousands of young people from other countries, holding various political convictions and political and religious views, swarmed over the Soviet capital, creating their own form of "diffusion." While disseminating the seeds of political doubt in the hearts and minds of their Soviet counterparts, the guests planted other seeds as well. Nine months later, Moscow's maternity hospitals reaped a harvest of newborns with skin color totally uncharacteristic for Moscow latitudes.

At the 1958 World's Fair in Brussels the Soviet delegation erected a massive Soviet pavilion, staffed by several hundred of its citizens. As a participant in this event, I can attest to the huge interest shown by Westerners in the life and people behind the Iron Curtain. Our pavilion was truly one of the more popular sights of the fair. Large numbers of curious visitors would often congregate outside the pavilion in the mornings before it opened.

It was obvious that Western intelligence had decided to study the pavilions and its employees. The counterintelligence operatives among the Soviet staff received many signals from our sources about the heightened interest shown by the other side toward the Soviet specialists, translators, and others working the stands. Special attention was accorded our presence by members of anti-Soviet organizations like the National Labor Alliance, the Organization of Ukrainian Nationalists, and others. But the employees of the pavilion had been thoroughly "filtered" in Moscow, and I do not recall any serious problems arising in connection with state security.

At the same time, a large number of tourist groups from various regions of the USSR traveled to the Brussels fair, where they learned a great deal about Western lifestyles as they were presented at the various pavilions. They then carried this knowledge home with them.

But the most audacious penetration of the curtain occurred in the summer of 1959 during an Soviet-American exchange of national exhibitions. The American exhibition opened in Moscow's Sokolniki Park, while its Soviet counterpart was held at the Coliseum in New York City. Vice President Nixon appeared at the American exhibition in Moscow, where he met with the Soviet leadership before visiting Leningrad, the Urals, and Novosibirsk. During the same period other mutual visits of high-level delegations, as well as tours by theatrical groups, took place. There was also an increase in tourism from the United States to the USSR and vice versa, along with a growing number of Soviet-American sporting events.

For KGB foreign intelligence the partial lifting of the Iron Curtain promised certain advantages as it increased the channels of intelligence contacts with the West, but for counterintelligence it was just the opposite. The sharp growth in direct contacts between a significant number of Soviet citizens with foreigners both abroad and within the USSR changed the situation and demanded new tactics and methods of operative activity.

The 1959 American exhibition in Moscow tested KGB resolve, while at the same time serving as a good proving ground for acquiring new experience in the changing demands made on our counterintelligence service. In Brussels, for example, it was enough to send a reliable team of personnel to our pavilion to counter any anti-Soviet actions or recruiting efforts by émigré organizations and enemy intelligence services.

At the Moscow Youth Festival the opposite situation existed. Here Soviet counterintelligence had to skillfully neutralize a rather large American team that was displaying great curiosity about the event. Their presence, and the propagandizing effect they could have on the citizenry, had to be kept to a minimum. To use boxing terminology, the situation differed from all the others in that it could have been called "close-in fighting" with the Main Adversary (the common KGB term for the U.S.A.), but in our corner of the ring.

Various subdivisions of the KGB were called on to "safeguard" the American exhibition, but since it took place in Moscow, all the daily operational work was placed on the shoulders of the Moscow regional directorate where I began my career as a counterintelligence officer in the Second Division.

A special group of our operatives staked out a twenty-four-hour watch from the police department, situated directly in Sokolniki Park, and maintained constant contact with headquarters. In addition to the professional operatives, the exhibition was "served" by numerous agents and confidential sources. Their functions ranged from translating at the pavilion stands to making regular weekly visits to the exhibit. Their overall goal, though, was very specific: to study the American workers and to observe their contacts with Soviet citizens. The information these "proxies" brought us on a regularly planned schedule was quickly subjected to analysis. If anything looked out of the ordinary, operative measures were immediately put into effect.

On one occasion it was reported to KGB headquarters that the police were detaining a young man, who had been observed holding an allegedly suspicious conversation at the exhibition with one of the American employees. During the course of their meeting the American supposedly dropped a parcel of money into the man's briefcase. We were immediately dispatched to Sokolniki Park, where we familiarized ourselves with the report of the "conspiratorial" rendezvous drawn up by two operatives who worked for external surveillance. Then we interrogated the frightened lad, who was not from Moscow but had come to the capital to take entrance exams. He insisted that he had asked one of the Americans at the exhibition for some fliers or brochures but categorically denied taking money from any of them.

He explained he had received the small sum found on him as the result of a bank transfer from his aunt. Further investigation into the episode revealed that the surveillants, after having observed the lad spending money in a park cafeteria, fabricated his "conspiratorial" meeting with the American "spy." Caught in their lie, they tried to justify their overzealousness by a desire to "distinguish themselves" and to earn a reward for their vigilance. They were both rewarded by being fired by the KGB.

Another battle between our service and the American side that was viewed as deadly serious at the time but which now seems rather silly involved U.S. publications. Some of our agents, whose goal was to intercept the dissemination of "ideologically harmful propagandistic literature" by the Americans, were assigned to visit the pavilion, become acquainted with the books, "seize" them, and thereby limit access to them by other Soviet citizens.

Within a few days of the exhibition's opening, a rather imposing mountain of American publications on the broadest of themes imaginable had accumulated in one of the offices of our department. Taking into account my knowledge of English and Spanish and some German and French, my superiors ordered me to look through the pile and determine what to do with it. Some of the books were given to foreign-language courses, while others were earmarked to be pulped. With my bosses' permission, I was allowed to augment my personal library with certain books that interested me. To this day, several volumes of Winston Churchill's memoirs, as well as publications on American history and government, like *A Pocket History of the United States* by Allan Nevins and Henry

Steele Commager and the U.S. Constitution, still sit on my book-shelves.

As far as I can remember, the flow of literature dried up. Apparently the organizers of the exhibition toughened their supervision of the stand and thereby complicated the work of our agents. As a result, though, we still "won" this skirmish because other Soviet citizens were also kept from acquiring so-called subversive materials.

In 1958 in Brussels, while working under cover in the "Culture and Art" division of the Soviet pavilion, I had to take part in a reverse action. We crammed our stand full of our own "harmful" publications, which foreigners from all over the world gladly took. In this instance, though, I cannot say for certain whether they also ended up in the offices of our enemy's intelligence services or if they served to spread our most advanced ideas among Western society.

Once I unexpectedly stumbled upon one of my "Brussels trails" at the exhibition in Moscow. For some reason I was looking over the list of American employees when I suddenly spotted the familiar name of a female member of the U.S. pavilion. She and I had been members of the International Youth Club of World's Fair Employees. After I reported this finding to my superiors, the decision was made to organize a "chance" meeting with her to study her more fully. At the time, she had already fallen into the category of individuals suspected of "affiliation with American intelligence" and was under surveillance in her hotel, during her movements about Moscow, and at the exhibition itself. For a while I also had to observe her, before running into her "by chance" at the exhibition, where she worked at the stand that displayed voting machinery.

She also displayed "genuine" joy when we met. We exchanged telephone numbers and agreed to call each other. What was interesting was that while we pleasantly chatted, as soon as I made a movement to grab my pen, a visitor standing a little off to the side hurriedly sidled up closer to me and politely offered me a pencil while straining to see what I was going to write. Our guys aren't sleeping on the job, I thought to myself.

To avoid creating the impression that operational activities at the pavilion resembled a musical comedy, I would like to cite an example in which our secret helpers comported themselves skillfully. This episode unfolded like a deftly plotted whodunit. If it had not, there might have been serious negative consequences for our country.

While facing the stand he normally worked at the pavilion, one of the "Americans" heard a soft voice behind him say, "Don't turn around, and put your hands behind your back. I'm going to give you something, and I want you to bring it to the address written on the package."

The "American" obeyed and felt a package thrust into his hands. Without turning around, he placed the package into his pocket and, understanding that his actions could be monitored, calmly stood and continued to work at his spot. After a while, he went to the bathroom and looked at the taped package, which read "Forward to the American embassy." A few hours later, the package sat on a desk at the Moscow headquarters of the KGB.

Skipping ahead, I can say that the author of the package had observed the pavilion employee on several occasions, and only when he had come to the conclusion that this employee was an American agent did he transfer the package. Not only was this "American agent" a Soviet citizen but a KGB agent who spoke English fluently. Thus began the operation I'll call the "Roman Affair."

The anonymous author wrote the American embassy that he had secret information about the anti-aircraft defenses in and around Moscow and its environs and was ready to part with this information for a price. He also demanded a series of conditions, in the form of proofs to convince him that his package had reached the right people.

The first condition called for a high-level "American embassy official" to appear at an agreed-upon time and day in a shop on Gorky Street near the center of Moscow and follow the instructions Roman called for in his letter. The scene was right out of the theater. Information regarding the meeting was not shared with external surveillance so that Roman would not get suspicious.

The second condition involved throwing a package of bank notes from the window of a commuter train at a predetermined time after it had left the platform of a suburban Moscow station. Preparations were made to satisfy this demand. This time, the surrounding area was filled with operatives from a surveillance unit and about a dozen members of our department. The plan was to capture our friend if he had been detected within the ambush zone.

Roman's actions suggested that he was familiar with intelligence procedures and could even be connected to a security organization. Therefore, only a very limited group of personnel was involved in the operation, and all measures were conducted with the utmost secrecy.

Exercising extreme caution, Roman appeared at the place where the money was to land. Approaching the drop point, he sensed danger and quickly returned to the platform. As frequently happens in surveillance work, Murphy's Law went into effect. It was a warm summer evening, and as Roman headed for the bushes at the drop point, he heard noises and quickly withdrew. The noises were produced by a young couple making love. Intelligence operatives have long known that the greatest threats to an ensuing operation are youngsters and passionate couples. It seems that extortionists, youngsters, and couples tend to pick the same spot for their activities.

External surveillance had secured the unpopulated platform by the drop point, but Roman managed to escape by jumping into a departing train just as the doors were closing. The operatives were able to get a sketchy description of the suspect. Shortly thereafter, Roman fell into another trap and again managed to escape. But he was finally identified, caught, and arrested. His work desk was secretly searched, and the material he used to prepare his package for the "American" was discovered. During the investigation and trial he admitted his criminal intentions, which were motivated by personal monetary considerations—he had to pay gambling debts.

The potential spy turned out to work in one of the KGB's Moscow regional divisions, just as we had hypothesized. He was tried and received a just punishment by being sent to prison.

Certainly the scale of counterintelligence work surrounding the Sokolniki and Coliseum exhibitions was significantly wider than the information I presented. My knowledge was limited by my neophyte status.

During this period the enemy, in order not to complicate political relations, was obligated to limit the scope of operations, and the

Moscow and New York exhibitions were concluded without serious incident.

The leaders of the two countries continued to "pull" toward each other. President Eisenhower invited a Soviet delegation, headed by Nikita Khrushchev, to visit the United States in September 1959. An accord was reached to hold a new meeting among the Soviet Union, United States, England, and France in May 1960. The expiring "Spirit of Geneva" was replaced by this agreement, called the "Spirit of Camp David," where it was reached.

The 1950s marked the first time that the political leaders of the two countries engaged in détente and expressed the mutual hope of reducing Cold War tension.

But for the intelligence services it was "business as usual." The American pilot Gary Powers continued U-2 reconnaissance missions over the Soviet Union. Colonel Abel, the Soviet agent, continued to languish in an American prison, and his place in America was ready to be filled by a new "invisible front" warrior.

In this climate, the old intelligence adage Don't Get Caught became especially important. It was better to operate judiciously than to invoke the wrath of the powers that be and end up being held responsible without even being guilty.

In the midst of this warming political trend, a train headed from Finland into Moscow, on its way toward the Iron Curtain. One of the passengers on board was a twenty-year-old American ex-marine hurtling toward the place of his cherished dreams. His name was Lee Harvey Oswald.

PART ONE

The Facts

The documentary practice of investigating crimes does not yet make literature.
—I. Burdenko, afterword to *Detective Stories*

It is a hallowed tradition that reports are written in a dry bureaucratic style, rigid and boring. They should be deliberately unemotional.
—Nicholas Freiling, *Death of a Smuggler*

Introduction

In Part I, I narrate the facts that I have at my disposal about relations between the KGB and Lee Harvey Oswald during his stay in the Soviet Union (Moscow and Minsk), his visits to the Soviet embassy in Mexico and the reaction of the KGB's headquarters in Moscow and its stations in Washington and Mexico to his intention to go back to the Soviet Union, and the KGB's activities after the November events in Dallas.

This information can be classified into three kinds:

1. Original documents of the KGB and other official Soviet organizations concerning the life of Lee Harvey Oswald and his family at that time. A number of documents are given in full. Others are excerpted.

2. Reminiscences of former KGB officers, who bore direct relations to Oswald's case at various times, and in various ways, direct contacts among them.

3. My original information concerning my meetings with Oswald in Mexico and the events resulting from those meetings.

In Part I, I have presented facts; authorial interpretation is reduced to a minimum. My task, as I see it, is to put the information in chronological order, tie the events together logically and explain some of the realities of that period and the specific actions of certain KGB units.

1

Tourist Non Grata: Oswald in Moscow (October–December 1959)

Before beginning the story of the "Moscow trail" of this book's main character, I would like to confess that as a professional spy and not a professional writer, I spent a good deal of time thinking about how to enliven this narrative. Ultimately, I decided I could inject some life into the tale and show, through classified KGB and other documents, how the same events were simultaneously viewed by the opposing sides. Therefore I beg the reader's forgiveness if the contents of this chapter and the manner in which it is laid out appear like an internal memorandum of a secret service. So, let us cut straight to the chase and describe the events which preceded American citizen Lee Harvey Oswald's appearance on Moscow soil.

On September 4, 1959, in view of his impending discharge from the military, U.S. Marine private Oswald asked the Superior Court of Santa Ana, California, to issue him a passport. From the questionnaire he filled out, it was clear that he was planning to leave the United States on September 21 to enroll in Albert Schweitzer College in Switzerland. From there he would go to the University of Turku in Finland, with additional trips to Cuba, the Dominican Republic, England, France, Germany, and the USSR. He received his passport in six days.

After his military discharge, Oswald returned to his home in Fort Worth, Texas, on September 14. He told his mother that he wanted to find a job on a ship or perhaps in an office that specialized in "import-export operations." After spending three days at home and visiting his brother, Oswald headed for New Orleans. On September 17, in a New Orleans travel bureau, he filled out a "Passenger Immigration Questionnaire" for people planning to go abroad. He listed his profession as as "shipping agent."

Three days later, on September 20, 1959, U.S. citizen Lee Harvey Oswald set sail from New Orleans on the freighter *Marion Lykes* and on October 8 disembarked at the French port of Le Havre. He immediately left for Great Britain, where he arrived on October 9. He told British customs inspectors that he planned to spend a week in England before traveling to his college in Switzerland. However, on that same day he boarded a plane to Helsinki, where he registered for one night at the Torni Hotel before moving on to the Klaus Kurki Hotel.

It was apparently on October 12 that Oswald asked the Soviet consulate in Helsinki to issue him a visa to the USSR. The visa, which came through two days later and was valid through October 20, allowed Oswald to take one trip to the Soviet Union for a period of no longer than six days. He also purchased ten Soviet "tourist vouchers," which cost thirty dollars a piece. The next day, October 15, he crossed the Finnish-Soviet border at Vainikkala en route by train to Moscow.

The *Warren Commission Report* describes the movements of the American tourist over the course of one month and a few days, until the moment when his name is pronounced for the first time on Soviet territory. Oswald's explanations for the purpose of his trip are curious, to say the least. In four different places—Santa Ana, Fort Worth, New Orleans, and Great Britain—he provided four different "legends," or fabricated stories, concerning his goals and itinerary.

The circumstances by which Oswald received a Soviet visa in Helsinki would later give rise to a number of speculations, reflected in the *Warren Commission Report:*

Speculation. It is probable that Oswald had prior contacts with

Soviet agents before he entered Russia in 1959, because his application for a visa was processed and approved immediately on receipt.

According to the Warren Commission:

> There is no evidence that Oswald was in touch with Soviet agents before his visit to Russia. The time that it took for him to receive his visa in Helsinki for entrance to the Soviet Union was shorter than the average but not beyond the normal range for the granting of such visas. Had Oswald been recruited as a Russian agent while he was still in the Marines, it is most improbable that he would have been encouraged to defect. He would have been of greater value to Russian intelligence as a Marine radar operator than as a defector.

Naturally, anyone has the right to speculate as much as he or she wants, but as far as the *Warren Commission Report* is concerned, I find no fault with their logic or reasoning.

In order to get a visa to the USSR at that time, a foreign tourist would have had to fill out two forms and submit two photographs to the same travel agency where he had obtained his tour package. The processing of the visa would be handled by the agency. Only on extremely rare occasions, such as in the event of an unforeseen flood of clients, would the agency send its clients directly to the Soviet embassy. Judging by the dates, it seems highly unlikely that this was the busy season for tourists.

The Soviet consulate in Helsinki issued visas quickly. This was attributable to the geographic proximity of Finland to the Soviet Union as well as to the good relations between Intourist, the Soviet national travel bureau, and the local Finnish travel agencies.

In 1992, in Minsk, I carefully studied Oswald's questionnaire, which the Belarus* KGB kept in their archives. On the line indicating present job, position, and basic profession, Oswald wrote "student." For the goal, length of stay in the USSR, and itinerary "Helsinki-Vyborg-Moscow. 5 days" is written. In general, Oswald wrote out all the answers in English, with the Russian equivalent

---

*Since the collapse of the Soviet Union, the former Soviet socialist republic of Belorussia has been renamed Belarus. For the time period under discussion in this chapter, Belorussia will be used when appropriate—trans. note.

alongside, but judging by a number of signs, they were not filled out by a native Russian. This could mean that the questionnaire had been completed and translated in the Finnish travel agency before being sent to the Soviet consulate. For "date of completing questionnaire," the answer, again in Oswald's handwriting, was October 13, 1959.

For the first time, on October 16, Lee Harvey Oswald stepped onto the platform of the Leningradsky train station in the capital of the Soviet Union.

According to the *Warren Commission Report:*

> He was met at the station in Moscow by a representative of Intourist. He was taken to the Hotel Berlin, where he registered as a student. That same day Oswald met with his Intourist guide, a young woman named Rimma Shirokova, who was assigned to accompany him during his stay in the USSR.

The USSR State Committee for Foreign Tourism, commonly known as Intourist, was the only organization at that time charged with handling both Soviet tourism abroad and foreign tourism in the USSR. Intourist travel bureaus were situated throughout the USSR, at all arrival points for foreign tourists. Employees of these bureaus met tourists at airports, train stations, and seaports and accompanied them to their hotels, where translator-guides, who were assigned to them from the day they arrived right up until the moment of their departure from the country, were already waiting for them. The Warren Commission reported, "In 1959, virtually all Intourist guides were KGB informants, and there is no reason to believe that this was not true of Oswald's guide."

The mass exchange of tourists began around 1956, when, as a result of Premier Nikita S. Krushchev's policies, the Iron Curtain between the East and West was raised slightly. The minor thaw in intergovernmental relations, however, was not accompanied by any corresponding change in the attitude the intelligence services showed toward one another, each hoping to use the exchange of tourists for their own ends.

Within the KGB there were two main subdivisions for handling foreign tourists: the First Chief Directorate, abbreviated in Russian as PGU (intelligence), and the Second Chief Directorate, known as VGU (counterintelligence).

Intelligence was interested in recruiting possible candidates who could be used as agents abroad. Counterintelligence was preoccupied with exposing enemy agents and preventing their subversive activities. Within the First Chief Directorate tourists were overseen by Department Fifteen, whose function was the recruitment of foreign targets within the USSR. Its counterpart in the Second Chief Directorate was Department Seven. These subdivisions of the KGB had complete access to all information gathered on foreign tourists, from their visa applications to the reports compiled by all the translator-guides.

The information provided by the Intourist guides was put to good use. All reports, which mentioned the wishes, recommendations, and observations of tourists, flowed into EMO, the acronym for the Excursion and Methodological Department. In turn, they were filtered by the KGB, which extracted from them all the pertinent information it needed for carrying out its specific tasks.

But the best method the KGB had for monitoring a tourist's behavior, exposing his contacts with Soviet citizens, and "feeding" him to the "right people" was to use its own agents. These it recruited from among the Intourist employees. The selection of candidates followed very strict criteria that determined one's capacity and suitability for engaging in operative activities. Barely half the Intourist personnel met these demands.

The work "on tourists" was carried out by intelligence and counterintelligence in various ways. Counterintelligence acted primarily on the basis of behavioral signs which might give cause to suspect that any given tourist was on a mission for the enemy's intelligence services. Intelligence made use of the data found in a tourist's visa questionnaire. The preliminary selection of possible candidates for recruitment was based on such criteria as social and professional affiliations, place of work, and residence. A tourist's residence was studied from the point of view of accessibility for Soviet rezidenturas, or foreign KGB stations, since the mobility of Soviet official representatives abroad, and their Western counterparts in the USSR, was limited to specific zones. This had to be taken into account while setting up "legal" rezidenturas under official cover for foreign intelligence operations.

The Western intelligence services functioned in approximately the same manner with regard to Soviet tourists. They maintained good relations with tourist agencies and had their own sources among the employees of such agencies. In turn, the foreign KGB rezidenturas studied these agencies from the point of view of counterintelligence. Any information about an enemy agent exposed "on the job" was immediately sent to the Second Chief Directorate. In this area, KGB intelligence and counterintelligence interacted very closely with one another.

Lee Harvey Oswald, until recently a U.S. Marine but now a "student," turned out to be more than the run-of-the-mill tourist. He had hardly stepped on Soviet territory when he began to exhibit unusual behavior. The day after he had registered at the Hotel Berlin, he and his guide, Rimma Shirokova, went out sightseeing. As described in *The Warren Commission Report:*

> Almost immediately [Oswald] told her that he wanted to leave the United States and become a citizen of the Soviet Union. According to Oswald's "Historic Diary," she later told him that she had reported his statement to Intourist headquarters, which in turn had notified the "Passport and Visa Office" (probably the Visa and Registration Department of the Ministry of Internal Affairs, the MVD). She was instructed to help Oswald prepare a letter to the Supreme Soviet requesting that he be granted citizenship. Oswald mailed such a letter that same day [October 17].

Such a serious and hasty statement made by a young American who had just arrived in the USSR obviously commanded the immediate attention of the KGB. This is how the events were reflected in a document emanating from the Fifteenth Department of the First Chief Directorate entitled "Report on the Stay in Moscow of American Citizen LEE HARVEY OSWALD":

Top Secret
Copy No. 2

On October 16, 1959, in the capacity of tourist, American citizen LEE HARVEY OSWALD arrived in Moscow.

On the very first day of his visit, he announced in a conversation with his translator SHIROKOVA R. S. that he had come with the intention of remaining in the Soviet Union and taking Soviet citizenship and, in this regard, expressed interest in where and to whom he should send the necessary application.

Soon after, he informed her that he had sent his declaration to the Supreme Soviet of the USSR and was awaiting its decision.

OSWALD showed absolutely no interest in sightseeing, but was completely consumed by the thought of staying in the Soviet Union.

He said of himself that he was alone and had no parents or close relatives; that he had attended school in Texas until the age of seventeen; and that, in connection with material hardships, he had joined the army in 1956 and served in California, Japan, and the Philippines. For some time he had nurtured the idea of taking a trip to the Soviet Union and becoming a Soviet citizen. According to his convictions, he is a Communist, although he does not belong to any organization, and because of his convictions he neither wants to, nor can he, remain in capitalist America and wishes to live and work in the first Communist country in the world.

Oswald could hardly have known that less than two weeks before he petitioned the Supreme Soviet, the newspaper *Pravda* had published the "Appeals of the Communist Party of the Soviet Union on the 42d Anniversary of the Great October Socialist Revolution" in its October 4 issue. One of the Appeals proclaimed that the peoples of the Soviet Union had entered into the period of "developed building of communism," and that all their strength and energy were to be applied toward fulfilling the tasks of building communism.

Thus, the "new builder of communism," in the person of Lee Harvey Oswald, could come in very handy.

Oswald's appeal for Soviet citizenship was like a booster shot to the circulatory system of Soviet bureaucracy. On October 17, 1959, a letter marked "urgent" was forwarded to the KGB deputy chairman, Aleksandr Perepelitsyn, from the chancellery of the Presidium of the Supreme Soviet: "In connection with our agreement,* I am sending you the statement of American citizen Lee Harvey Oswald, in which he asks for Soviet citizenship." The letter was signed by the deputy head of the chancellery, V. Vysotin. An appendix to the letter from the KGB suggested that the First and Second Chief directorates jointly examine Oswald's request.

That same day, the Registry and Archives Department (UAO) of the KGB requested information from the First and Second Chief directorates and immediately began a *spetsproverka,* or "control file," on Oswald.

In those days such files were usually kept on any Soviet citizen who had traveled abroad at least one time via the so-called private exit channel, that is, at the invitation of relatives or friends. (The latter was extremely rare.) The *spetsproverka,* or as we called it, the "exit file," was a dossier that kept personal and other biographical data on a person, information about the reasons for his trip, the results of background checks culled from special card files maintained by the KGB and MVD (Ministry of Internal Affairs), reports from his place of employment regarding the extent of his knowledge of state secrets, the correspondence of KGB organs, and other documents. Operative documents rarely made their way into such a dossier—only when foreign *rezidenturas* reported on the "figurant's" "bad" behavior abroad.

The spetsproverka, accompanied the "traveler" for his whole life. Additional material was added to it each time another trip was made. These files were maintained and held by the Registry and Archives Department. In reply to the department's request for materials to add to Oswald's file, the department heads of both the

---

*Indicating that prior to the memorandum's being sent, telephone conversations on the matter had already taken place between the officials.

First and Second Chief directorates wrote back, stating that they "had no interest in American citizen Lee Harvey Oswald," and, in their opinion, it "was not advisable to grant him Soviet citizenship." The letter was dated October 20, 1959.

Judging by their answer, the KGB had obviously determined that despite his claims to everyone that he was a dedicated Communist who wanted to become a Soviet citizen, Oswald held little intelligence potential. Still, he would have to be kept under observation, a burden of unspecified duration that would require physical and material expenditures without any payback. Since he did not hold any operative interest, the KGB's attitude most likely was to send him packing as quickly as possible.

I have nothing specific to back up my contention that that was what the Second Chief Directorate was thinking at the time, but a certain knowledge of the mechanism of KGB decision making in similar circumstances allows me to draw such an inference.

As far as the reaction from the First Chief Directorate, the request from the Registry and Archives Department had apparently forced them to "feel out" the "dedicated builder of communism" before supplying their answer. The initial debriefing of Oswald by an intelligence officer with Oswald was held on October 20. Insofar as the pretext for the meeting was his solicitation of Soviet citizenship, the conversation was conducted under the cover of OVIR, the Russian acronym for the Visa and Registration Department.

The debriefing, which lasted approximately one and a half hours, touched upon Oswald's life, the circumstances of his trip from America to the USSR, and his motives for requesting political asylum. The results of the talks were summarized in the following report from the Fifteenth Department of the First Chief Directorate:

> On October 20 of this year, OSWALD, in a conversation with OVIR regarding the reasons that led him to submit a statement about refusing to return to the United States and becoming a Soviet citizen, said that he was born in 1939 in the city of New Orleans, state of Louisiana. His father had been an insurance agent and died in 1939. Together with his mother, he moved

to the city of Fort Worth in the state of Texas, where she lives to this day at 3124 West Fifth Street.

In October 1956 he entered the military service and was enlisted as a private in the U.S. Marine Corps. During the period of his military service, from March 18 through May 5, 1957, in the city of Jacksonville, state of Florida, he took courses in electronics at the Naval Air Technical Training Center and from May 4 through June 19, 1957, courses for radar operators at Keesler Air Force Base.

Concerning the motives that caused him to submit a statement to the Supreme Soviet of the USSR, he repeated what he had earlier told the translator, that is, by his convictions he is a Communist, that the Communist party in the United States is persecuted, that it is demoralized and is virtually nonexistent, that he does not see any future for his life and activities in America and therefore he does not want to, and cannot, return there, and that he has firmly and seriously resolved to remain in the Soviet Union, become a Soviet citizen, and make himself useful in building a new Communist society.

He told no one in the United States, not even his mother, of his decision. His mother, as he supposed, would have been against it.

On September 11, 1959, in Santa Ana, California, he was discharged from military service and asked for a passport to travel abroad to Europe. After receiving his passport, he purchased a ticket with money he had saved during this military service. He left for Europe by way of New Orleans. In Helsinki he obtained a visa for a five-day tour to the USSR and arrived in Moscow, from which place he does not intend to leave.

He was told at OVIR that on the following day, that is, the twenty-first, he would be called and informed of the decision taken on his statement and that, considering the motives he had set forth, it was unlikely that his request could be satisfied at the present time and that in all probability he would have to return to the United States.

Oswald's interloculator was Abram Shaknazarov, who had worked in the organs of state security since the 1920s and knew several foreign languages. He was this author's supervisor in the KGB's Moscow and Moscow regional directorate in 1958–59. Shaknazarov later returned to the First Chief Directorate and worked with tourists in the Fifteenth Department. It was he who authored the aforementioned report of Oswald's trip to Moscow in the fall of 1959.

Judging by the nature of the conversation, Oswald did not create the impression of being a source of valuable intelligence information. Giving him Soviet citizenship and permanent residency in the USSR would provide the KGB no benefit. And to use him in active propagandistic activities during warming periods in Soviet-American relations was also hardly worth the trouble. Presumably, the deputy head of the First Chief Directorate concurred with his counterpart at the Second Chief Directorate that "it was not advisable to give [Oswald] refugee status in the Soviet Union."

Based on the replies from intelligence and counterintelligence, the Registry and Archives Department informed the secretariat of the Presidium of their conclusions in a memorandum dated October 22, 1959, and signed by deputy KGB chairman Aleksandr Perepelitsyn.

Thus, in the eyes of the Committee for State Security, the KGB, Lee Harvey Oswald had been declared a "tourist non grata." It is plausible to assume that most any other individual in his position would have quietly accepted his fate and returned to the United States to continue working on his mastery of Marxism. But this tourist turned out to be a tough nut to crack.

After his petition was rejected, Oswald turned to more dramatic means of gaining attention. In the same internal KGB document already cited the consequences of his refusal are set out in the dry prose of bureaucratese:

> On October 21, a phone call was placed from OVIR to the Hotel Berlin with a message for OSWALD and his translator to appear at OVIR at around three o'clock in the afternoon. OVIR wanted to know if tickets for OSWALD's departure had been purchased and, learning that they had not, suggested that they

be ordered immediately, since the time of his stay in the country had expired. To the question of whether it made sense to extend his tour for one to two days, the reply was negative.

At twelve o'clock noon the hotel informed OSWALD, in the presence of his translator, that he must be at OVIR at three o'clock and that train tickets to Helsinki had been ordered for him.

Oswald said that he would come down at 2:45 and went back to his room. When he did not appear at the appointed time, the translator became worried and went to his room. The door was locked from the inside, and no one responded to the sound of knocking. When the door was opened with an emergency passkey, OSWALD was discovered lying in his bathtub unconscious and with a cut vein on his left arm.

Before opening his vein, he had written a note of the following content: "I have made such a long journey to find death, but I love life."

Oswald was taken to Botkin Hospital, where he remains at the present time undergoing treatment.

On October 23, OSWALD was transferred to ward 7 of Botkin Hospital. In a conversation with the translators Zhuravlev and Shirokova, DR. TRATAKOVSKY said that OSWALD is a strong-willed individual and that if his request is again denied, he can repeat his attempt at suicide.

An investigator paid a visit to OSWALD and had a talk with him about what had happened. OSWALD repeated everything he had said earlier and added that if it was learned in the United States that he wanted to stay in the USSR, he would be put in jail.

When Oswald was taken to Botkin Hospital, a search of his belongings was conducted in his hotel room. Among Oswald's personal papers, a letter was found written in English. There was no addressee on it:

I, Lee Harvey Oswald, hereby request Soviet citizenship. This request, written by me, has been carefully and seriously thought out, with full understanding of the responsibilities and duties connected with it. While my citizenship is being processed, I also ask that I be granted asylum in the Soviet Union as a Communist and Marxist.

After this unpleasant suicide incident involving this particular American tourist, Intourist was the first of the state organs to wake up. Formally responsible for his fate, as, incidentally, it was for the fate of all foreign tourists in the USSR, the head of Intourist, [name] Ankudinov, took it upon himself to transfer the "disturber of the peace" to other hands. He had an excellent reason for doing so: This had all happened after Oswald's request to change his category from foreign tourist to that of Soviet citizen was rejected. Now he was someone else's problem.

KGB archives report that on October 22, Ankudinov sent the report of its Excursion and Methodological Department, which laid out the circumstances of Oswald's stay in Moscow, to the Central Committee of the Communist Party, the Ministry of Foreign Affairs in the name of Andrei Gromyko, and the KGB in the name of Aleksandr Shelepin. In particular, this report mentioned Oswald's petition for Soviet citizenship, his suicide attempt after his request was turned down, and his lack of interest in sightseeing.

The stubborn tourist had become a hot potato. The KGB, which obviously knew of the suicide attempt without having to be told by Intourist, now kept an extremely close eye on events. KGB archives contain the following:

On October 24 Oswald was greatly alarmed. There was one other American in ward no. 7, *who was often visited by his friend, an employee of the American embassy* [author's emphasis]. The latter used to ask Oswald if he had registered with the embassy and what had happened to him. Oswald did not tell him the truth. *On that same day, someone called from the embassy and asked when he would be released* [author's emphasis].

On October 27 the stitches were removed from OSWALD's arm. His health was good, but he was visibly agitated. No one from the American embassy showed any more interest in him.

On October 28, OSWALD was released from the hospital and

registered at the Hotel Metropole in room 233. He had already been given a train ticket to Helsinki and advised that on October 29 he would be called down to OVIR at twelve o'clock.

On October 29, OSWALD was received by the head of OVIR, COMRADE RYAZANTSEV. OSWALD repeated his request for permission to stay in the USSR.

COMRADE RYAZANTSEV said that the matter was still unresolved and that he could remain for the time being in Moscow and wait for a definitive answer from the Supreme Soviet.

OSWALD left OVIR in a good mood. He said that he hoped his request would be granted.

At the present time OSWALD resides at the Hotel Metropole, does not go out and spends whole days in his room.

He has to pay 30 rubles a day for his room, beginning October 28. He has 800 rubles left in his possession.

On November 1 OSWALD, in a conversation with his translator, said that if he is refused he will not leave but will again appeal to the Supreme Soviet and in such fashion will get his request satisfied. "I don't think," he said, "that the Supreme Soviet will be so cruel to me."

The translator Shirokova R.S. continues to work with OSWALD.

On November 5, 1959 OSWALD, in a conversation with his translator, said that he had been to the American embassy on October 31, where he renounced his American citizenship and informed the embassy that he was going to ask the Supreme Soviet for Soviet citizenship. The employee of the embassy who had received him "did not express any particular joy and said that it did not concern him," although he reported it to journalists.

On November 1, 2, and 3 many journalists, including STEVENS, visited OSWALD, but he refused to speak with them.

On the 5th one of the journalists sent him a letter with tickets to the Puppet Theater. OSWALD said that he was going to send the ticket back.

On November 4, an intelligence employee had another meeting with Oswald. This time it was not an "employee of OVIR" but an "employee of Intourist," who called himself

"Andrei Nikolayevich," who spoke with Oswald. They again talked about the reasons that had prompted Oswald to petition for Soviet citizenship, about Oswald's political views, and his plans for the future.

Andrei Nikolayevich promised to help Oswald get settled in the USSR and suggested they meet after the November holidays, that is, in five days. The holidays passed, but Andrei Nikolayevich did not reappear. Oswald attempted through his translator to arrange a meeting with "Andrei Nikolayevich" from Intourist, but he was told that there was no such employee there by that name.

With its guard up, Intourist sought clarification from the Seventh Department of the Second Chief Directorate of the KGB, responsible for foreign tourist counter-intelligence control. Soon after, counterintelligence agents explained that Oswald had met with a representative from the First Chief Directorate and had spoken with him "on the subject of possible use abroad."

In my opinion the lack of coordination between the subdivisions of intelligence was a rather common occurrence. Most likely someone from within the First Chief Directorate, who had access to a list of foreign tourists, took an interest in the American student and decided to arrange a meeting with him so that he could be questioned. It is possible that in the process of "becoming acquainted," Oswald spoke about his plans and his visit to the American embassy to renounce his citizenship. Perhaps after that conversation had already taken place, the operative realized that "he was barking up the wrong tree" and therefore was no longer interested in continuing the contact with Oswald. The fact that the promised second meeting with "Andrei Nikolayevich" never happened supports this view.

Generally speaking, as soon as KGB foreign intelligence became aware of Oswald's visit to the American embassy, they ceased accumulating materials on his Soviet stay. As U.S. authorities knew about his desire to become a Soviet citizen, what interest could the intelligence service have in him? He had exposed himself forever to

American intelligence and therefore became useless to KGB intelligence.

If it had been known that the American U-2 spy plane was housed at the U.S. Air Force base in Atsuga, Japan, where Oswald had served as a radar operator, more likely than not the KGB's attitude toward him would have been different. But all indications are that our intelligence was unaware of this. It is also clear that Oswald never volunteered such information in any of his conversations with Soviet officials, but he did use it to blackmail the American embassy in his meeting there on October 31, 1959.

The news of Oswald's visit to the embassy, in conjunction with his attempt at suicide, upset the people who ran Intourist even more. Now the Western mass media were clued in to events, which could lead to reports that in the Soviet Union tourists are "driven to commit suicide." This could damage the image and commercial interests of Intourist by scaring away potential tourists to the USSR. Therefore, the Intourist brass again began to sound all the alarms. This time it sent another strictly confidential message on November 12 straight to Anastas Mikoyan, deputy chairman of the USSR Council of Ministers.

As first deputy chairman, Mikoyan was in charge of all Soviet foreign trade organizations, including Intourist. In this capacity he could issue orders to the Ministry of Foreign Affairs and the chairman of the KGB. Mikoyan forwarded the letter to the head of the Seventh Department of the Second Chief Directorate, the division of counterintelligence that handled tourists.

While all this correspondence back and forth was going on, with suggestions made in regard to the stubborn American tourist's fate, information flowed into the Seventh Department about Oswald's behavior and contacts, rather scanty considering his lifestyle and rare meetings with representatives from OVIR.

Oswald's diary describes the period from November 2 to November 15, during which he continued to isolate himself, as "days of utter loneliness." The Warren Commission reported:

> For the rest of the year, Oswald seldom left his hotel room where he had arranged to take his meals, except perhaps for

a few trips to museums. He spend most of his time studying Russian "eight hours a day," his diary records. The routine was broken only by another interview at the passport office; occasional visits from Rimma Shirokova; lessons in Russian from her and other Intourist guides.

Oswald's passive lifestyle did not allow counterintelligence to arrive at any conclusions about his nonaffiliation with the American intelligence services because, in theory, he could have been assigned a long-term goal of becoming an agent in place. Time would be needed before any final conclusions could be reached.

Meanwhile, Mikoyan's instructions were being worked on at the Ministry of Foreign Affairs and at the KGB. The result of this effort was a top-secret joint memorandum to the Party's Central Committee which laid out in abbreviated form "the Oswald problem," from his request for citizenship to his slashing his wrist, to his continuing refusal to leave the USSR. The memo, dated November 27, 1959, ended with a concrete proposal:

> Considering that other foreigners who were formerly given Soviet citizenship (Sitrinell, Afshar) left our country after having lived here awhile and keeping in mind that Oswald has not been sufficiently studied, it is advisable to give him temporary residency in the USSR for one year, with a guarantee of employment and housing. In this event, the question of O.'s permanent residency in the USSR and granting of Soviet citizenship can be decided during this term.

It was signed by Andrei Gromyko, minister of foreign affairs, and Aleksandr Shelepin, chairman of the KGB.*

There is no doubt that the KGB did not change its position vis-à-vis Oswald, and it is even possible that recent events had strengthened their view of him, but after the unambiguously worded directive was sent down from the deputy chairman of the Council of Ministers, the organs had no choice but to comply.

In the conditions of the time, the proposal was "Solomonic" in

---

*The full text of the memo appears in the appendix to this book.

its wisdom: Mute the situation, which by now had received international publicity, remove the petitioner from Moscow, and observe him carefully for one year in order to understand just who he considers himself to be and how suitable he is for the role of "builder of communism" which he so stubbornly persists in claiming to be.

According to KGB archives, a resolution by the Central Committee was appended to the memo:

In regard to the petition by American citizen Lee Harvey Oswald for Soviet citizenship, let it hereby be resolved:

1. To agree with the proposal of Ministry of Foreign Affairs and the KGB to grant U.S. citizen Lee Harvey Oswald temporary resident status for one year and to resolve the questions of his permanent residency in the USSR and Soviet citizenship during this period.

2. To oblige the Belorussian National Economic Council to place Oswald in a job in electronics and the Minsk City Council of Worker's Deputies to assign him his own small apartment.

3. To instruct the executive committee of the Societies of the Red Cross and the Red Crescent to assign five thousand rubles for equipping the apartment for Oswald and to issue him an allowance of seven hundred rubles a month over the course of one year.

For the Central Committee it was all the same whether it was Lee Harvey Oswald, John Smith, or someone else. It was evident that a "problem" existed which could have possible negative political consequences and become an irritant for the highest echelons of the government. The proposals of the Ministry of Foreign Affairs and the KGB seemed perfectly reasonable. On December 1, 1959, Oswald was granted temporary residency status in the Soviet Union for one year.

It is interesting to note that the Warren Commission's analysis, cited below, almost completely came to the same conclusions as to how events had evolved in Moscow in those days:

The information relating to Oswald's suicide attempt indicates that his application to remain in the Soviet Union was probably rejected about six days after his arrival in Moscow. Since the KGB is the Soviet agency responsible for the initial handling of all defectors, it seems likely that the original decision not to accept Oswald was made by the KGB. That Oswald was permitted to remain in Moscow after his release from the hospital suggests that another ministry of the Soviet government may have intervened on his behalf. The most plausible reason for any such intervention may well have been apprehension over the publicity that would follow the rejection of a devout convert to the Communist cause.

This conclusion virtually coincides with the information given the CIA on the Oswald affair by the KGB turncoat Yuri Nosenko (whom we will meet later), including the KGB's attitude toward Oswald's request for citizenship. Since the CIA decided not to allow Nosenko to testify before the Warren Commission, on the suspicion that he was a KGB "plant," it can be posited that the CIA consultants equipped themselves nonetheless with his information in order to heighten their prestige and demonstrate the degree to which they were knowledgeable about "Soviet reality."

In answering one of the "speculations" about the Soviet authorities' relationship to Oswald, the Warren Commission again draws a completely correct inference:

> Speculation—Soviet suspicion of Oswald is indicated by the fact that he was sent off to work in a radio plant in Minsk as an unskilled hand.
>
> Commission finding—The Soviet Government probably was suspicious of Oswald, as it would be of any American who appeared in Moscow and said he wanted to live in the Soviet Union.

While the Belorussian National Economic Council and the Minsk City Council of Workers' Deputies were busy meeting the demands of the Central Committee resolution to arrange Oswald's new life, the KGB, though it did not like the decision, was also carrying out its assignment, but in its own way.

The KGB had no concrete grounds whatsoever for suspecting Oswald of ties to American intelligence. But insofar as the KGB had to be directly involved in deciding Oswald's fate, it had to ensure the best conditions for effectively studying him. And the only way to do so was to assign his case to the so-called highest category, that is, one involving espionage. Nothing was more serious than cases involving American espionage. All means of available surveillance and countersurveillance technology were at the KGB's disposal, in addition to as much manpower as was needed to carry out round-the-clock observation of the subject. On December 21, 1959, the Seventh Department of the Second Chief Directorate began an espionage file on Lee Harvey Oswald.

Thus, by his persistence and stubbornness, Oswald had crawled under the "shroud" of the KGB on his own.

At the same time, across the ocean, the FBI, CIA, and other U.S. intelligence agencies, as soon as they learned of Oswald's moves in the USSR and his visit to the American embassy, scrambled to do virtually the same as their Soviet counterparts, that is, put a constant watch on him. During the course of two weeks, October 16–31, Oswald attracted the attention of many people by his indefatigable quest to change one citizenship for another, thereby setting into immediate motion the bureaucratic machines of the two great powers.

Four days after the first year of the new decade was ushered in, Oswald was called in to OVIR and issued a USSR residency permit for "stateless persons." Since he had left his American passport in the American embassy, he was now formally a "stateless person." He was told at OVIR that the city of Minsk, capital of the Soviet Socialist Republic of Belorussia, had been chosen for his residency and that he was to leave for there within the next few days.

On the following day, the Red Cross, in accordance with the resolution, counted out five thousand rubles as a onetime stipend to help Oswald get his new life in order.

On January 5, the "tourist non grata" left Moscow, and on the following day he arrived by train in Minsk. On January 13 he became an apprentice at a Minsk experimental radio plant.

His Moscow file followed him by special delivery to Belorussian

KGB counterintelligence and the Belorussian Second Chief Directorate. Considering the gravity of his case, the first step taken by Belorussian counterintelligence was to compile its own dossier on Oswald and draw up future plans for working with him.

In the summer of 1992 I asked Vladimir Semichastny, former KGB chairman from 1961 to 1967, the following questions relating to Oswald's Soviet period:

Q: Did the KGB have any direct contacts with Oswald during his stay in the Soviet Union?

A. Officially, no one from the KGB ever talked with Oswald. While he was being studied, those who met with him were under the cover of different organizations: Belorussian Ministry of Foreign Affairs, USSR Ministry of Internal Affairs, OVIR. In general, we studied Oswald's biography.

Q. Was the KGB interested in Oswald from the point of view of intelligence missions?

A: Based on the initial meetings with Oswald, it might have been understood that he possessed information of interest to us. But as the then head of the First Chief Directorate, Sakharovsky, told me, it became clear in the course of conversation with him, especially to those who touched upon his military service, that the level of his knowledge was extremely low and that knowledge of his specialty, according to Sakharovsky, was "very primitive and did not extend beyond the textbooks." Therefore, there was a lack of interest in him on the part of intelligence.

Q: Whose decision was it, and why, to send Oswald to Minsk?

A: From talks with responsible employees of the KGB, who at the time were dealing with Oswald, I found out that the question of place of residence in the USSR was decided simultaneously with the question of granting him "stateless person" status. After preliminary agreement, the Baltics or Minsk was chosen.

This is probably as good a place as any to wrap up the "Moscow trail" of Lee Harvey Oswald in 1959. But I am troubled by the contradictory information concerning certain circumstances of that

period for which I cannot find a proper explanation. I am referring
to the episode which, for lack of a better name, I shall call the
"Botkin incident."

I will remind the reader that in the KGB's report, which has been
quoted here and there throughout this chapter, mention was made
of one other American who was placed in ward 7 of the Botkin
Hospital, where Oswald was transferred from the psychiatric ward
following his unsuccessful attempt to take his own life. This American, according to the report, "was often visited by his friend, an
employee of the American embassy." It further states that on October 24, Oswald became agitated when this employee asked him if he
"had registered with the American embassy and what had happened to him. Oswald did not tell him the truth. That same day,
someone phoned from the embassy and asked when he would be
released." And then, after the stitches were removed, Oswald, who
had physically recovered, remained noticeably anxious. The KGB
report adds, "No one from the American embassy took any more
interest in him."

In the Minsk file on Oswald it says only that the other American
in the ward was a "businessman."

In the Warren Commission Report the episode is presented in a
somewhat different light by Oswald himself:

> Judging from his "Historic Diary" [Oswald's], the only
> complaint in the new ward was that one of the patients, an
> "elderly American," was distrustful of him because he had not
> registered at the American Embassy and because he was eva-
> sive about the reasons for his presence in Moscow and con-
> finement to the hospital.

In his "Historic Diary" entry for September 26, Oswald makes
absolutely no mention of the visits to the "elderly American" by an
American embassy employee.

The most interesting bit of information about the episode, in my
opinion, is what Edward Jay Epstein reported in his book *Legend:
The Secret World of Lee Harvey Oswald,* which I quote in its
entirety:

In order to determine whether or not Oswald was ever actually in the hospital, the CIA asked the FBI to search for the elderly American Oswald had identified in his diary as having been in his hospital ward. After an intensive search the FBI located Waldemar Boris Kara-Patnitsky, a seventy-five-year-old Russian-born New York businessman who had been hospitalized for a prostate condition during a business trip to the Soviet Union. Mr. Kara-Patnitsky, however, insisted that he had never seen or met Oswald or any other American when he was in the hospital.

Each piece of information on its own illuminates one and the same fact. Taken together, they produce a kind of mystical *labyrinth* which I find virtually impossible to fathom.

My attempts to gather additional data on the "New York businessman" have thus far met with failure. A check of the KGB files on Mr. Kara-Patnitsky has divulged nothing. Equally unsuccessful was a search of the Botkin Hospital, where any archival records on patients from the 1950s have been destroyed.

Someone might ask just what is so particularly mysterious about the incident and why I find it so intriguing. Who cares now whether a businessman spoke with Oswald in the hospital and whether Oswald lied to him or not?

The episode attracted my attention chiefly because of one detail, which I would like to have explained: Was the American embassy in Moscow involved? I shall try to explain why I think this is significant.

There is very little reason to doubt the authenticity of information which reached the KGB about Oswald's stay in the hospital. He ended up there as the result of an emergency. Without a doubt, the medical staff there was instructed to pay especially close attention to everything that happened to him and around him. It must also be taken into account that Oswald was transferred to the so-called diplomatic ward of the hospital, where foreigners were treated and where the KGB obviously maintained a strong presence. Naturally, the fact of Oswald's contact with another patient, an American "businessman," and his "friend," a visitor from the

American embassy, was noted, and signals were sent to the organs of state security.

The same can be said about the embassy's telephone call concerning Oswald. It follows from the report that someone intercepted subsequent phone calls, since it says that "no one from the embassy took any more interest in him." This, in my view, serves to confirm that the earlier call from the embassy to the hospital had taken place; the call was a fact.

Thus, a fact asserts itself: Someone in the embassy already knew of Oswald's stay in Moscow, at least a week before he showed up there himself on October 31. Yet the Warren Commission has this to say:

> Oswald appeared at the American Embassy in Moscow on October 31, 1959, three days after his release from the Botkin Hospital. He did not give the officials at the Embassy any indication that he had recently received medical treatment. Oswald's appearance was the first notification to the American Government that he was in Russia, since he had failed to inform the Embassy upon his arrival, as most American tourists did at the time.

It is possible that the American government truly learned of Oswald and his misadventures in Russia only after October 31, but what about the American embassy in Moscow? Since it is clear from the KGB document that *someone* there knew about his stay in the hospital, it cannot be excluded that the reason for his being there also became known. In spite of all the instructions, someone from among the hospital staff could have "leaked" to the other patients in the ward, which in turn reached the ears of an anonymous embassy employee, who had visited his friend the businessman.

If these suppositions are true, then the American embassy in Moscow had a week's time to obtain specific information on Oswald from the proper American organizations, particularly his recent discharge from the marines and his knowledge of military secrets. In this case, they would have been ready for his possible visit to the embassy. Then the patience and restraint shown by the consular officer, a Mr. Richard Snyder, during his conversation with Oswald on October 31, becomes perfectly understandable. Although the visitor was extremely defiant and even aggressive, threatening to hand over to the other side information having "special interest for Soviet intelligence," which clearly constituted an attempt to blackmail the consul, Snyder was very polite and well mannered in return. The skillfully scattered seeds of doubt in the correctness of Oswald's intentions, in my view, bloomed a year and a half later, when he again showed up at the embassy, but this time with directly opposite goals.

So, was the embassy in Moscow prepared for Oswald's "unexpected" visit or not? A whole bouquet of other questions is arranged around this central one concerning the "Botkin incident":

Why did the CIA, and not the Warren Commission, ask the FBI to establish the identity of the "elderly American"?

Did the CIA possess information about the "elderly American" through its station in Moscow?

Did the FBI establish the identity of precisely that "elderly American" Oswald mentions in his "Historic Diary"?

Have the materials relating to Mr. Kara-Patnitsky's questioning been preserved?

Why was Mr. Kara-Patnitsky not included among those called to give testimony to the Warren Commission? After all, his testimony would refute Oswald's "Diary" entries and at the same time put to doubt his "Diary" as a credible source of information.

The testimony of Mr. Kara-Patnitsky does not jibe with the KGB's and Oswald's data about the Botkin episode. If he were a "businessman" and an "elderly American," why does he deny ever having talks with Oswald?

The Warren Commission says:

> The most reliable information concerning the period Oswald spent in Moscow in the latter part of 1962* comes from the records of the American Embassy in Moscow, the testimony of Embassy officials.

*In both Russian and English versions of the *Warren Commission Report,* the year is given as 1962. This is clearly a typographical error, for it is commonly known that at the time Oswald was not in Moscow but in the United States.

But is there any possibility now of obtaining any kind of testimony from those officials concerning the participants of the "Botkin incident"?

After having spent a little more than two and one-half months in Moscow, American citizen Lee Harvey Oswald was granted new status—stateless person—and remained in the Soviet Union.

It would have entered hardly anyone's head at the time to imagine that almost four years later to the day he was allowed to remain in the Soviet Union, the issue of his obtaining Soviet citizenship would surface anew. This time, though, it would be as the result of other circumstances and not on his own initiative but that of the U.S. government.

But more about this story in the chapters to come.

2

Oswald in Minsk
(January 1960–May 1962)

> He looks about in amazement; he is entirely in his
> own world, where lemons ripen and figs suddenly
> crack open.
> —Nickolas Freling, *Death of a Smuggler*

> Bureaucracy is terrorified of human beings, and
> since policemen deal with human beings, they are
> tempted to imprison a live being within the suf-
> focating straitjacket of their labels."
> —Ibid.

If we continue to use boxing terminology and call Oswald's stay in Moscow the first round in his relationship with the KGB, then the former marine won it on points. He acted with an enviable stubbornness, raised the stakes by attempting suicide, and placed the highest Soviet government organs in a difficult position. For a month and a half he persisted and forced a decision regarding his stay in the Soviet Union. It was a compromise decision, since Oswald was given permission to live there but not offered the political asylum and citizenship he so desperately wanted since his arrival in the Russian capital.

The bell rang for round two in January 1960. The KGB posed the following questions: Is he a spy? Can he be of any use to us? Do we let him stay? Oswald's visa permitted him to live in the Soviet Union for one year; during this period, the KGB had to formulate its conclusions and report to the Central Committee of the Communist party of the USSR.

Based on available information, the KGB and Oswald did not even spar with each other. The following is an excerpt from a conversation between the author and former KGB chairman Vladimir Semichastny:

Q. How was Oswald handled in Minsk?
A. With the usual control measures. Routine surveillance, involving agents, observation, and standard operative techniques.
Q. Did control methods involving Oswald vary from techniques used with other defectors?
A. Yes, we didn't even involve our most skilled surveillance agents, because we didn't want to risk compromising them for future, more important use. But as I already stated, the rest was standard operating procedure, using all means of surveillance, including agents and informants.

Oswald kept to himself during his first months in Minsk. He studied Russian with that characteristic doggedness he exhibited in trying to reach his goals. As he gradually felt more secure in his surroundings, he began to make friends, mostly at work. He become quite close with these acquaintances and continued relations with some after his return to the United States. Oswald noted in his diary that he enjoyed Minsk and that work was pleasant.

As his friendships deepened and his Russian improved, Oswald would enter into philosophical discussions. For example, concerning the role of the individual in history, he attributed a great deal of significance to personality and defended this position with passion and conviction. Discussing the relationship of "result" and "method" with a friend, he stressed that "the method is more important; a good method can be repeated and achieve good results." During this period, Oswald showed no inclination to further educate himself. Based on these recurring observations, the KGB felt that Oswald would not be useful for propagandistic purposes.

He was not well educated, and his ideological ideas were rather simplistic. His use as a propaganda instrument could actually backfire.

The state of euphoria which Oswald felt in the first months of his stay gradually passed. His image of an ideal Communist society did not mesh with Soviet reality. Semichastny made this comment to me:

> Oswald knew little about Soviet reality. Almost everything he saw was completely unexpected by him. While living in the Soviet Union, he made no effort to augment and deepen his theoretical knowledge of Marxism. He was incapable of adapting himself to our reality. Incidentally, based on this, we concluded that he was not employed by any special intelligence service. Oswald's actions in Minsk were not those of a foreign agent. His primary interest was in attending dances.

The possibility of returning to the United States began to crop up in Oswald's conversation in midsummer, 1960. In August he was heard to say at work, "Well, I'll return to America and write a book about all the wonderful Soviet people who have shown such concern for me."

He no longer expressed any desire to enroll in a "VUZ," a Soviet institute for higher learning, although he had mentioned doing so to friends in the past. Despite his secrecy and almost pathological lying, faint notes of nostalgia appeared in Oswald's speech. By November he no longer concealed his mood and told a friend that he was "homesick." In December, co-workers asked where he would spend his vacation, and Oswald, half in jest, replied, "In America." It should be noted that Oswald had a sense of humor and joked with his friends. He used this ability to laugh off political discussions and thus avoid expressing his feelings.

Oswald was reevaluating his socialist ideas. Early in 1961 he participated in an argument regarding socialism versus capitalism. Oswald stated that he was not sure that "socialism was a more progressive phenomenon." He "did not see a method or reason for objectively evaluating the advantages of socialism over capitalism.

No one here can be objective because each person's judgment is subjected to their upbringing, which completely defines the person's view."

Conversation turned to comparing the systems of government in the United States and the USSR. Oswald said that the Soviet Union possessed many limitations which he didn't like and which made the country unattractive. He gave as an example the fact that its citizens were forbidden to leave the country. Undoubtedly, this example reflected his own inner turmoil. As an example of the problems Oswald found in America, he mentioned that he disliked "the fact that blacks could not sit on benches designated for white people."

These are observations of Oswald's co-workers after a year's acquaintance:

> He did not have a close relationship with anyone, and he expressed no particular interest in his work. Asked about his job, he would limit his answer to "Work is work." He didn't talk about his past or his plans for the future. On the surface he seemed suited to, and satisfied with, his work. He didn't take part in political discussions or factory meetings. His relations with the people around him seemed normal. He seemed more interested in having a good time.

KGB surveillance also meant taking precautions to avoid unpleasant situations. During a lunch break, a worker fooling around with Oswald kicked him. For his action, "the worker was rebuked by the collective and subsequently apologized to Oswald." The "potential American spy" had to be treated with kid gloves.

The year 1960 ended with a reevaluation by Oswald of his idealization of the Soviet Union. Meanwhile, the KGB continued to analyze him. Oswald's diary mentioned "drabness" and the lack of places, such as bowling alleys, to spend his money. He had "had enough." The KGB concluded that he was neither a spy nor a builder of socialism.

In the beginning of 1961, Belorussian counterintelligence sent the following letter to Moscow Center:

In the process of working on "Nalim,"* data supporting the
suspicion of espionage activity was not obtained. It has been
established that he purchased a rifle in August and went hunting with co-workers. Nalim was not observed "hunting" on
his own. He did not contact individuals who could be of
interest to foreign espionage.

Nalim's lifestyle includes frequent cinema, theater, and concert visits. He enjoys the symphony. He has a radio receiver
and record player in his apartment and frequently invites girls
to listen to music.

He shows little interest in his work or in improving his
abilities in this area.

Nalim was on vacation from December 22 to January 5. He
spent this time in Minsk, and no suspicious activities were
observed.

He does not express any concrete plans for the future, although he mentioned "missing America." His temporary refugee status expired on January 4, 1961. He visited the passport
department of the Minsk city police and inquired if a Soviet
passport in his name had come from Moscow. Nalim announced that he had processed all necessary documents for
Soviet citizenship in Moscow in October 1959. Asked whether
he would take up permanent residence in the Soviet Union,
Nalim explained that before he answered the question he
wanted to know Moscow's decision in connection with his
status.

The passport division extended his residency permit for one
more year and sent an inquiry regarding his citizenship to the
division of the Ministry of Internal Affairs in Moscow, responsible for all visas and registration.

The Belorussian KGB concluded that Oswald intended to correspond with the American embassy in Moscow about the possibility
of his return to the United States. The Belorussian KGB expressed
the opinion that Oswald should be denied Soviet citizenship.

All the information gathered in the last year on Oswald's inten-

*Nalim was the KGB code name for Oswald. In Russian it means turbot, or river fish.

tions and stability supported the initial decision of the Communist party of the Soviet Union. He was only given temporary residence because "other foreigners had been granted Soviet citizenship in the past but after having lived a certain time in the USSR quit our country." It was clear to the KGB that Oswald fit this description.

The decision to extend his stateless-person residency was implemented to give him time to establish relations with American authorities. He had to ascertain the legal ramifications of his move to the Soviet Union. Step one in this process occurred in the beginning of February, when he wrote to the American embassy.

There is no possibility that Oswald's correspondence with the embassy was not monitored. During this period, the embassies of the two superpowers were considered bastions of subversive activity. Counterintelligence paid constant attention to their activities. Any mail was routinely intercepted, opened, and checked for its content and any possible hidden text.

Oswald's contact with the American embassy led the Belorussian and Moscow KGB to work out plans for dealing with the situation in the event he maintained or furthered his relationship with his own people. In boxing parlance, Oswald took the initiative, and the KGB resorted to counterpunching.

One KGB response involved the continued study of Oswald's behavior in which information about his past was gathered and his military service verified. When friends became interested in the reasons for Oswald's defection to the Soviet Union, he tried to wave off the question. But he finally answered, "I'm a lonely person, and I don't really care where I live." He made no mention of his desire to return to America. Several days later, another friend asked about his experience in the military service. Oswald willingly told him that he served from October 24, 1956, through September 2, 1959. He explained that he was a private and had spent months studying radio electronics and radar. He showed documents verifying that he had taken these courses, his honorable discharge, his soldier's ID, a map of some city in Japan, and a pass to a bar where he spent his free time. Asked about marine corps drill formations, he enthusiastically demonstrated them for about an hour.

Oswald was at a party with friends, and the conversation turned to sweets—candies, cookies, and halvah.

"I like halvah very much," he said. "In America we have all kinds of candy, but no halvah. You know what I'm going to do? When I return to America, I'm going to open a shop that makes and sells halvah."

"You'll be very successful, for there won't be any competition," someone said.

"Yes, I won't have any competition," he said, and realizing his mistake, he began, "But I'm not going to Amer—" He stopped in mid-sentence and asked, "Do you know how to make halvah?" He was intent on not letting his friends know of his desire to return to the United States.

In February, Oswald suddenly began to study German. He purchased two dictionaries and a textbook. He became interested in foreigners in Minsk and paid particular attention to West Germans and Americans. In the middle of March, the Michigan University symphonic band was on tour in Minsk. Oswald rushed to contact the arriving Americans.

According to the *Warren Commission Report:*

> Sometime in the second week of March, Miss Katherine Mallory, who was on tour in Minsk with the University of Michigan symphonic band, found herself surrounded by curious Russian citizens. A young man who identified himself as a Texan and former Marine stepped out of the crowd and asked if she needed an interpreter; he interpreted for her for the next 15 or 20 minutes. *Later he told her that he despised the United States and hoped to stay in Minsk for the rest of his life* [author's emphasis]. Miss Mallory is unable to swear that her interpreter was Oswald, but is personally convinced that it was.

Based on reliable information in Nalim's operative files, the author is prepared to swear that Miss Mallory's translator was indeed Oswald.

While the symphony performed in Minsk, Oswald spoke to many of the Americans who had traveled there with the orchestra. Initial contacts were made in stores and on the street. He not only conversed with his countrymen; he helped them shop. He became acquainted with two girls, spoke with them for a long time, showed them the city, and helped them purchase candy.

On the day of the first concert he went to the Hotel Minsk and spoke to a number of Americans. Miss Mallory was among them. Oswald attended the orchestra's concert. After their performance, several orchestra members walked out on the stage to speak with the remaining members of the audience. Oswald also remained and served as interpreter, giving the Americans the spectators' programs to autograph. He struck up a conversation with a tall American in glasses. The American had studied Russian for more than ten years. Oswald praised the orchestra and told this American that, to Oswald, he seemed to come from another planet. In further conversations with the orchestra members *Oswald observed that he "would like to go home"* (author's emphasis).

Obviously this confession does not agree with Miss Mallory's recollections. It is entirely possible that Oswald still did not want people to know his intentions. He considered it appropriate to say one thing in the hotel lobby but expressed his true feelings after the performance. While the orchestra remained in Minsk, he sent another letter to the embassy, asking for permission to return.

Despite his campaign to return to the United States, Oswald's lifestyle did not really change. He remained indifferent to his job, invited friends to his apartment, attended parties at various institutes, and struck up acquaintances with girls.

On March 17, 1961, Oswald attended a dance at the Medical Institute. He met a girl named Marina who would become his wife after a short courtship. Marina Prusakova was only twenty-one years old when she met Lee Harvey Oswald for the first time. Her biography was short, and the KGB checked her background quickly and efficiently. Inquiries were sent to her former residences and places of study. Information about her relatives, her political views, and her lifestyle was compiled. The only secrets she kept were her own. There was no reason to oppose the marriage.

When Oswald applied for a marriage license at city hall in Minsk, a letter was sent to OVIR in Moscow. No objection was registered, and they were legally married on April 30. Marina, naturally, was included in the KGB's continuing surveillance.

Despite indications that Oswald wanted to return to America, he did not mention his desire to Marina during their courtship or the early days of their marriage. After they were married for two months, he told her of his wish. She was startled but supportive.

Oswald once again managed to introduce a new element in his relationship with the KGB. His desire to return to America was viewed positively, for he was an annoyance and they would be glad to get rid of him. The new development concerned his marriage to a Soviet citizen who had become pregnant. The question now was whether to let the young couple leave. A new plan had to be developed to deal with this event.

Surveillance indicated that the Oswalds had a normal family life. They spent their free time together. Marina's uncle's family accepted Oswald warmly. They did not seem to mind that he was a foreigner, much less an American. Marina confided to a friend that they lived amicably but that Lee could be extremely stubborn at times.

A check of the workplace showed that Oswald was well behaved. He did not have a drinking problem, though once he went to a restaurant after hunting with his friends and got drunk. The system for overseeing Nalim sprang into action. The incident became known at the factory, and his drinking companion was held responsible and reprimanded.

In July, Oswald inquired about the price of round-trip plane tickets to London. While this information was being analyzed, Oswald visited the American embassy in Moscow with his wife. She was allowed into the building. When friends inquired as to the reason for his trip, he replied that they had gone to a film festival.

It was clear that Oswald wanted to return to America and take his wife with him. The KGB feared that Marina might be used for anti-Soviet propaganda in America. Russian intelligence also did not want to set a bad precedent for her friends and acquaintances. The KGB decided, therefore, that it would be preferable if Marina remained in the Soviet Union. Preliminary steps were taken to achieve that goal. Her friends noticed that she had become more irritable and withdrawn. They tried to dissuade her from leaving the Soviet Union. People at work told her that if she moved to America she would be used to make slanderous statements about life in the

Soviet Union. Indignantly, she answered, "I love my husband, I am expecting a child, and I must go with him. But what you're afraid of will never happen. I will not allow myself to slander our life."

Efforts to pressure Marina continued. In July she was expelled from the Young Communist League. Her uncle's family severed relations with Marina and Lee, but these efforts backfired. Marina's anger made it easier for Oswald to influence her. She, too, became more stubborn in her desire to emigrate.

By August, when Oswald had filed all the necessary documents for processing their exit visas with OVIR, it became clear that any further attempts at dissuading Marina would only have negative consequences. Such tactics ceased.

Oswald's initial arguments for becoming a Soviet citizen were no longer taken seriously. The next step for the KGB was to consider what occurred during his visits to the American embassy, including the possibility of his being given an espionage assignment in exchange for the right to leave. Surveillance was heightened to ensure that he did not "gather any information of a military and economic character." Conceding the likelihood of the couple's return to the United States, the KGB prepared measure to prevent them "from being used in anti-Soviet activities upon completion of their journey."

This strategy involved treating him well at work. A transcript from the radio factory indicated how Oswald's behavior changed:

> After his July trip to Moscow he began to show complete apathy toward his work. Often he did not work at all. Such behavior provoked the indignation of the workers, who were not satisfied with his idleness. The foreman of the shop demanded that he work like everyone else. Oswald did not like this and felt that the foreman had offended him. The party organization politely explained that he was violating the work ethic. After all, he was being paid for his labor.

It appears that those who were assigned to handle Oswald at the factory were more successful than Marina's colleagues had been. Despite his refusal to work, they did not make any superfluous demands and did not insult him. They paid close attention to him as part of the plan to minimize the chances of his being used for anti-Soviet activities in America.

Marina's uncle was also persuaded to soften his stance toward his niece and her husband. After relations had resumed, Oswald was asked why he wanted to go back. He stated that his decision was based on the fact that Soviet law prohibited such a return and he felt that this was unfair. He said that the American embassy had promised to pay for the trip. He was also told that he would not be arrested in the United States for defecting to the Soviet Union and that he believed this to be so. Oswald was uncharacteristically forthright about his future plans. If he had any difficulty finding work, he planned to live with an uncle. He also promised Marina's relatives to reconsider his decision. In the fall of 1961, Marina began to waver in regard to their departure but was swayed by her worry about what kind of life she could have with Oswald's child in the Soviet Union.

Oswald still did not tell his friends about his decision to leave. He lost all interest in his job. When the foreman asked him why he wasn't working, Oswald rudely answered, "I do what I want." The factory's administration continued to treat him gently. Oswald was still paid. Only once did they display any vindictiveness. In November a group from the factory planned an excursion to Moscow. Oswald signed up for the trip, but the shop's party secretary did not permit him to go. Oswald's reaction was sharp and negative.

The period from late summer to early fall was characterized by Oswald's growing irritation with the Soviet officials' silence regarding his request for an exit visa. He complained to the American embassy, to relatives in America, and to OVIR. He also wrote to U.S. senator John Tower of Texas, intimating that he was held against his will in the Soviet Union.

Oswald became more open in his feelings toward America. When his relatives sent books and magazines, he gave them to girls and stressed that they were from America. Previously he had condemned discrimination, and now he announced, "I'm a southerner. I don't like Negroes, anyway." For the KGB the logical conclusion, based on all their observation, was to give him the visa and let him go. On November 21, 1961, the Belorussian KGB reached the same conclusion. The Second Chief Directorate of the KGB and the Council of Ministers of the USSR still had to give their approval. It was not known how long this would take, but in the beginning of January, Oswald's residency permit had again expired. Once more he had officially become a stateless person.

The Minsk police department began to gather the necessary documents to renew his permit to reside in the Soviet Union. A character reference was needed from the factory. When contacted, the following report was submitted:

> Employed from January 13, 1960, Oswald has not sufficiently mastered his qualifications. He displays no initiative in increasing his skill.
>
> Citizen Oswald has been oversensitive to foremen's remarks and careless in his work. He does not take part in social activities in the shop and is very withdrawn.

Clearly, Oswald had made no effort to strengthen his Marxist ideas or to improve his work skills. At the same time, he certainly had not endeared himself to Soviet officials.

During this period a change in KGB leadership occurred. Vladimir Semichastny replaced Aleksandr Shelepin as chairman. I talked to Semichastny thirty years later.

Q. When did you first encounter Oswald? Who made the reports and suggestions? What was decided regarding him?
A. This happened literally during the first days of my administration. At the end of 1961 the question concerning Oswald's return arose. Minsk concluded that permission be granted. But before making a final decision we had to take into account the opinions of the First Chief Directorate of the KGB, responsible for foreign intelligence, similar to the CIA. The head of that agency told me that Oswald was of no interest to intelligence. A week later the same opinion was expressed by the Second Chief Directorate, responsible for counterintelligence within the Soviet Union. When I asked him how to proceed, he answered, "Who the hell needs Oswald?" Both directorate heads briefed me on Oswald's complete history. It

was clear that he was of no use as an operative. Their impression of him was that he was a gray, mediocre personality.

We had no relationship with Marina; Oswald found her himself. Why he married her was incomprehensible to us; Marina was also of no use to us. There was absolutely no need to set any obstacles in their way and to let them go. By this time we were certain that this kind of person could not be a U.S. intelligence agent. We decided that his actions were based on individual motivations. Operatives tracking him in Moscow were actually offended. They wondered if the enemy considered us so stupid that they would send us this "garbage."

I recommended to the Supreme Soviet that no obstacles be placed in front of Oswald and his wife on their way to the United States.

In judging the second round up to this point, Oswald scored by obtaining permission to leave the USSR. The KGB knew that the former marine was not a spy and that he was of no use as a Soviet spy.

The family received permission to leave on December 25. If this was their joyous Christmas present from the KGB, then Oswald came up with a New Year's surprise in return. Days before the new year, operatives had uncovered that Nalim had a new pastime. He had decided to build bombs. This was not a hypothetical hobby, since he had already built two iron casings, one box-shaped and the other cylindrical. Each contained two compartments; one filled with shot and the other with explosives. He had also prepared paper-tube fuses, 4–5 centimeters long and 2 millimeters in diameter. They were to be filled with gunpowder, with the fuse designed to last approximately two seconds. Nalim concealed his new toys from his wife and stored them at home. Nothing related to the construction of the bombs was done at the factory, where it would have undoubtedly attracted attention.

As recently as November it had been decided at the highest levels that Oswald was not involved in espionage activities. Now this bizarre activity. The KGB did not quite know what to make of it. The possibility could not be excluded that Nalim would commit a last hostile act before his departure from the Soviet Union. Based on this development, surveillance levels against Nalim had to be increased, especially before different celebrations, congresses, and high-level political meetings.

On January 3, 1962, Oswald was observed leaving his apartment with a wrapped parcel, which he clutched tightly to his chest. The parcel clearly contained his single-barrel rifle. To the consternation of his fellow passengers, he boarded a streetcar with the rifle in plain sight. He ended up pawning it at a sporting-goods store for eighteen rubles. This rifle had originally been prominently displayed on a wall in his apartment, but lately it had been gathering dust in a closet. Oswald told his friends that he had tired of hunting and preferred fishing.

Just as it appeared that Nalim's behavior had become more quirky and unsettling, it was learned that he could not obtain sufficient powerful explosives for his "home-made toys." He ultimately threw out the bomb housing, thereby bringing his "hobby" to an unclimactic close. The KGB was greatly relieved, but it did not discount the possibility of another weird act before his departure.

After Oswald obtained Soviet consent for an exit visa, he exchanged "enemies" and began focusing all his attention on America. His daily concern now was to gain permission for his wife to leave. He continued to work on making financial arrangements. To borrow and mix a metaphor from another sport, he became both toreador and bull. He waved his goal like a red cape and charged, using all his strength and not stopping for anything.

On February 15, Marina gave birth to a daughter, whom they named June. Now Oswald was not so eager to pursue his departure. He wrote his brother Robert and told him that he would like to stay until the fall, for he enjoyed spring and summer in Russia. In April he took his vacation. He had expressed the desire to take a trip, probably to Vilnius, since it was inexpensive and nearby. He remained in Minsk and frequented parties, often without his wife. He continued to befriend new girls. His relatives from America sent him reading material, mainly science fiction.

As to Oswald's married life, within a few months of his marriage he had already begun to show features of abusiveness in his relations with his wife. In one such family scene, the pregnant Marina asked Oswald to open the window to allow some fresh air in. In response he snapped that *he* was cold. In spite of his wife's pleas, he did not appease her. He was also very choosy about his food. He demanded that she prepare only certain favorite dishes. And God forbid that Marina should forget his clean laundry! If he was without some specific piece of clothing, she was immediately reprimanded. Such family scenes characterized their life together until their departure for the United States.

As early as March, Oswald became particularly interested in Gary Powers's interrogation upon the pilot's return to the United States. Oswald noticed an article about Powers in *Izvestia* and read it carefully. He asked friends what they had heard about this case and told them that he intended to follow it by listening to the Voice of America. Evidently he connected his fate to Powers's. He wanted to learn how Powers was treated in America, because he felt it would affect his situation. He intimated that he knew something about U-2 flights.

American officials notified Marina in March that she had been issued a visa. In May, the Oswalds were scheduled to appear and sign the final papers. Lee quit his job on May 18.

The KGB's plan remained the same: to watch Oswald carefully for anything unexpected and pay special attention to ensure that he had the proper impression of "Soviet reality."

Oswald received his Soviet exit visa on May 22. The family was scheduled to leave for Moscow on the twenty-third. Oswald finally told his friends about his departure. He spent his last evening in Minsk visiting these friends and saying good-bye. The couples' closest friends were invited to a party at his apartment. This group accompanied them to the train station. KGB operatives stood by to make sure that they boarded the train.

Other operatives said the final good-bye at the border. They carefully checked the departing family's luggage. Notes describing Oswald's stay were not found. It seemed that he intended to publish a book upon his return to the United States. His notes totaled fifty pages, but their contents could not be determined.

On August 10, 1962, the head of Belorussian KGB signed a

decree that "the case was concluded with his departure and that the files be placed in the archives."

The bell sounded. Round two, two and a half years in duration, was over. Apparently the judges and the participants felt that not only was the round over but the entire bout as well. But the future will show that although one of the opponents left the ring, he did not take his gloves off for long.

3

Oswald in Mexico City: Provocateur or Visitor? (September 1963)

My method of joking is to tell the truth. In this world there is nothing funnier.
—George Bernard Shaw

Caveant consules! (Be watchful of consuls)
—a Latin saying

On Friday, September 27, 1963, at approximately twelve-thirty in the afternoon, someone rang the buzzer outside the Soviet embassy gate to the sentry's booth situated near the entrance to the compound. Peering through the window, the sentry saw a stranger standing there. He pressed a button, which automatically opened the gate, and went out to meet him. Upon entering the embassy grounds, the stranger turned to the sentry and said in Russian, "I'm an American and would like to speak to someone from the consulate."

"Come in and wait here." The sentry led the visitor into the consulate area and stepped into the consul's office. "Valery Vladimirovich, there's someone outside. He speaks Russian. Says he's an American and wants to speak to one of the consular officers."

"I'll be out in a minute. Let him wait."

Valery Vladimirovich Kostikov was one of the consulate employees who on that particular day was receiving visitors from eleven in the morning until one in the afternoon. After a few minutes, Kostikov went out into the reception area. Rising from his chair to meet him was a young man about twenty-five years old. When asked in English the purpose of his visit, the stranger looked skeptically at Kostikov and said, "I would like to speak with one of the *Soviet* consular officers." He emphasized the word "Soviet," obviously doubting Valery's nationality. Indeed, Kostikov looked more Latin American or Arabic than Russian. Amused by the stranger's request, he pulled out his diplomatic ID and showed it to the visitor. He then invited him into his office.

Kostikov took his seat behind the consul's desk, while the stranger sat down at another desk attached to it. The young man spoke first, announcing that he had come to Mexico from the United States to ask for a visa to the Soviet Union. He said that he had lived there a few years ago and had married a Soviet citizen who was now in the United States with their child. He explained that he was under constant surveillance in the United States by the FBI, and as a result, he wanted to return to the USSR He then said that the "local authorities" were also persecuting him and his wife, making life in America unbearable.

To support his claims, the stranger presented his American passport, issued in the name of Lee Harvey Oswald, and pulled a rather hefty package of other documents from his jacket. He then offered the package to Kostikov. As he quickly glanced at the contents, Kostikov saw certain papers that corroborated the visitor's claim of having lived in the Soviet Union. Kostikov interrupted the American and said that another consular officer would have to address his particular question and asked him to wait outside again in the reception area. Kostikov closed the door behind him and rang the embassy. The consular department was situated in a small one-story building off to the side of the embassy. I was working in the office of the *rezidentura* when Nina, our secretary, called me to the phone.

"Listen, some gringo is here," Kostikov said at the other end of the line. "He's asking for a visa to the Soviet Union. Supposedly he already lived there, married one of our girls. They live in the States, but the FBI is harassing them. Come over here and get to the bottom of this. It seems to be more in your line of work. I'm in a hurry."

"Okay, I'll be right over." An American in my field. Hmm, this could be interesting, I thought, as I began putting away my papers for the day. Back then the consular division consisted entirely of the consul and two employees with diplomatic status. Outside the embassy we passed ourselves off as the consul and the two vice consuls. All responsibilities of the consular division were divided equally among the three of us, as were the duties that made up our main "lines" of work. Our jobs in the consulate were merely a cover. In fact, all three of us worked for KGB foreign intelligence and belonged to various subdivisions of Moscow Center.

The head of the consular office, Pavel Yatskov, and I were from the same subdivision—foreign counterintelligence—responsible for security abroad. Therefore, whenever we had any dealings with a foreign visitor, and especially with an American, that involved a consular matter, we would view that individual through that specific lens of our intelligence interests and decide how to proceed in our further relations with him. As a rule, we would help each other out and "transfer" our visitor to the one among us who might have the most interest in him.

On the way over to the embassy, my wife, who was taking our children for a walk in the garden, joined me, figuring that I was heading home on my lunch break.

"Wait for me at the entrance," I told her. "We have a visitor, and I might be delayed."

As I approached the small building that housed the consular division, I saw a stranger, apparently twenty-five to twenty-seven years old, standing on the steps and leaning against the doorpost. He appeared to be European or American. He was of medium height, with a longish face, a narrow chin, and a high forehead that clearly tended toward baldness. I would have called him a brunet.

The first impression I had of this stranger was his aloofness. He seemed to be looking beyond me, absorbed in his thoughts, and did not even react as I approached him. He was clad in a light jacket, a sport shirt with an unbuttoned collar, and either gray or brown slacks that were wrinkled. I greeted the stranger with a nod. He responded in kind.

"Is this the gringo you're talking about?" I asked Valery.

Valery nodded. "He keeps saying the FBI is after him and that he lived for a while in the Soviet Union. Those are his papers over there. That's why I called. I thought he might be of some interest to you. Listen, I gotta run. I have a date in the city. I'll see you later this evening. If there's anything to this, tell the sentry or leave a note."

Valery opened the door to the reception area and invited the stranger into the office. Without mentioning my name, he introduced me as the vice consul who would handle his question and then beat a hasty retreat.

The visitor, who appeared to be in a state of physical and mental exhaustion, accepted my offer to sit down. But he suddenly became more focused as he explained to me the reason for his visit. He repeated everything he had already told Valery. Over the course of our conversation, the visitor's mood changed from discomfort to a state of great agitation, creating the impression of a high-strung, neurotic individual. In order to give him a chance to calm down, I paused in my questioning and looked over his documents. Everything seemed to be in order regarding his American passport. Other documents testified to his stay in the Soviet Union. One of them was a marriage certificate to a Marina Prusakova. Among the others, one that stood out was a letter to the Soviet embassy in Washington that had something to do with travel for his family to the USSR and, it seems, the embassy's refusal to grant his request. Seeing that Oswald had cooled off a bit, I renewed our conversation.

When I asked him to provide specific information about the FBI's following him, he replied that it all began after his return from the USSR, where he had gone as a Marxist sympathizer. When the couple returned to the United States, both were interrogated. His wife was still being questioned in his absence, and he claimed that the FBI had even been in contact with his friends. When I then asked him the reason for his return to the United States, Oswald fidgeted, changed the subject, and avoided answering the question. I realized that he did not want to state the reason, which put me on my guard.

From the very outset of our conversation, I had no doubt that Oswald had been within the sights of my colleagues while in the USSR. But the thought of the KGB's having any operational connection to him quickly disappeared. From my first impressions of him it was clear that he was not suitable agent material.

Oswald maintained that as a result of the FBI's activities he could not find a good job and that the situation at home had become intolerable. Even though I had seen the letter to our embassy in the United States, I nonetheless asked him if he had appealed to the Soviet embassy in Washington. Oswald said that he had already sent a letter there and had been turned down. He later mentioned his fear that the FBI would arrest him for establishing contact with our Washington embassy. So as not to give the FBI additional cause to seize him, he decided to come to Mexico to follow through on his plan. Moreover, in the event that he should be allowed to return to the Soviet Union, he wanted to travel to Cuba first. In Mexico he could obtain visas to both countries at the same time.

The more I learned about Oswald and the more I observed him during the course of our conversation, the less I was interested in him. I silently cursed Valery for "transferring" him to me and decided that it was time to bring this meeting to a close. I had more important items on my agenda. I explained to Oswald that, in accordance with our rules, all matters dealing with travel to the USSR were handled by our embassies or consulates in the country in which a person lived. As far as his case was concerned, we could make an exception and give him the necessary papers to fill out, which we would then send on to Moscow, but the answer would still be sent to his permanent residence, and it would take, at the very least, four months.

Oswald listened intently to my explanation, but it was clear from his gestures and the expression on his face that he was disappointed and growing increasingly annoyed. When I had finished speaking, he slowly leaned forward and, barely able to restrain himself, practically shouted in my face, "This won't do for me! This is not my case! For me, it's all going to end in tragedy!"

I shrugged my shoulders and stood up, signaling the end of our meeting. Oswald's hands shook as he put the documents back into his jacket. I led Oswald through the reception area and showed him the way out of the compound. He departed, obviously dissatisfied with the results of our talk. He appeared to be extremely agitated. This was how Oswald's first visit to our embassy in Mexico ended.

Our meeting had been conducted primarily in Russian, but Oswald, possibly from the strain of being overly excited, often experienced difficulties in finding the proper Russian word and would switch to English. His pronunciation was bad, and he really mangled the grammar, but overall he was able to express his thoughts in our language. Not once during our conversation did he show any interest in knowing my name or who I was. This struck me as odd, because our American visitors usually wanted to know with whom they were dealing. I suspected the reason for this was that Oswald was so consumed by his own problems that he couldn't care less which Soviet representative listened to him. This suited me just fine.

I glanced at my watch. Oswald's visit had taken up almost one hour, and I had to be somewhere soon. On my way out of the embassy, I instructed the sentry to tell Kostikov that I had not promised our visitor anything. Then I stopped off at home for a bite to eat. My wife had grown used to my showing up late for lunch or missing it altogether and to my early departures and late arrivals. Resignedly, she rewarmed my meal and asked what time to expect me that evening. "Probably not too late," I said, and kissed her. I decided to check on our children in the other room, who were napping after lunch. Hearing their peaceful breathing, I left the apartment and headed toward the car.

As I drove along a specially chosen route to make sure that I was not being followed by anyone prior to meeting my contact, I inadvertently began thinking about our visitor to the embassy. I have to admit that his problems meant little to me. In fact, it was I who was disappointed at having spent time with another uninteresting American. For the slightly more than two years that I had been posted to Mexico, beginning in August 1961, I had received several American citizens at our embassy and therefore had already had some experience with them. The reasons for the visits were varied and, in some cases, amusing.

We were once called upon by an elderly and respectable-looking gentleman who said he had come to Mexico as a tourist and, after seeing the sign outside the embassy gate, simply decided to come in and talk to some real-live Russians, whom he had never met before in his life. He and I had a very pleasant chat in my office for about fifteen minutes, after which we firmly shook hands good-bye. On another occasion, I had to receive an American visitor who handed me six thick notebooks, completely scribbled over in tiny and absolutely illegible handwriting. He told me that they represented the record of his ongoing talks with Khrushchev. In the middle of our meeting, he suddenly cocked an ear and said, "Just a minute . . . Khrushchev is speaking to me again."

There were other visitors whom we waited for but whose appearance nonetheless was unexpected. These were individuals who lived and worked in the United States in interesting places, from the point of view of our intelligence, and who, in their visits to the embassy, offered us various bits of information or announced their readiness to cooperate with us.

The interest shown in such visitors was not exclusively confined to the former Soviet intelligence service. It was one of the functions of "legal" rezidenturas of many intelligence services under the cover of official representations, such as embassies or other institutions. Each had its tactics and methods for handling such cases, in addition to its own criteria for determining whether a visitor was a "well-wisher" or a "declarant," to put it in intelligence terminology. What guided us most of all—and I do not think I am mistaken in assuming that it was the same for all intelligence services—in working with such foreigners was the principle of "fifty-fifty." This meant that the probability of obtaining a source of good, possibly even valuable, information was equal to the probability that the source was a "plant," that is, a trap set by the enemy with unpredictable consequences.

As I thought about that day's visitor and weighed the criteria of one "fifty" against another, I came to the conclusion that he fit neither category, meaning that he did not have any interest for us, and certainly not for my own subdivision of counterintelligence, which included the United States, Canada, and Latin America. It was perfectly clear that our internal counterintelligence back home had already studied him. Now that he was under FBI surveillance, let him be their headache, I thought.

The meeting with my contact went smoothly. Toward evening I

returned to the embassy to make a few notes, and then prepared to go home. A light was burning in the consular division, so I decided to investigate. Valery was sitting in the office playing chess with one of the employees from the Ministry of Foreign Affairs. He had nothing to do with our intelligence operation.

"What's up, Valery? How come you're not going home?"

"The sentry told me you were here, so I thought I'd wait for you. I'll win this game in a minute, and then we'll leave together. Watch me beat him."

Valery was an extremely skillful chess player. Rarely did anyone in the embassy manage to win against him. While I leafed through the evening paper, Valery's opponent, under threat of impending checkmate, resigned. Valery suggested we go to one of our favorite local cantinas for a beer.

Valery and I had both graduated from the translation faculty of the Moscow State Teacher Training Institute. He finished a year ahead of me, even though he was one year younger than I. Valery spent two years at intelligence school, after which he became an operative in the First Chief Directorate. Six months after completing the institute, I joined the staff of the Moscow Directorate, also as an operative, but in the counterintelligence division. During our time at the institute we knew each other only by sight. Since we both enjoyed sports, we would occasionally see each other at athletic events. Valery was good at track and field, especially in the sprints and hurdles. Indeed, an offer was made to him to turn "professional" sportsman.

One day we bumped into each other in one of the KGB's buildings. We struck up a conversation, reminiscing about our relatively carefree student years, and shared our impressions, as much as we could under the circumstances, about the nature of our work. It seemed we had several things in common, and soon after we were thrown together on the same case. Thus, our personal and professional lives had merged. After I was transferred to foreign intelligence, we began seeing quite a bit of each other on the job. Subsequently, we found ourselves preparing for an extended stay in Mexico in our respective subdivisions, but both under cover of the consular division. We arrived separately in Mexico in the summer of 1961. Our wives got to know one another, and our young daughters, who were of the same age, quickly became friends. Our families often spent free time together.

"Listen, Oleg," Valery began after we had sat down to our first mug of beer in the noisy cantina, a favorite spot among the local blue-collar crowd and a perfect place for us to discuss sensitive issues. "As soon as I came back from lunch and the sentry passed on your message to me, I got a call from the Cubans. It was Silvia Duran from the consulate. It turns out that our 'friend' had been to see them after us and supposedly told them that we had promised him a visa, so she decided to call and double-check. She asked specifically for me because this guy had given her a name that sounded like mine. I'd shown him my ID when he doubted I was Soviet. I told her we hadn't promised him anything and that even if we did begin processing his visa, it would take at least four months. She thanked me, and that's it. When he told me had lived in the Soviet Union, I decided not to probe too deeply. What do you think? Is our man schizoid?"

"I don't think so, judging by our conversation. But there's no doubt he's neurotic. That's for sure. You know, I don't think he's especially afraid of being followed. It seems like he's not telling everything. Do you think we should report this to Moscow Center? Since he already lived there, the VGU [Second Chief Directorate] is bound to have a file on him."

"Let's do it tomorrow morning, before volleyball," Valery proposed. "We'll report it to the Chief and make a decision then."

"Right. I got so wound up with all these meetings that I completely forgot about our game. Okay, let's drink up and go home, or else we won't be able to jump at all tomorrow."

Wednesdays at the Soviet embassy were set aside for sports. We would finish our work toward lunchtime, after which we would get together for the activities. The most popular sport in those days was volleyball, and we would play it literally to the point of exhaustion and at a height of more than two thousand meters above sea level. As a team, we took part in the city tournament and garnered one of the top spots against teams made up of university and college students, who were in their early twenties and used to the climate. In contrast, not one of our players was younger than thirty.

Weekends were free. On Saturday mornings we would participate in intense volleyball games on the embassy grounds until lunchtime. On Sundays we went for rides with our families into the country or to places that had swimming pools, which was a favorite pastime for our children.

On Saturday, September 28, 1963, a serious volleyball match was scheduled between the diplomats and a combined team from the military attaché and the trade mission. Essentially, it was a match between two rezidenturas: ours—the KGB—and GRU, military intelligence, since both teams were comprised almost entirely of officers from both services. All three of us, employees of the consulate, played for the "diplomats." The head of our consulate, Pavel Yatskov, although considerably older than us, kept himself in excellent physical shape and played like a professional in both volleyball and tennis. In chess he and Valery were fierce opponents.

We usually changed into our playing clothes in one of the offices belonging to the consulate. The entire consulate consisted of three rooms: a reception area; the consul's office, where meetings with visitors were held; and another room, communicating with the consul's office and connected to it by a door, where Valery and I had our desks. It was this office that also served as our dressing room on the days we played sports. This office would also play an integral role in the events that followed.

Pavel Yatskov was the first to show up at the embassy on this Saturday morning. He arrived around ten and went to the office to get ready to play. The games usually began after ten o'clock. Soon thereafter the sentry on duty knocked on the door and said we had a visitor, not Mexican in appearance, who asked to speak with the consul. The sentry had explained to the visitor through the embassy gate that today was not a workday and refused to let him enter. Pavel ordered the sentry to bring the visitor to the office. Shortly, the sentry opened the door, and the stranger entered.

Yatskov recalls his immediate perception of the stranger:

"A thin subject, of medium height and nondescript appearance, age twenty-five to twenty-seven, appeared in the doorway. He was carelessly dressed, in a gray suit. His pale features and the extremely agitated look on his face were especially noticeable. I told him to take a seat at the attached desk, and I sat down at my own. The visitor, without waiting for any questions, spoke to me in English. My limited knowledge of English nonetheless allowed me to understand that my guest was an American, a Communist, pro-Cuban, and that he was asking for a visa to Cuba and the USSR. I was also able to discern that someone was persecuting him and that he feared for his life. When I asked him if he spoke Spanish, he shook his head no. While relating his story, the foreigner fidgeted in his chair, and his hands trembled, as though he didn't know what to do with them. The conversation was strained due to the language difficulties. Then the door opened again, and Valery, obviously looking forward to the upcoming volleyball battles, stood smiling in the doorway. I was happy to see him, since I knew Valery spoke English.

Valery picks up the story: "I arrived about nine-thirty in the morning with my wife and daughter. I let them into the grounds, then headed toward the consulate to change my clothes. I flung open the door to the first office, and there I saw Pavel sitting at his desk, and at the attached desk to the right, his back to the window, was the American who visited us the previous day. He was disheveled, rumpled, and unshaven. He had the look of someone who was hounded and he was much more anxious than the day before. I greeted him, and he nodded in response. Pavel also seemed tense. He turned to me and said, 'Listen, help me out. I don't fully understand what it is he wants.' Without engaging Oswald in conversation, and it *was* he, I explained to Pavel that the visitor had been here the previous day. I had spoken with him. He requested a visa for an immediate trip to the Soviet Union, where he had already lived and where he had married a Russian woman. As a result, U.S. authorities were victimizing him, and the FBI was on his trail. Therefore, I turned him over to Oleg, who spent time explaining everything to him.

Valery continues, "At this point Oswald, on his own initiative, turned to me and quickly began to retell his story, which I had already partially heard from him and then from Oleg. He reported that he had been discharged from the U.S. Army a few years before, had traveled to the Soviet Union as a tourist, where he had remained for political reasons, and had lived for a while in Belorussia, where he married a Russian and returned to the United States. *He even dropped some hints that he had supposedly carried out a secret mission.* He announced that he was a Communist and a member of an organization that defended Cuba. Pavel interrupted his monologue and said, since he had been in the Soviet Union, lived and worked there, that he could probably explain himself in Russian and looked at him disapprovingly. Without answering, he switched over to broken Russian, in which the rest of the conversation was conducted, except in a few instances when Oswald experienced difficulty in expressing certain thoughts in Russian and inserted English words.

"While telling his story, Oswald again, as he had the day before, tried to support it by showing various documents, which I would have trouble listing now but as far as I can remember included some that had been issued in the Soviet Union. Looking over these documents, I took his American passport and asked him how he had come by the rather strange sounding Chinese name of Lee. Oswald answered that it was a fairly common name in America.

"Continuing the conversation, Oswald repeated his desire to quickly obtain a visa to the USSR, where he wanted to clear up questions about his living there on a permanent basis. He said he was motivated by the fact that it was very difficult for him to live in the United States, that he was constantly under surveillance, even persecuted, and that his personal life was being invaded and his wife and neighbors interrogated. He lost his job because the FBI had been around his place of employment asking questions. In recounting all this, he continually expressed concern for his life.

"In his words, he dreamed of returning to his former job in the Soviet Union and living quietly there with his family. He spoke with noticeable warmth about his wife and child.

"Throughout his story, Oswald was extremely agitated and clearly nervous, especially whenever he mentioned the FBI, but he suddenly became hysterical, began to sob, and through his tears cried, 'I am afraid . . . they'll kill me. Let me in!' Repeating over and over that he was being persecuted and that he was being followed even here in Mexico, he stuck his right hand into the left pocket of his jacket and pulled out a revolver, saying, 'See? This is what I must now carry to protect my life,' and placed the revolver on the desk where we were sitting opposite one another.

"I was dumbfounded and looked at Pavel, who had turned slightly pale but then quickly said to me, 'Here, give me that piece.' I took the revolver from the table and handed it to Pavel. Oswald, sobbing, wiped away his tears. He did not respond to my movements. Pavel, who had grabbed the revolver, opened the chamber, shook the bullets into his hand, and put them in a desk drawer. He then handed the revolver to me, and I put it back on the desk. Oswald continued to sob, then pulled himself together and seemed indifferent to what we had done with his weapon. Pavel poured Oswald a glass of water and handed it to him. Oswald took a sip and placed the glass in front of him.

Valery concludes: "At this moment Oleg literally flew into the room with his athletic bag and stopped in his tracks when he saw all of us sitting there. I looked at my watch. It was a little after ten o'clock, meaning we were already late for our volleyball game."

Pavel Yatskov picks up the story: "When I unloaded the revolver, it had a short barrel, but it was of impressive size, with a wooden handle. I think it was a Smith and Wesson, though I don't recall now if the chamber held five or six bullets. Oswald began to droop. Most likely the peak of his tension had passed, but his eyes were wet with tears, and his hands shook. I poured him a glass of water and offered it to him. Oswald, without thanking me, took a few swallows and placed it down in front of him. I began to console him, saying that it might all seem terrible to him, since the reasons for his being victimized were not immediately evident. Valery repeated a few of my sentences in English. Regarding his visa to the Soviet Union, we explained our rules once again, but in view of his condition, I offered him the necessary forms to be filled out. If he thought this was acceptable, we would send them on to Moscow, but it was absolutely out of the question that we would issue a visa to him at that very moment.

"In response to his persistent requests that we recommend that the Cubans give him a visa, as an alternative to obtaining our visa, we told him that Cuba was a sovereign nation and decided visa questions for itself. Oswald had explained his desire to travel to Cuba earlier in the conversation saying he wanted to help the Cubans 'build a new life.'

"He then discussed his correspondence with the Soviet embassy in the United States, in which he sought to return to the USSR. He spoke of the employees of the consulate as apathetic bureaucrats who 'looked at his report officially and simply did not want to understand him.'

"Oswald gradually calmed down, evidently after having understood and reconciled himself to the fact that he was not about to get a quick visa. He did not take the forms we offered him. His state of extreme agitation had now been replaced by depression. He looked disappointed and extremely frustrated. Valery and I exchanged glances and let it be known that the subject of this conversation had been exhausted and that it was time to break it up. I rose from the table. Oswald got up from his chair, and simultaneously grabbed the revolver and stuck it somewhere under his jacket, either in a pocket or in his belt. Turning to Valery, he once again said something about being followed. I bent down to get the bullets from the desk drawer. I then handed them to Oswald, who dropped them into a pocket of his jacket. We said good-bye with a nod of our heads. Valery also stood, calmly opened the door leading into the reception area, and after letting him go first, followed right behind him. At the same time Oleg came in through the other door."

In recalling my own impressions: "Lidia [my wife] was delayed in getting the kids together to go to the embassy, so I hurried them along. It was almost ten. As we lived practically across from the embassy, all we had to do was cross the street and turn down the nearest lane. The entire walk took only a few minutes. As soon as we entered the grounds of the embassy, I quickly headed toward the consulate. Voices and the sound of the ball being hit were already coming from the volleyball court. It was clear that everyone was warming up. I swung open the door to the first office, where I saw the following picture: Sitting behind the desk looking quite serious was Pavel; behind the adjoining table, turned halfway toward the entrance, his back to the window, sat the American visitor of the previous day. Papers which he had shown me the day before were spread out on a table in front of him, and to his left lay a short-barreled revolver with, I think, a brown handle.

"At the same desk, across from Oswald, sat Valery, who was explaining something to him. The American seemed to me more worked up than he had been the previous day. He hardly reacted at all when I showed up, only slightly turning his head and glancing in my direction. Then he began talking again. I saw that his eyes were red from crying. Having exchanged glances with my colleagues, I realized that it was a difficult conversation and that my presence was superfluous. But taking into account the unusual situation and knowing from yesterday's conversation the easily excitable nature of our visitor, I decided to stay and give my friends some backup. I shut the door, walked out into the embassy courtyard, and warned the sentry standing at the entrance not to let anyone into the consulate. If the volleyball players asked about us, he was to tell them that the three of us were occupied with certain consulate matters and to start without us. Then I went into the second room of the consulate from the side of the courtyard and stood near the door to the neighboring office where the conversation was being conducted. The door was slightly ajar. Pavel was doing most of the talking, while Valery repeated a few sentences in Russian. Oswald only interjected a few brief answers, something having to do with the impossibility of living any longer in the United States. I understood that the conversation was almost over and that my colleagues were bringing it to a close.

"Soon after I heard the sound of two chairs being moved back and almost simultaneously the sound of a drawer in the desk being opened. The desk was metal, and the opening and closing of its drawers made a specific noise. I opened the door a bit wider and observed that Pavel, who was standing, took something out of the drawer. Oswald had also stood up. Valery was standing off to the right. At that moment I distinctly heard Oswald say that he was afraid to return to the United States—where he would be killed. 'But if they don't leave me alone, I'm going to defend myself.' Valery confirms that these were Oswald's words.

"It was said without mentioning anyone in particular. At the time this phrase meant nothing to us. What happened to him in his own country was his problem. We recalled these words only on that fateful November twenty-second. When I led Oswald out of the reception area into the courtyard and showed him the way to the gate, he pulled his head down, and raised the collar of his jacket to conceal his face and thus attempt to avoid being clearly photographed. After he walked outside the gate I saw him turn to the right.

"After Oswald had left, the three of us remained in the consulate and exchanged our impressions about this strange visitor. As a result of our two-day conversations with him we decided we could not take Oswald seriously. His nervousness during the conversations, his rambling and even nonsensical speech at times, his avoidance of answering specific questions, and the shifts from strong agitation to depression gave us reason to believe that his mental state was unstable or that, at the very least, he suffered from a serious nervous disorder. As far as fearing for his life in the United States, it was difficult for us to judge because he had declined to give us a direct answer as to who was behind this threat to him. *However, he linked the FBI with all the adversities and difficulties of his life in America.* From Oswald's stories and the documents he had shown us relating to his recent past, it was obvious that he must have been under observation by our internal intelligence organs in Moscow and Minsk, and it is possible that he was also known to our rezidentura in Washington. Although we had evaluated this trip to Moscow as just another whim on his part, we nevertheless decided to inform Moscow Center about his visits in general terms.

"It was agreed that Pavel and Valery would immediately send a report about today's visit to the rezident and would also report it in a coded cable to Moscow Center. On that day the report went to the Center, but we received no response. For us this telegram subsequently became a 'life preserver' which we had thrown to ourselves. After November 22, all three of us, plus the rezident, could have become the same kind of patsies that many still consider Oswald to be in this drama, but I'll speak more about this later.

"Thus we reported to the rezident. That is, instead of reporting the meeting with Oswald before the volleyball game, we had to put off the game and file the report instead. The team of 'diplomats' lost, which was possibly attributable to our absence, but we could not have known then that by not participating in the embassy volleyball game we would become participants in a tragic international enigma still unresolved after thirty years."

4

Time-out

The bond which holds all civilization together implies the exchange of emotions, facts, ideas or knowledge.
—C. Northcote Parkinson, *Parkinson's Law*

We felt a sense of guilt for the defeat of our volleyball team, a game in which we could not play because of our talks with Saturday's psychotic or maybe schizoid visitor. But this feeling did not last for long, for in the beginning of October we received news from Moscow that Yuri Gagarin and Valentina Tereshkova, the first man and woman in space, were coming to Mexico later in the month. The ambassador convened a meeting of the diplomatic corps and assigned each diplomat specific tasks for the upcoming visit. A similar meeting was held in the rezidentura. The consular division was to meet the cosmonauts at the airport and deliver them to the embassy. The order from Moscow Center to the rezidentura was the usual one—provide security for the delegation. The main burden would fall upon counterintelligence, that is, upon Pavel Yatskov and me.

Life inside the Soviet colony began to buzz with excitement as soon as we learned about the cosmonauts' impending arrival. The children in the embassy school learned some poetry by heart and prepared a musical composition for the grand welcome of our illustrious guests. The women were busy with their hair and clothes, trying to squeeze out extra money from their husbands for new outfits. Meanwhile, the men calculated how many cocktail parties they would have to attend. But Pavel and I were preoccupied with one thing—security.

Days before the visit, Pavel represented the embassy in negotiations with the Mexican Ministry of Foreign Affairs to coordinate the efforts of both sides, with the aim of avoiding any untoward incidents during the cosmonauts' stay. I was working out the logistics of their reception at the airport, where, under consular cover, I had spent a great deal of time meeting and accompanying diplomatic messengers, members of the Soviet colony, and various groups. As a result, I had established good contacts there. Valery, as a consular employee, also spent entire days working on security-related questions.

On the eve of Gagarin and Tereshkova's arrival we were informed that the Mexicans had assigned a couple of men from the Federal Directorate of Security (Dirección Federal de Seguridad). The main service among Mexico's numerous police organs, it fulfilled the functions of counterintelligence and political police. In those days, the security officers had not yet been introduced into Soviet foreign institutions—embassies. Therefore, all contacts with the local security forces and special services in case of need fell upon the consular staff, heavily made up in the majority of foreign countries of counterintelligence agents. On the one hand, these encounters allowed the local special services to get a rather quick fix on the kind of "consuls" they were dealing with. On the other, it also gave us a perfect opportunity to establish and, in separate cases, develop the necessary contacts among their employees. If one of them suddenly had the urge to "share" some confidential information with us, he would know where to turn.

We entered into direct contact with our Mexican colleagues the day before the cosmonauts' arrival from Cuba. Some of them we already knew from before. They all belonged to FDS-a, which concerned itself with counterintelligence "servicing" of foreign embassies, especially Soviet and Cuban, and kept tabs on the Mexican Communist party and political emigration from other Latin American countries into Mexico. We were constantly bumping into certain members of the group at the airport while meeting and escorting our diplomatic couriers from Cuba.

Back then the only method of transportation linking Cuba to the outside world was the weekly flights on Mexican and Cuban airlines. Without exception, all passengers had to pass through strict control at the Mexican airport. They were photographed, and the information contained in their passports was recorded in a special list. It was precisely this procedure that was carried out by some of the FDS-a employees. Copies of the lists and photos were then handed over to the American embassy. The head of the group was someone named S, who maintained regular contact with representatives from the CIA and FBI working in Mexico under cover of the embassy.

On October 11, the day of the delegation's arrival, Pavel and I went to the airport on an "inspection" trip a few hours before its expected appearance. We were met there by one of the police officers responsible for maintaining order. The three of us then checked out the forces assigned to the task. A formation of police-academy students was positioned in ranks inside the airport. They had formed a human cordon from the runway to the cars waiting outside. It looked as if their safety would be guaranteed. We thanked the officers and continued with our inspection.

A crowd had already gathered inside the airport. All the newspapers had reported on the visit of the Soviet cosmonauts, especially Gagarin, who was popular the world over. Representatives of the press, cinema, and television gradually assembled near the entrance to the runway. In general, the situation did not cause us any particular concern, but we soon realized that our evaluation was erroneous. As the time of the flight's arrival approached, Mexican officials began showing up. Our ambassador was present. Embassy employees, along with their wives, were visible in the crowd, and someone had brought the children, even though we had strongly advised against it.

When the announcement was made that the Aviación Cubana flight was preparing to land, the crowd began buzzing in anticipation. Shortly before nine, I spotted my wife among the elegantly dressed and stylishly coiffed women from the embassy. I went over to her, handed her my movie camera to record the event, then pushed my way back to the airplane's ladder. Our ambassador,

Mexican officials, officers from the rezidentura, and our colleagues from FDS-a were already standing there. As soon as the airplane touched down and began taxiing toward its specially designated parking spot, the surrounding crowd began pressing in. To keep the crowd from pushing aside the VIPs on hand to meet the guests, we had to isolate them—and ourselves—from the crush.

After pushing the ambassador onto the ladder, we rushed toward the aircraft's door. Pavel and I stood near the entrance, exchanging greetings with the crew. Soon after, Gagarin, smiling as always, appeared in the doorway, followed by Tereshkova, the ambassador, and other members of the delegation. To free up the passageway, I stepped onto the top of the stairs, looked down, and instantly felt a little dizzy. Down below, the huge, faceless, dark mass, bristling with telephoto lenses and movie cameras, swarmed about, totally engulfing the bottom of the ladder. In another minute or two we would have to dive into this human sea and fend it away from our invaluable guests. And I had no idea how we were going to do it.

The ambassador was first down the stairs, followed by the head of the cosmonauts' party including the famous aviator Lieutenant General Kamanin, Gagarin's wife, Valentina, and others. Then the first man and first woman in space stepped out of the doorway together, raised their hands in greeting, and began their descent down the stairs.

As soon as they made their appearance, the crowd exploded with a deafening cry of welcome and applause. Bouquets of roses were thrown at Tereshkova. At the foot of the stairs I caught sight of my comrades from the rezidentura and our Mexican colleagues, their faces straining with tension, as they tightly locked arms and formed a small cordon around the ladder. I immediately joined the chain, and with great effort we managed to move away from the stairs in the direction of the entrance into the airport. At one moment it seemed as if the crowd picked us up and carried us there. I figured that the situation would be easier once we got to the entrance, since dozens of brave guards would be waiting there to help us. Meanwhile, the gap between us and our charges now disappeared completely, then increased just enough to give everyone a chance to breathe. Looking at Gagarin, I noticed that something resembling a smile was still on his face, but his eyes registered anxiety. The other guests were not smiling at all.

Finally, we reached the building and squeezed our way inside, where, as part of the program, the cosmonauts had to sign the guest book for honored visitors and be greeted by the city's municipal officials. While this ceremony took place, we continued to hold off representatives of the press and the public who were trying to force their way into the building. Several floodlights and the large concentration of people made the place incredibly hot. An uninterrupted barrage of camera flashes created the impression of a noiseless round of gunfire.

The first official ceremony ended, and we led our guests into the main area of the airport. It became immediately evident how wrong we had been. The guards we had expected no longer existed. Instead, their ranks had been squashed and mixed in with the crowd. We plunged into the human maelstrom, but because we were in an enclosed area, it was even more difficult to move forward here than out on the street. The crowd wanted to touch our visitors and shake their hands.

The Mexicans in general are very warm and open people, but they have this tendency to think that once they have shaken some VIP's hand, they are friends with that person forever. On a number of occasions this led to trouble for our young operatives (or case officers). For example, they would gleefully inform Moscow Center that they had made a contact who claimed to be close to high-ranking and potentially interesting individuals. As it turned out, though, these "connections" were based on nothing more than a handshake. Every person at the airport obviously wanted to take advantage of the opportunity to become acquainted with the "First Man and Woman of Space."

As we finally made it to the exit and burst out onto the street toward the waiting cars, we heard behind us the sound of breaking glass and loud cries for help. Apparently the glass walls and doors of the airport had not withstood the crush of people. The cars were also surrounded. After we somehow managed to get the cosmonauts seated in the large, open vehicle reserved for them, Valery and I simply threw the ambassador over the side of the same car.

He tried to protest, shouting, "What are you pushing me for!" Forgetting all rules of protocol in the heat of the moment, Valery and I snapped back at him. "Sit down, motherfucker!" After that he didn't argue anymore.

We hopped onto the sides of the vehicle, Valery to the left behind Gagarin and I to the right of Tereshkova. As our automobile, followed by the rest of the entourage, slowly pulled out into traffic, youngsters ran alongside, grabbing at the car and trying to shake the cosmonauts' hands. We had to fend them off, fearing that the cosmonauts could be thrown from the car or that someone could fall under its wheels. As I recall now, every step of the way, from the landing of the airplane to the cars outside, was accompanied by Mexican mariachi music.

Journalists estimated that the size of the crowd that day was at least fifteen thousand people, approximately one-third of them inside the airport. The newspaper *El Día* describes the scene as madness.

We were all able to breathe a little easier as our entourage picked up speed and headed downtown to our embassy. Along the way people would stop and wave and clap their hands as we passed.

A press conference was held immediately after we arrived at the embassy. Our colleagues from FDS-a had been invited, and together we raised toasts to the cosmonauts, to Soviet-Mexican friendship, and to our further cooperation. On the whole, the contacts we made with these people turned out to be very useful for our basic work in Mexico. But one of them subsequently became director of FDS-a and worked diligently with the CIA station to make life there as unpleasant as possible for us.

The rest of the cosmonauts' stay passed without further incident. Our main concern was to guarantee their safe passage through groups of people wherever they went and to keep their hands from coming unscrewed from all the many handshakes.

I remember two amusing incidents that occurred during their visit to the renowned Aztec pyramids in Teotihuacán. The Mexicans had organized a luncheon in a restaurant that is located in a cave near the pyramids. Gagarin and Tereshkova sat in the middle of a long table, flanked by our ambassador and Mexican officials.

A few of us from the rezidentura, along with our friends from FDS-a, sat at an adjoining table. At the very outset of the lunch, a waiter who was standing behind Tereshkova lifted a bottle of Coca-Cola over her head, apparently getting ready to open it. At just that moment a photojournalist prepared to get a picture of the scene. But the planned "provocation" did not escape our vigilant eyes. No way could we allow the first woman cosmonaut, a Soviet woman, to be used in an advertisement for a bourgeois soft drink! Our Mexican colleagues immediately roared at the waiter, who beat a hasty retreat, and the photographer was threatened with expulsion from the restaurant if he did not move farther away from the table. The incident passed without diplomatic protest.

After several toasts had been made, the Mexican colleagues at our table expressed a desire to treat the Soviet cosmonauts to a very popular national dish—fried bulls' testicles. We quietly informed Gagarin of the Mexicans' gesture but kept the nature of "the Mexican national dish" a secret from Tereshkova. Gagarin helped himself to a portion and passed the rest to Tereshkova, telling her that it was "delicious." After she had indecisively cut and tasted a small piece, Yura, with a bewitching smile on his face, leaned over and whispered in her ear what part of the bull she had just consumed. Her reaction was instantaneous. Choking, she sharply pushed the plate away, said something under her voice to Yuri, and turned away from him. He burst into laughter, while everyone at our table buried their faces in their plates.

The remainder of the cosmonauts' stay in Mexico went smoothly. As soon as we had seen them off to New York on the next leg of their journey, it was time to make preparations for the anniversary of the Great October Revolution of 1917. Whenever an important holiday or event took place in the Soviet Union, such as a party congress, the procedure was for Moscow Center to send long-winded, coded directives to all the foreign KGB rezidenturas.

Their contents varied little from one year to the next. Each one would explain the significance of the date, evaluate the situation in the world, and emphasize that the happiness of the Soviet people during these events could be overshadowed by provocations on the part of the imperialist enemies of socialism. It was therefore necessary to heighten political vigilance. A list of measures would then be given which needed to be adopted for ensuring the safety of Soviet institutions and citizens abroad. They would end with congratulations and wishes for success in our work.

These directives were written in standard Soviet boilerplate; only the names of the holidays and a few realities of the international situation changed. The long list of measures was virtually the same each time. When I was younger, I could not understand why money had to be spent on these coded "messages" when it was just as easy to send regular holiday greetings.

Only years later, when I had mastered the bureaucratic working of the Center, did I comprehend the "wisdom" of such documents. If something were to go wrong in one of the foreign posts during a holiday, who would be held accountable? By sending specific orders and a list of instructions, the Center covered its back. In the days before and after each event, these same directives virtually paralyzed the intelligence-gathering activities at the rezidenturas by forbidding any meetings with agents and "dubious and unverified contacts." For this particular anniversary, the situation in the world was relatively quiet, so no unusual security precautions were required.

The November holidays came and passed. The time approached for every operative of the rezidentura to submit his year-end report, along with his plan for the upcoming year, to the rezident. By the end of December the individual reports would be signed and sent to the corresponding departments of Moscow Center for which each agent of the rezidentura worked. These reports detailed our work with foreign agents, recruitment techniques, and the establishment and development of new contacts. We also reported on the information we had obtained and put to use during the course of the year.

At the same time, we had to draw up reports on the activities carried out under our assumed jobs within the embassy. Usually Pavel, Valery, and I would put our heads together and divide the report equally, each according to his responsibilities, before tying it all up into one cohesive report for the ambassador's perusal.

As a result of all these pressing matters during the final two months of the year, we completely forgot about our strange visitor in September. At the time, we had thought it advisable to inform the Center of his visit and let it go at that. We had no idea that our communiqué would save our careers and lives. Nor did we have any inkling that our report was being bounced back and forth in Moscow from one organization to another.

5

How the Buck Was Passed

It has been said that a former president carried a
sign on his desk that read "The Buck Stops Here."
This phrase, and perhaps the idea itself, originated
in the United States, but it had long been in circula-
tion in Britain and friendly countries. It means that
the one passing the buck shifts responsibility to
another person, who will be the one blamed in the
event of a mistake.

—C. Northcote Parkinson, *Parkinson's Law,*
"The Art of Passing the Buck"

In the early 1960s, the KGB's foreign counterintelligence unit—
Service 2—occupied several offices in the famous building on Lubyanka Square. This same building served as the headquarters for
the All-Russian Insurance Company before the revolution. Workers called this building "House 2," located at 2 Dzerzhinsky Square,
to distinguish it from KGB offices across the square.

The department of foreign counterintelligence concerned itself
with providing security to Soviet citizens and businesses located
abroad. It watched over delegates, those on business trips, and the
handful of tourist groups. The rare individuals who were on so-
called private visits, at the invitation of their relatives, were more
carefully monitored.

This division also was concerned with those people entering the
country. Material from Soviet embassies and rezidenturas were sent
to Service 2. Documents from tourists wishing to visit relatives or

return permanently to the Soviet Union were processed here and at the Ministry of Foreign Affairs.

All this material created a vast amount of paperwork and made up the routine aspect of the Service 2's work. It was time consuming and thankless. If a person whose documents were processed became the object of further investigation, security rules prohibited informing or "thanking" the worker responsible for uncovering the need to investigate. Naturally this process created feelings of alienation and excessive formality and procedure in the use of the gathered material. Since foreign counterintelligence was given the responsibility of gathering this information and passing it on to other departments, it would decide whether the subject might first be of interest to its own department.

In marked contrast to this bureaucratic paper mill, Service 2 was also involved in the penetration of American intelligence. In the world of counterespionage there is a sacred law: To ensure your own safety, you must have sources of information on the enemy side. Operating out of a rezidentura is one of the most effective means of penetrating foreign intelligence operations. Here counterintelligence operatives work in enemy territory under consular cover. They perform two basic functions: infiltrating American intelligence and protecting their own people and so-called clean, nonespionage Soviet citizens from being seduced.

Reconnoitering networks are established, and information about the enemy's counterintelligence is gathered. This work can be excruciatingly complicated, since it involves colliding with like-minded professionals on their own territory. But it is intellectually stimulating and very rewarding. An operations officer works out a combination of events that results in a new, valuable contact. Every tiny step, the slightest movement, can absorb months and even years in the attempt to recruit an agent from the enemy's special services.

A colleague and close friend, Yura Mostinsky, began his career at Service 2 in the 1960s. Yura was a novice at the time but became involved in this exciting aspect of counterintelligence. The department leadership felt that it was imperative to have new people develop their skills in this area. The "youngsters" learned how to analyze material coming from the rezidenturas and make recommendations based on it. They learned through the right steps and the blunders made by the operatives. Service 2 was the training ground for working as a rezidentura operative.

Yura and other novices were supervised by their more experienced colleagues, specifically those that had previously handled the same assignment. This way security was not breached, and the new people were able to learn how to answer an inquiry from the rezidentura, make a recommendation without offending the operative, and were taught how to edit drafts of letters signed by their bosses. This was the interesting part of the job and provided the possibility of promotion and recognition. All the young workers spent as much time as they could concentrating on this area.

Yura also had his share of routine paperwork. He did not find it stimulating, nor did it require a great deal of concentration, but it did teach him how to coordinate actions between the various security and governmental agencies, including the KGB and the Ministries of Internal and Foreign Affairs. Yura's assignment was to conduct correspondence concerning exit and entry visas of Soviet citizens from and into the United States. He also examined and distributed the documents of foreign tourists.

Sometime in the late summer of 1963, a pile of these documents arrived at his desk. The section head called him in to discuss one of the documents. Yura did not have a chance to read it, only to glance at the name in question: Prusakova-Oswald.

The head of Yura's section, Pavel Aleksandrovich, was a corpulent, fifty-year-old, no-nonsense type of person. He had worked in the KGB for many years and came to the American division of foreign counterintelligence because of his intuitive, almost uncanny ability to instantly detect what files to peruse. He was one of the few people in his position who did not speak English and had not lived abroad.

He told Yura, "This is a special case. It involves a Marina Prusakova asking to return to her relatives in Leningrad. But her husband's an American; she married him in Minsk and left for America a year ago. He was a former marine who came here as a tourist and didn't want to leave. Over a year ago, they asked us about his return to America, and we said he was of no interest to us. This appears to be a second request to return here. Clarify the situation in Leningrad; let me know what they think. Give me the report as soon as you've gathered all the pertinent information."

Back in his own office, Yura carefully read the file, which stated that Marina Prusakova had a stepfather and other relatives in Leningrad. Together with her husband, Lee Harvey Oswald, she requested permission to return to Leningrad permanently. The trip was planned for November–December 1963.

I met with Yura in the spring of 1992, and he told me about his involvement with the Oswalds.

"I came up with a plan for handling the inquiry. The first thing to do was to understand the reasons for Prusakova's request and then figure out which departments should be informed. I found background information in the archives. The Prusakova file, like most 'exit' files, was thin. It consisted of the usual special investigative material, that is, letters, place of birth, employers, schools, and so on. As I remember, it was started on her husband, and then her paperwork was included.

"My next step was to ask Leningrad KGB to utilize the local OVIR office to ascertain whether Marina's relatives were willing to let the Oswalds stay with them. Clarification of this question was standard in connection with an immigration request.

"The information about the husband chronicled his stay in Minsk. So I also informed the Belorussian KGB of Marina's request. I don't remember how much time elapsed before I got a reply from Leningrad. Local authorities learned that her stepfather had no interest in taking them in. The gathered data indicated that their relationship was strained. He characterized Marina as a woman of loose morals. In his words, her main goal was to marry a foreigner and leave the country with him."

Yura continued: "Intelligence had no interest in Oswald and his wife. If there had been any, it would have come through my department. All the information I had gathered pointed to the inadvisability of allowing the Oswalds to return in the current year. I presented a draft to Pavel Aleksandrovich, who edited it slightly and signed it rather quickly. All that was left for me to do was to send the document to the consular division of the Ministry of Foreign Affairs, which I did.

"Then we received a reply from the chairman of the Belorussian

KGB granting permission. I don't remember any weighty operational arguments being advanced in this letter. It's entirely possible that Minsk was already informed that the answer was no. It was too late to stop the process. If the letter had come sooner, it might have influenced the decision. When I was young, I thought it strange that if KGB Center showed no interest, why should a republic branch division create a fuss. Who needs the extra headache?

"After Kennedy's assassination, I learned that the FBI, after having searched Oswald's apartment, found the official Soviet rejection of his immigration request. Imagine what the reaction would have been if permission had been granted and it coincided with the assassination! It would have been taken as firm evidence of Soviet involvement, offering to shield the assassin after he completed his mission. It would be difficult to image a better propagandistic gift for certain groups!

"But this is speculation after the fact. After I sent my conclusion in regard to Prusakova, I forgot all about it. I was preparing to leave for an assignment in the United States."

I discovered documentary evidence of Yura's reminiscences in the Nalim, or Oswald, file in Minsk. Central foreign counterintelligence did ask the Belorussian KGB their opinion regarding the advisability of admitting the Oswalds, based on the applications made in the Soviet embassies in Washington and Mexico.

On October 8, 1963, Deputy Chief Dryakhlov of the Registry and Archives Department wrote a letter to the Ministry of Foreign Affairs, addressed to the head of the consular division, Vlasov. It concerned Special Communication No. 550 from Mexico, dated October 3, 1963, and asked that the Oswald's petition requesting immigration be checked over.

On the back of this letter there is a report that Marina petitioned for her own return to the Soviet Union. It further states that the Ministry of Foreign Affairs, agreeing with the Leningrad KGB's decision, refused her request on October 7, 1963. The Ministry of Foreign affairs had not yet received Lee Harvey Oswald's petition. The report is dated November 16, 1963.

On October 25, KGB deputy chairman of the Secretariat, S. Bannikov, sent the Ministry of Foreign Affairs the following letter:

To Deputy Minister of Foreign Affairs, Comrade V. V. Kuznetsov:

Comrade Bazarov (Soviet ambassador to Mexico) reports that an American citizen, Lee Harvey Oswald, came to the embassy in Mexico to request permanent immigration to the Soviet Union.

The letter continues with Oswald's history from 1959 up to his return to the United States. It concludes by stating, "In our opinion, it is inadvisable to permit Oswald to return to the Soviet Union."

These are the impressions former KGB chairman Vladimir Semichastny retains of that period:

Q: Were you aware of the attempts made by Oswald or his wife to return to the Soviet Union? What did the KGB do in connection with this?

A: I remember it being reported. But we clearly stated, "Not under any circumstances." We were against their return not so much for political reasons as for material considerations. We did not want to waste money on him with nothing in return. He was of absolutely no interest to us. Moreover, his scurrying about caused us headaches on more than one occasion.

Q: Did you know about Oswald's trip to Mexico in September 1963?

A: I learned of Oswald's visit to our embassy in Mexico only after Kennedy's assassination. Sakharovsky was asked the same question. He confirmed it and said that a coded telegram had come from our rezidentura there.

Immediately following the news of the assassination of President Kennedy in Dallas, the following memorandum was sent from the KGB to the deputy chairman of the USSR Council of Ministers:

TO: Comrade MIKOYAN, A. I.

DATE: 23 November 1963

In connection with the reports of foreign information agencies and the mass media about the arrest by American authorities of Lee Oswald, allegedly involved in the murder of the president of the United States, I can inform you of the following established data.

There then ensued the familiar litany of information about the circumstances of Oswald's arrival in the Soviet Union, his desire to become a Soviet citizen, his attempt at suicide after being denied that citizenship, his marriage to a Soviet woman, their departure for the United States, and their subsequent efforts to return to the USSR. But as far as I was concerned, the next paragraph of the memorandum was the most important one, and for obvious reasons:

In October 1963, Oswald visited the Soviet embassy in Mexico and again asked to be given political asylum in the USSR, citing the fact that, as secretary of a pro-Cuban organization, he was *being harassed by the FBI* [author's emphasis]. Oswald's solicitation was reviewed by the Ministry of Foreign Affairs and the KGB and rejected for the same reasons his previous requests had been denied.

The memorandum was signed by KGB chairman Vladimir Semichastny.

Thus, only while working on this book, almost thirty years after the fact, did I see for myself how far our "life preserver"—the information we had forwarded to Moscow about Oswald's visit to our embassy in Mexico City—had "floated" and what role it played at the time.

A former co-worker, retired colonel Vitaly Alekseevich Gerosimov, vice consul of the Soviet embassy, was stationed in the Washington rezidentura and relates the following:

"In 1963–64, I worked in the rezidentura under the cover of consular functions. I worked for counterintelligence and was responsible for the safety of Soviet citizens living in America permanently. In the summer of 1963, I was assigned Marina Oswald's case. I began to correspond with the petitioner. Although these letters were signed by the consul, I was responsible. She filled out all the necessary consular questionnaires, and I was prepared to forward them to the consular division in Moscow when Consul Reznichenko suggested that I find out why she wanted to return. This request needed the embassy's approval and the preparation of an inquiry to the Ministry of Foreign Affairs. This procedure was followed when there were further questions for the petitioner. As far as I remember, she never replied to this letter, and I can't venture a guess as to whether we sent her declaration with all the other documents to Moscow.

"In corresponding with Prusakova, we paid no attention to her husband. We had no information on Oswald prior to the assassination. If such material had been sent from Moscow Center, it would have come to me in my cover job. We were also very surprised by Prusakova's request, since there were only a handful of people like her living in the United States."

My colleagues, however, err slightly in their recollections. One did not know that her petition to return to the USSR had indeed reached Moscow Center and passed him by. The other, since he did not discover materials regarding this matter, decided that he was the first to work on the problem. Within the bureaucratic structure it is entirely possible that somebody sent Prusakova's request to the Ministry of Foreign Affairs, from where it automatically reached the Second Chief Directorate and sat in a cubbyhole gathering dust.

On April 9, 1963, an inquiry was sent from the PGU to Belorussian KGB. The contents of this inquiry clearly show that the person who sent it had no knowledge of the archival contents on the Oswalds. This operative did not find the time to check and in his letter to Minsk asks for information already available to him.

Nevertheless, Belorussia responded on April 16. The information is restated, and the Oswalds' correspondence with friends in the USSR is mentioned. In a letter that Lee had written, he stated that when he returned to America he was not under surveillance, but on one occasion two FBI agents *came to his apartment and "asked a lot of stupid questions."* Marina's letters were extremely reserved. She was satisfied with being in America but was not overly enthusiastic about the American way of life.

The document from Belorussian KGB noted that "while in Minsk, Oswald's and Prusakova's married life was unhappy. They often quarreled, as they were both quick-tempered."

The report continues that "we have no information about Oswald's behavior in America."

The Belorussian KGB's letter concludes with the following sentence: "I see no reason to impede Prusakova's return to her homeland." It was signed by the chairman of the Belorussian KGB.

The next letter from Belorussia was received by the PGU on October 21, 1963, in reply to the inquiry of October 8. This letter stated that the return of the Oswald family, after their brief stay in America, could be used for propagandistic purposes and put our nation in a favorable light. This question was approved by the Central Committee of the Communist Party of the Belorussian Soviet Socialist Republic. The letter was again signed by the KGB chairman of the Belorussian Council of Ministers.

However, since Moscow Center had already decided that the Oswalds' return was undesirable, the following response was made to Minsk:

> The decision of the Ministry of Foreign Affairs, dated October 7, 1963, denies Marina Oswald/Prusakova permission to return to the Soviet Union. This decision is based on her stepfather's refusal to take her into his home in Leningrad.
>
> Prusakova's husband, Lee Harvey, did not declare his intention to immigrate to the USSR.
>
> Your letter has been sent to the Archival Department of the KGB in the event that there may be further questions connected with this case.
>
> Chief, PGU Service 2
> November 22, 1963

Pay special attention to the date of this letter.

6

Tragic Days: The Reaction in Mexico City, Moscow, Washington, and Minsk (November 1963)

Now weigh within your own intelligence
how will and violence interact, so joining
that no excuse can wipe out the offence.
—Dante Alighieri, *The Divine Comedy*

Mexico, KGB rezidentura
Le mataron!
Mataron al presidente de los Estados Unidos!
Mataron a Kennedy!
(They killed him!
They killed the President of the United States!
They killed Kennedy!)

T hese words reached my ears from the street through the open
window of the consular division's office. Bounding into the embassy

courtyard, I saw a middle-aged Mexican woman convulsively grab at the bars of our gate, racked with sobs and shouting that President Kennedy had been killed. I ran back inside and turned on the radio: "President of the United States John F. Kennedy has died in a hospital in Dallas, assassinated during his ride through the city in an open limousine."

I have to admit that I do not recall this news having an immediate emotional effect. The president of the United States was too abstract for me as a human being, but I did view him as a formidable politician. I had respect for him as a confident and intelligent adversary.

A little more than a year before, during the Cuban missile crisis, when Kennedy played a leading role, if not the central role, our rezidentura in Mexico found itself in a critical zone, on the boundary of the triangle formed by Moscow-Washington-Havana. Moscow relentlessly demanded information from us. I had cultivated a source who was able to mingle among the anti-Castro émigrés in Mexico and the United States. Naturally, I had to make use of him even if doing so meant bending the rules of security. The world stood on the brink of disaster. I had to meet with him not just every day but sometimes twice a day. Everyone in our rezidentura during that dramatic moment in history ran around like hamsters on a treadmill.

As I listened to the report on the radio, the word "assassination" focused my thoughts: How? What? Why? At the same time, I thought of the international consequences and our safety here in Mexico. I decided to speak to our rezident about additional measures we should take for the embassy's security. I can't remember if I found him, but I do recall moving about the embassy, listening to the radio in different offices. Now it was being reported that the new president, Lyndon B. Johnson, had taken the oath of office inside Air Force One. One of our diplomats said that a suspect had been arrested, but he could not recall the name. I returned to the embassy and busied myself with some papers. Suddenly, Valery, his eyes bulging, flew into the office.

"Oleg, they just showed the suspect in Kennedy's death on TV! It's Lee Oswald, the gringo who was here in September! I recognized him!" he blurted out in what seemed like one breath.

"Him?"

We dashed out of the consulate toward the embassy, where the entire staff gathered around a television set in the first-floor lounge. Rudely pushing someone out of the way, we stood next to the screen. There, surrounded by police, was the suspected assassin. Valery and I looked at each other. Neither of us had any doubts. It was he, Lee Harvey Oswald. We could not take our eyes off the television set. When the report ended, we went outside and again exchanged a long, silent glance before exclaiming in unison, "Holy shit!" We were in a state of shock.

After a pause, Valery said, "You know, I felt something was wrong while I was driving around the city and I heard the name 'Lee' over the radio. When I returned, I ran into Pavel and told him of my suspicions. Now it's perfectly clear that it's him. Listen, I'm gonna run up and see the chief. He still doesn't know anything about this."

"Good idea," I replied. "I'll give instructions to the sentry. It's difficult to say what might happen now. After all, they know he lived in the Soviet Union, and they'll raise a stink about that. If it gets out that he was here, too, then we're really fucked. I'll join you in a bit."

Against all norms of standard protocol, Valery dashed into the office of the chief, who was in the midst of listening to a report from another agent. Forgetting even to excuse himself, Valery shouted, "It's him, him! Oleg and I just recognized him on TV. It's the same guy that was here twice in September."

The rezident raised his eyes and stared at Valery, his whole face registering displeasure at his presence in his office. "What are you doing bursting in like that and making a ruckus?"

Valery repeated what he had seen on television.

The rezident, a normally severe and scowling man, began to chuckle. "Well, what the hell, friends? It's our good fortune that we informed the Center about those visits on a timely basis. Prepare a telegram quickly, and don't forget to mention our cable number so-and-so from such and such a date in which we reported on Oswald's visits. Sit down and write it, Valery. Where's Pavel and Oleg?"

Valery said, "Oleg went to give instructions to the sentry, and Pavel, I think, is with the ambassador."

"Tell Oleg to get up here, too. We have to determine what additional safety measures should be taken." The rezident then picked up the phone and rang the ambassador on an internal line. Confirming that Pavel was indeed in the ambassador's office, he asked that Pavel be sent to him immediately.

Soon a coded cable marked "Top Priority" was dispatched to Moscow reporting that the alleged assassin of President Kennedy had been recognized by us as the visitor to our embassy in Mexico in September of this year. Naturally, we did not omit the fact that we had informed them of his visits in a previous telegram. As I noted earlier, this was our lifesaver.

At the same time, we informed Moscow Center that additional measures would be taken to guarantee the safety and security of the embassy and other Soviet institutions in Mexico as well as the "Soviet colony" within the country. Orders were immediately issued through the ambassador to the heads of the various institutions to limit the trips by their employees and family members into the city. Additional sentries were posted to guard the diplomatic corps on the embassy grounds. Fire extinguishers and backup power sources were checked. In short, we prepared for the worst.

To any observer it may seem strange or incomprehensible now why we did what we did back then, but one must remember the significance of that historic moment in which we were participants. After all, we did not know what was behind the assassination of the American president—a conspiracy of internal forces, the participation of international organizations or other governments, and so on. Even if it turned out that Oswald was a lone assassin, it would be enough in the strained atmosphere of the Cold War to point a finger at him and scream:

"He lived in the Soviet Union. He married a Soviet citizen. He corresponded with the Soviet embassy in Washington and the Communist party of the United States. He's a member of the Fair Play for Cuba Committee, and two months before the assassination he visited the Soviet and Cuban consulates in Mexico."

This would be enough "evidence" to conclude that the Russians or Cubans were guilty. Perhaps it was precisely for this reason that Oswald was chosen? However, we had absolutely no doubt that Soviet operatives were not involved in any way.

After we had sent the telegram, the three of us got together and repeatedly attempted to resurrect the details of our meetings with Oswald and to weigh all the pros and cons vis-à-vis his possible involvement in the assassination.

It was not such an easy thing to do. Oswald had been in our "field of vision" for only two days in September, and then only for a total of approximately two and one-half hours. Each of our contacts with him varied in duration. Of the three of us, Valery had had the greatest opportunity to observe him. He first met Oswald on September 27, during which time he spoke with him for about ten to fifteen minutes and then spent practically the entire second session with him. I spoke with Oswald for about forty to forty-five minutes on the first day but became an inactive participant in the second conversation. Pavel conversed with him only at the second meeting, but it was for more than an hour. Thus, Valery and I could compare Oswald's condition and behavior over the two visits, but Pavel had only his impressions from the second meeting.

Oswald's visit for all of us was unexpected; we had no prior information about him at our disposal. Everything that we knew about him came from what he told us himself. Generally speaking, he avoided answering any direct questions of a specific nature. True, the documents he carried with him, whose authenticity we had no reason to doubt, confirmed he was the person he said he was. Thus, the basis for our analysis of his personality came entirely from the short biographical data he gave us and his condition and behavior over the course of two meetings.

Judging by his story alone, this individual's actions were extraordinary for those times: A former U.S. Marine, supposedly a Marxist sympathizer, travels to the Soviet Union and asks for political asylum. There he gets a residency permit, but then, this time with a Soviet wife and child, he returns to the United States and again becomes an American citizen. (At the time we were unaware that he had not been stripped of his American citizenship.) Now he is supposedly being persecuted by the "local authorities" and fears his assassination by the FBI and as a result wants to return to the

USSR or go to Cuba. What conclusions could we draw from all this? There is no doubt that he was under KGB surveillance while living in the Soviet Union, but of which subdivisions? Internal counterintelligence for certain, but what of intelligence? If yes, then the rezidenturas in the United States could have been clued in to his actions by the Center. But the circumstances under which he appeared at our embassy in Mexico, in addition to his behavior, gave us reason to feel certain that Oswald did not belong to our intelligence services. As to precisely why he could not have been our agent, I will attempt to explain in greater detail in a subsequent chapter.

In the annals of our intelligence practices it has sometimes happened that an agent who has lost his contact in his own country, or as the result of counterintelligence maneuvers is deprived of the possibility of maintaining that intelligence contact there, leaves for another country, usually one where security is not so tight, and attempts to reestablish the contact by, among other things, visiting the embassy or other Soviet offices. There were such cases in Mexico.

But nothing of the sort happened with Oswald. His behavior was evidence to us of the opposite—that he had no contact at all with intelligence. His murky allusion during the second meeting to having carried out some kind of "special mission" and his avoidance of a concrete answer to the follow-up question of what and for whom were seen as an attempt to lend weight to his persona and possibly to influence our decision to issue him a visa.

As far as arriving at some kind of conclusion based on his personality, here we had greater difficulty. Our only source of information, as already noted, consisted of our visual observation of his condition and behavior during two and one-half hours. Perhaps such a brief period is sufficient for a highly qualified professional psychoanalyst or psychiatrist to come up with a diagnosis. But here again our opinions meshed, and we gave Oswald our unconditional evaluation, perhaps not very scientific but one widely used in our everyday life: psychotic. We were also of the unanimous opinion that if this was not a person suffering from mental disorders, then he was unbalanced at the very least or had an unstable constitution.

Finally, we all agreed that he was more hysterical than aggres-

sive, someone who rids himself of tension through emotional out-
bursts rather than through actions. When he spoke about the threat
to his life, he used such expressions as "I'm afraid," "I can't take
it anymore," and "It's unbearably difficult" that reflected a passive
position, as opposed to offensive expressions such as "I'll show
them," "I'll give them what-for," and so on. That is why, when he
said during the second meeting "that if they don't get off my back,"
he was going "to defend himself," it sounded more to us like a
forced defensive reaction than an active threat to a certain definable
"them." For many years now the thought has remained with me:
Did Oswald pronounce the same phrase and accompany it with
shots when he met Dallas police officer J. D. Tippit, whom Oswald
allegedly killed some ninety minutes after the assassination. And
were those not the same bullets in the chamber of his revolver that
were returned to him before he left the Soviet consulate on September 28? But who can answer these questions now?

As the three of us reflected on the assassination, we simply could
not picture Oswald as being capable of making rapid-fire, precise
shots at a moving target. We all remembered his teary eyes, trem-
bling hands, and overall nervousness. Is it possible that he could
have pulled himself together to shoot like that?

We still did not have enough detailed information concerning the
circumstances of the assassination to go on, but virtually everyone
in the rezidentura believed that it was the result of a conspiracy and
that there were several shooters.

During his two visits to our embassy Oswald never once mentioned the name of President Kennedy and, in general, did not get
involved in conversation about the politics of the Kennedy administration.

The following day, November 23, was a Saturday, but all athletic
and cultural events usually held on such days were canceled. Only
those persons whose presence was absolutely necessary were to be
found at the embassy. No reaction had come from the Center to our
telegram. We continued to pay close attention to the development
of events over radio, television, and through the newspapers.

Here is how our rezident described the problems faced by the
rezidentura: "That Oswald visited the Soviet and Cuban embassies
in Mexico became widely known in the United States and Mexico

by the second day following the assassination. Journalists began converging upon the embassy in an effort to get "firsthand" information. Our situation was not an easy one. Any answer we gave them might not mirror Moscow's position and might reflect badly on us. If we admitted that the alleged assassin of the president had visited the embassy in connection with a visa inquiry, the question would be: Why had he done this in Mexico and not at the Soviet embassy in Washington? If we tried to deny that he had ever appeared at the embassy by saying that visitors to our consulate are not officially registered by the Mexican authorities, it would be pointed out that the CIA's stationary observation point across from the embassy had clearly identified him. It was difficult to say which answer for us was worse.

"The main thing was that we were in the dark concerning Oswald's stay in the USSR except for what he told us. We also possessed no information on possible talks between our authorities in Moscow or Washington and the Americans. Under those circumstances, we decided to ask Moscow Center for immediate instructions. In the meantime, all the 'consular' employees who had any contact with Oswald, and they were all agents of the rezidentura, were ordered to stay away from journalists and not even leave their apartments.

"During the entire day we did not hear one word from Moscow Center. The answer we finally did receive on Sunday literally infuriated us, for it was perceived by our rezidentura not only as a bureaucratic, formal reply but even as direct mockery. It had turned an alarming situation for us into one that seemed idiotic. Ignoring our precisely worded request, the Center, for no reason at all, advised us in an official address to 'be guided in your answers by the reports from the Associated Press,' which, in essence, offered no more details than what was already known. Naturally, we did not explain to the journalists how the AP was reporting everything so well and correctly. There was nothing left for us to do but to continue hiding from reporters. How could the reaction from the Center be explained? Bungling at the bottom? Confusion at the top in an extraordinary situation? Expectation of a decision from the 'very top'? Probably all of these reasons together."

It seems that by the end of Saturday, Valery's name began ap-

pearing in the mass media as the representative who had received
Oswald during his visit to the Soviet embassy in Mexico. We immediately understood that this was evidently the result of his telephone
conversation with Silvia Duran from the Cuban consulate being
intercepted by the CIA station. We still did not know that Oswald
had told his wife, Marina, about "Kostin," which is how he remembered the surname Kostikov after Valery presented his identification to him. This is the name to which he referred in the letter he
had sent to the Soviet embassy in Washington and in the rough
draft of his manuscript which the FBI turned up in a search of his
belongings.

The rezident ordered Valery to be brought to the embassy for the
time being until the situation cleared up. On Sunday morning we
brought him, his wife, and all their necessary belongings to the
embassy and put them up in the same room with the television set.
Since we knew that on the following morning Oswald would be
transferred from the police station to a local jail, we gathered
around the television set to observe the proceedings. Everything
that happened next took place right before our eyes. The dispas-
sionate television cameras showed to all, "live," the murder of the
alleged murderer of the president.

At first completely numb, we suddenly began to talk all at once.
All our comments boiled down to one clear conclusion: This was a
conspiracy, and further actions could also be expected. Time after
time we fixed our attention on the repetition of frames showing
Ruby shooting Oswald. We simply could not understand how this
could happen right out in the open in a police station in the presence of so many intelligence service employees and policemen. The
entire day was spent in anxious anticipation of something else
about to occur. True, that evening we had a little "housewarming"
party to celebrate Valery's move to the embassy, but the chief came
along and broke it up, even though he also understood that we had
to relieve the tension somehow.

It is understandable that the foolish position the Center had
placed us in would bewilder and irritate the press. In order to fill in
the informational vacuum, they began to come up with their own
theories and versions as to the reasons for our silence, which put us
at a considerable disadvantage. However, as best I can remember

it now, the press cooled rather quickly toward us, possibly as a result of our inaccessibility. The situation in general around the embassy remained rather calm, and we did not experience any hostile actions. Gradually, our fears began to subside, and we returned to our daily chores. Valery's incarceration in the embassy lasted three days, after which we moved him and his wife back to their apartment. Life returned to its normal routine. The Center kept up a modest silence. And we certainly were not in any hurry again to contact them. Apparently they did not want to be bothered with us.

We observed the president's burial on television, feeling profound human sorrow for his family and regrets that this outstanding man and prominent, respected politician had left this life in such a senseless way.

KGB Center, Moscow

At KGB headquarters in Moscow, Oswald's dossier was immediately plucked from the archives and rushed to Pavel Aleksandrovich's office, the same head of the American desk of foreign counterintelligence who, ironically, did not speak English. All the materials relating to Oswald and his wife, the memoranda recently sent back and forth between the subdivisions in connection with their requests to return to the Soviet Union, were laid out on his table and carefully examined. A report, based on these materials, would have to be drawn up immediately for the KGB leadership. The goal of the report was to show that Oswald and his wife held no interest for the KGB, which the documents clearly demonstrated, and that no operative actions were being carried out with them. Pavel Aleksandrovich quickly wrote the report himself on three sheets of paper, barely consulting the documents. It was out of his hands now. Let the Second Chief Directorate deal with it—it was their problem.

All KGB employees were tense and nervously awaited further events, especially after Oswald was shot by Jack Ruby before the eyes of the world. Such was the mood of those on the lower rungs of intelligence. In order to get the reaction of the bosses, I again turned to the former head of the KGB, Vladimir Semichastny:

"My first, personal, reaction was that something tragic and senseless had happened. My first professional reaction was that this was clearly the result of a conspiracy.

"When Oswald's name was mentioned, my suspicion became all the stronger that there was something rotten going on. We were convinced that Oswald was incapable of such actions. I even had the idea of asking our country's leaders to send a group of agents to take part in the investigation of the assassination. But then a propagandistic anti-Soviet campaign in connection with Oswald began. The atmosphere became supercharged, which prompted us to conduct a serious analysis of the materials we had on him. Since the new documents in the Center were meager, we asked Minsk to send us what they had. We asked Sakharovsky, head of KGB intelligence, to prepare materials for presenting to the Politburo of the Communist Party of the Soviet Union.

"All coded telegrams from our embassies and rezidenturas were sent immediately to the Politburo. Khrushchev was quickly informed of the data on Oswald's Soviet period. We gave him our evaluation of Oswald as an average person and expressed doubt that he was the assassin. Following the assassination, at my initiative, I reported to Khrushchev on the circumstances of the president's death as well as the versions and rumors then circulating. He listened to it all very attentively and without interruption, commenting only that it was a very dark matter. He expressed his genuine regret at the death of President Kennedy.

"Anastas Mikoyan, deputy chairman of the Council of Ministers, was chosen to represent the Soviet government at the president's burial. He had visited the United States exactly one year before, during the Cuban missile crisis, and was personally acquainted with many members in the American administration. Sakharovsky asked me to 'arm' Mikoyan with our materials from Oswald's stay in the Soviet Union, just in case. Mikoyan agreed to take the materials with him to give to the Americans."

There is, however, one curiosity in the memorandum. In one of the paragraphs comprising the conclusion, it states that Oswald visited the Soviet embassy in Mexico in October 1963 and requested political asylum in the USSR. In the previous chapter there is a reference in one of the cited documents to "special report from

Mexico no. 550 dated 3 October 1963" concerning this visit. It is difficult to determine now why the coded telegram, the drafts of which were prepared by the Ministry of Foreign Affairs and the KGB on the day of Oswald's last visit to the embassy, that is, September 28, made its way to Moscow Central so late. But it can be assumed that since these cables were not priority reports that required Moscow's immediate reaction, the decoders only began working on them in the beginning of the following week (the twenty-eighth was a Saturday) and were then presented to their bosses for signature. No other explanation for this clearly comes to mind.

The KGB memo to the Central Committee concludes:

> During the time of Oswald's stay in the USSR, and after he left our country, the Committee for State Security exhibited no interest in him.
>
> One can posit that the fuss raised in connection with Oswald's name is dictated by the aspiration of certain circles within the USA, who possibly were accessory to the murder, to lead world opinion on a false trail and to give the case an anti-Soviet, anti-Communist orientation.
>
> Chairman of the KGB
Semichastny

It may also seem utter nonsense or an attempt by the KGB to deliberately deceive the Central Committee of the Communist party for Semichastny to mention, as if in passing, that the KGB has no interest in an individual who was watched closely for suspected espionage ties for more than two years and who was the subject of eight months of correspondence between various internal and foreign agencies.

But what it really means is that Oswald was not used as a source for intelligence or counterintelligence information and was not viewed as a possible candidate for KGB recruitment either in the USSR or abroad. Moreover, the KGB chairman had already explained in greater length to Khrushchev the KGB's position toward Oswald in a private meeting.

On a cool October day in 1992, I found myself sitting in the reading room of the periodicals section of the former Lenin State Library, now renamed the Russian State Library. Spread out before me were bindings that contained the November 1963 issues of *Izvestia* and *Pravda*. As I turned the pages, already yellowed with time, chronicling those long-ago days, I became a little excited and even felt my pulse quicken slightly. Almost thirty years had passed, half a life! How much water had passed under the bridge since then! No matter how many events I've been a party to, no matter how many countries I've visited, it is the memory of those days that is engraved forever in my mind.

The first reports about President Kennedy's death appeared in the central Soviet newspapers on Sunday, November 24. The front pages ran a portrait of the president, followed by a short piece on his murder and condolences of the Soviet leadership sent to the Kennedy family. On that day the Soviet people learned the details of the assassination from a report by *Izvestia*'s special correspondent in New York, S. Kondrashev:

> . . . At 12:30 three shots thundered around the president's vehicle. The shooter hit his target with sniperlike accuracy, using a *large-caliber Mauser rifle* [author's emphasis] with a telescopic sight. The weapon and remains of the murderer's breakfast were found among the boxes of textbooks on the sixth floor of the book depository. *A bullet struck the president in the right temple* [author's emphasis]. Covered with blood and unconscious, Kennedy fell into the arms of his wife. A second bullet hit Governor Connally. Surgery was performed on him, and he is listed in satisfactory condition.

All subsequent issues, until the end of the month, contained information about the events in Dallas, along with reports from Soviet correspondents accredited in the United States, commentaries on the sundry versions concerning the organization of the assassination, the views of Soviet Op-Ed columnists, and so on. Yet not a single published article in any of the newspapers mentioned Oswald's two-and-half-year stay in the Soviet Union, his marriage to a Soviet woman, or his most recent fuss about returning to the

USSR. Our country's leaders obviously did not think it necessary to call the Soviet people's attention to those details of the alleged killer's biography. At the same time, however, all Western mass media were widely discussing precisely these facts about Oswald's life as well as his visits to the Soviet and Cuban embassies in Mexico.

Such information naturally reached the eyes and ears of the Soviet people through the foreign press and radio. Therefore, the official policy of stonewalling only strengthened the version making its rounds in the West of the KGB's possible involvement in Kennedy's death. In such instances the iron logic of the Soviet people went into effect: If our leaders are telling us one thing, it must mean that the exact opposite happened. This calculated failure to report the entire story created fertile soil for planting the most outrageous rumors and establishing the most "genuine" details.

I closed the bindings of the newspapers from that era and begin to think. The "wise" reaction by the Center to our requests from the rezidentura on how to conduct ourselves with foreign correspondents in the first days following the assassination now became clear to me.

Washington, KGB Rezidentura

In the days immediately following the assassination the mood of anti-Soviet propaganda intensified. Some newspapers accused the Soviets outright of involvement; anonymous phone calls like "Why did you kill our president, Commie bastards?" were made to the embassy. The rezidentura's chief concern was for everyone's safety within the embassy. Their worries only increased with the arrival of Minister Mikoyan at Andrews Air Force Base, where they had to team up with their counterparts from the American side for his safety. After Oswald's murder, the assumptions of a far-flung conspiracy took on extra steam.

K, who at the time occupied a top post in counterintelligence in Washington's KGB rezidentura, remembers those days:

"Prior to the assassination, the KGB rezidentura in the Soviet embassy in Washington did not even have a clue as to the existence of Lee Harvey Oswald. There was no information from the Center on either him or his wife. Vitaly Alekseevich Gerasimov, vice consul in Washington, was the only employee of the rezidentura who knew the name from his correspondence with Marina Oswald in connection with her petition to be allowed to return to the Soviet Union. The resident agent, Fomin [Feklisov], most likely handed these materials over to the Americans after the assassination, but I am not one hundred percent certain of it."

Another former intelligence officer, a retired colonel, recalled:

"I came to Washington on an extended mission in late November, 1963. As I worked undercover, posing as a journalist, I was met by our media representatives accredited in the U.S.

"Early on November 22 a Tass correspondent and I went there to take a look at an apartment I was thinking of renting. Some time after we arrived, one of the owners came up to us and said, 'Our president has been shot . . .' We rushed down the elevator, climbed into the car and turned on the radio. Broadcasts about the President's assassination accompanied us all the way to the hotel.

"In the hotel we sat glued to the television screen while also listening to the radio. Suddenly the broadcasts were interrupted to announce that a suspected assassin had been arrested and was being identified. It was also said that he had allegedly shot officer Tippit.

"By the evening of the same day a photograph of Oswald was shown on television. I told my wife that he had a somewhat strange and silly-looking face. I also noted that in a very short period of time they had managed to provide a lot of information about the suspect. A little later we went to the Tass bureau and reviewed Oswald's biography. Then we went to the embassy. The situation there was tense. All the women were crying, as everybody had warm feelings toward the Kennedys.

"Then the word *war* became part of the conversation, since the impressions of the previous year's Caribbean crisis were still fresh in our memories. The American media were already full of information about Oswald's stay in the Soviet Union and his Russian wife. They were linking Marina's uncle, allegedly a colonel of the Ministry of Internal Affairs, with the KGB, thus hinting the KGB's involvement in the assassination.

"I went up to the third floor, where our rezidentura was located.

There the atmosphere was also tense. What worried us most was the persistent attempts of the media to link Oswald's stay in the Soviet Union with his probable contacts with the KGB. The lack of any additional information on Oswald from Moscow Center put us in an uncertain position.

"On November 23, we saw Oswald 'live' on television for the first time. It is worth noting that while passing the television cameras and reporters' microphones he kept crying: 'I didn't kill anyone. I'm innocent.' Later, these frames were removed, never to be shown again. As I observed these events, I could not help myself and began to predict aloud that Oswald himself would soon be killed and that his killer too would be removed from the picture. Everyone hissed at me to be quiet.

"The next morning we again took our seats in front of the television, anticipating the 'live' broadcast of Oswald's transfer from the police jail to the county jail, as had been announced the previous day.

"When the screen showed the procession, I noticed that Oswald was not surrounded by detectives but even seemed to be pushed out in front of them—'set up' in other words. I managed to say, 'Now he's gonna get it,' before someone's back appeared on camera and a shot was fired. 'What did I tell you!' I exclaimed. 'And now this one's a goner!' There are several witnesses who can corroborate my statements.

"Soon after Mikoyan's arrival, we noticed that the anti-Soviet hysteria in solid publications like the *Washington Post* and *Time* and on television died down. We realized why after we learned that Mikoyan had brought with him certain documents about Oswald's life in our country that he turned over to the U.S. State Department. We all breathed a sigh of relief. Such a step on Moscow's part meant that we were not accountable for Oswald's actions, but it still took a great deal of effort to convince the average American otherwise. And back then there were plenty of them who did not want to have their minds changed.

"As far as our evaluation of the events was concerned, we were of the unanimous opinion that Oswald had not killed the president, that he was set up to be a scapegoat.

"Even before those uneasy days security at the rezidentura had

always been strict. But now everybody had to be especially careful.
Everyone was prohibited from leaving the embassy except for emer-
gencies. The whereabouts of every officer had to be reported. Even
I was ordered to come to the embassy every day. However, it must
be noted that in those days none of the intelligence officers noticed
any surveillance."

Lieutenant General Z., still on active service, recalls that time:

"After the attempt upon Kennedy's life the atmosphere at the
embassy became very tense and alarming, especially when the mass
media reported that the suspect had once lived in the Soviet Union
and was married to a Soviet girl.

"The situation at the rezidentura was similar: the operational
officers were on alert, as it was difficult to predict in what way the
events could influence the operation of the rezidentura, though they
would undoubtedly require special measures. Before the event we
had no idea who Oswald was. An inquiry was sent to Moscow
Center. Soon an answer was received saying that our intelligence
had nothing to do with Oswald. It somehow encouraged us, though
we were still uncertain and worried about possible developments. It
must be emphasized that the relationship between both countries
was complicated and the international situation left much to be
desired.

"Naturally, we were closely watching the reaction of the American side. It must be said they were rather quick to take the right
course. I mean, they let up on the anti-Soviet campaign in which
they had indicated the KGB's alleged involvement during the first
days following the president's death. We were relieved because it
was hard to bear the thought that the service we represented had
been accused of such charges."

The news that Lee Harvey Oswald, who until recently had
worked in the Minsk radio electronics factory, was held in connection with the death of President Kennedy, hit everyone who knew
him like an avalanche. It seemed as if everyone was caught up in
discussion of the news. The KGB determined from the information
they gathered then that there was not a single fellow employee of
his at the factory who believed that the assassination was the work
of Oswald.

As one employee of the factory put it, "If it's the Oswald who worked with us, he was the secretive type, but then he openly expressed his feelings against our system." There were many who recognized him as soon as his photograph was published in the newspapers.

In the Minsk medical institute, where Oswald had many contacts in one of the departments, a lively meeting was held to discuss the events. Some of the gathering, who maintained rather close relations with him in the past, now tried to downplay their friendship with Oswald to the level of mere acquaintance.

A smaller circle of friends expressed doubts that Oswald was capable of killing the president and clung to the opinion that "he was probably murdered at the hands of a group."

Then there was this kind of reaction: One of the students from the department went to the KGB on his own and told them of his friendship with Oswald. After Kennedy's murder, and then Oswald's, those who had corresponded with him in the United States began to feel anxiety about their friendship with him.

The information about the reaction of the KGB headquarters, its stations abroad, and other Soviet people to the Dallas events, together with the information taken from various publications about the reaction within the United States, gave us grounds to point out the following versions of the Texas assassination.

- The majority of the people were apt to consider that the president's death was the result of a plot, the quick death of the suspect being a confirmation of this.
- Many of the people were of the opinion that Oswald had become a tool if not an innocent scapegoat in the plotters' hands.
- A few thought he was a lone killer.

In fact, none of the three versions, nor even their proportional relations, have changed so far. I think this diversity of opinion was based on marked information rounds. The volume of information on John Kennedy's domestic and foreign policies was great and available to anybody, even behind the Iron Curtain. It was clear that the energetic political activities of the president in different directions were sure to offend somebody's interests and that "somebody" was ready to remove him from the helm of power. Hence the first version of the plot.

As for Oswald, by November 1963 information about him was available from numerous official organizations on both sides of the Atlantic. But the simple thought is that by November 22 *nobody,* and I emphasize it, could see him whole.

Those at the KGB who had been watching him during his two-and-a-half-year stay in the Soviet Union had very limited data on his earlier and later life in the United States. Moreover, he himself was the source of this information.

On the other hand, the American's intelligence services—I mean the FBI, the CIA, the Office of Naval Intelligence—had more information on the early periods of his life, up to his service in the marines, and some information on his life after his return to the States, but they did not have any trustworthy information on his stay in the Soviet Union. And again Oswald himself was the source.

The State Department and the Immigration and Naturalization Service knew him only by the paper correspondence that piled up during the four years when he was trying to settle his personal problems.

His relatives, even his mother and his brother, knew of his service in the navy and his stay in the Soviet Union only through the fragmentary information that he himself gave them.

His friends and acquaintances in both the USSR and the United States knew him by their personal contacts. As for us, the three Soviet intelligence officers who met him in Mexico two months before the assassination, we were in the same boat.

Thus, everybody judged Oswald's role in the Dallas drama by the fragmentary information received about him during a certain time frame and depending on one's personal likes and dislikes.

To my mind, all this provided a rich breeding ground for numerous deliberate speculations and honest errors about Oswald's part in the attempt on John Kennedy's life. We are still harvesting the aftermath.

I must admit that my opinion, which resulted from my personal encounters with Oswald, had been changed radically as my information about him enlarged and my interest in the Dallas problem deepened.

Now I daresay—and it is not my supposition but a conviction— that even now, after thirty years have passed, not a single person, not a single organization on earth, is able to claim that it possesses overwhelming information about Lee Harvey Oswald. I say "so far" because I am sure that this problem can only be solved by the combined efforts of the people who possess the information and a precisely organized complex analysis of the facts.

Then the key in the keyhole of the Dallas mystery will turn in the right direction.

7

"It Has Come to Pass"

A journey of a thousand miles begins with a single
step.

—Lao-Tzu

Post mortem, nihil est. (After death, there is nothing.)

—Latin saying

Ambassador Dobrynin sent a coded telegram from Washington
to the Ministry of Foreign Affairs on March 25, 1964. He had
received a hand-delivered note from U.S. Secretary of State Dean
Rusk, with an attached letter from Earl Warren, head of the Warren Commission. The note expressed gratitude to the Soviet embassy for providing information about Oswald, specifically the
correspondence between Lee and Marina and the Soviet consular
division from 1962 to 1963. The note further requested supplementary material about Oswald from 1959 to 1962.

Earl Warren's letter stated that the commission had gathered
testimony from Oswald's mother, wife, and brother. The commission found material received from the Soviet leadership very useful. The letter went on to say that the commission needed certain information about Oswald's life in the Soviet Union. It would
be extremely valuable if the Soviet Union could provide information about this period, including any official documents. It was

stressed that this was necessary for the commission's work, and a list of requested documents was enumerated.

A copy of the coded telegram was sent to the leadership of the KGB. These instructions were written on the telegram: "Request time to prepare our thoughts." It was signed by Vladimir Semichastny, head of the KGB.

The FCD and the SCD issued a joint memorandum with concrete suggestions about how to give the United States the following information on Oswald and his wife:

On March 24, Comrade Dobrynin received a note from Secretary of State Dean Rusk with an attached letter from commission chairman Earl Warren. The contents requested that the Soviet Union provide any supplementary information in connection with Lee Harvey Oswald's period in the Soviet Union from 1959 to 1962 and include any and all official documents concerning Oswald and his wife, Marina Pruskova.

It has been determined from Warren's letter that the United States is interested in the following information:

—copies of documents concerning the medical, and especially the psychiatric, examination and treatment of Lee Harvey Oswald and his wife;

—copies of documents attesting to any hooliganism or other indecent behavior on Oswald's part.

The Warren Commission expressed its desire to receive copies of official documents concerning Oswald's stay in the Soviet Union, his efforts at obtaining Soviet citizenship, records from residences and places of work, and the couple's efforts to immigrate to America.

There is also a request to provide copies of any statements made before or after the assassination by Soviet citizens who knew Oswald during his stay in the Soviet Union.

The following documents have been gathered:

—Oswald's medical history during his stay in the Botkin Hospital, October 21–28, 1959, including his stay first in the psychosomatic and then the surgical divisions;

In the opinion of the chairman of the Central KGB Poly-
clinic, Comrade B. N. Sokolov, who is familiar with these
documents, there are no signs of psychiatric impairment or
illness in Oswald during this period. On the contrary, the
clarity of his mind is stressed. He understood all the questions
he was asked. Sokolov reiterates that Oswald's self-inflicted
wounds, resulting from his October 21, 1959, suicide attempt,
could not have been fatal.

—medical documents pertaining to the period that Oswald
lived in Minsk. There is no reference in these documents to
any psychiatric illness;

—documents from places of work and residences;

—documents from the visa divisions from Minsk and Moscow;

Documents concerning Marina Oswald include those connected with the legalization of her immigration and Minsk
Medical Institute records of her checkups. There is no mention
of any psychiatric illness.

There were also documents from the Special Investigative
File, SCD, and from the file of the Passport Division of the
Ministry of Internal Affairs. There exist documents presented
by Marina Oswald regarding her emigration.

Photocopies of the following can be forwarded to American
representatives:

A. Material of a Medical Nature
   1. Records from the psychosomatic and surgical
   divisions of the Botkin Hospital.* Outpatient records
   from the Minsk Second Clinical Hospital.
   2. Medical and outpatient history of Marina Oswald in
   Minsk.

B. Material Concerning Oswald's Residence and Employment
   1. Oswald's declaration to the Visa and Registration
   Department to obtain a visa.
   2. Receipt signed by Oswald acknowledging his
   stateless-person status.

*Oswald was under medical observation there following his 1959 suicide attempt.

3. Oswald's declaration to the Minsk police to extend his permission to stay (from January 1961 to 1962.)

4. Receipt signed by Oswald when he obtained permission to remain.

5. Oswald's declaration and autobiography written in conjunction with his job application. His employee identification card, certificate of passing the medical exam, and a card stating that he had been instructed in job safety.

6. Registration from his employer from July 15, 1961.

7. Registration for his residence from July 15, 1961.

8. Character reference from his place of employment.

9. Pages 1, 2, and 3 from Oswald's job record.

C. Material Related to the Oswald's Emigration From the USSR

1. Lee Harvey Oswald's declaration to OVIR in Minsk requesting permission to obtain an exit visa.

2. Marina Oswald's declaration to the Visa and Registration Department agreeing to her husband's emigration from the USSR.

3. Marina Oswald's declaration to receive permission to emigrate and the supporting documents.

4. Oswald's agreement to assume financial responsibility for his wife in conjunction with their emigration.

With regard to other documents, it is advisable to inform the Americans that:

—documents witnessing any hooliganism or indecent behavior on Lee Harvey Oswald's part;

—any observations of nervous disorder in Marina Oswald; and

—other observations regarding the questions in the Warren Commission letter

are not in the possession of Soviet authorities.

First Chief Directorate	Second Chief Directorate
Lt. Gen. A. Sakharovsky	Lt. Gen. O. Gribanov
April 1964	April 1964

The author does not know who received this information within the KGB, but the Nalim files contain photocopies of this material.

Another inquiry made by Dean Rusk, the American Secretary of State, to the Soviet government at the beginning of December 1963 concerned the circumstances behind the Soviet's denial of Oswald's request for citizenship. Rusk sought the answer to the question one week after Lyndon Johnson had appointed a commission, under the chairmanship of Supreme Court Justice Earl Warren to investigate the assassination.

This sensitive question obviously troubled the minds of the esteemed members of the commission and was one of the first inquiries that demanded a persuasive response: Why did the American Marxist not become a Soviet builder of communism?

The Central Committee, the Ministry of Foreign Affairs and the KGB, the same Soviet organizations which had decided this issue exactly four years earlier, once again undertook to provide the answer. The following documents were the result:

Top Secret
Copy No. 4

Central Committee of the Communist Party of the Soviet Union

In conversation with Ambassador of the USSR Dobrynin, A.F., Secretary of State Dean Rusk asked him to report, if possible, the reasons for denying American citizen Oswald Soviet citizenship (telegram from Washington No. 2054).

MID USSR (Soviet Ministry of Foreign Affairs) and the KGB deem it advisable to instruct the Soviet ambassador to inform Rusk orally that American citizen Oswald did not meet the criteria necessary for satisfying his request of Soviet citizenship.

A draft of the resolution is appended hereto.

We ask that you* examine it.

A. Gromyko   V. Semichastny
6 December 1963

*Central Committee

This was followed by two appendixes: the drafts of the resolution and direct instructions to the Soviet ambassador:

Top Secret
Copy No. 4

The Resolution of the Central Committee of the Communist Party of the Soviet Union concerning the reply to Secretary of State D. Rusk to his interrogatory about the motives for denying the request of American citizen Oswald for Soviet citizenship. Confirm the draft of instructions to the Soviet ambassador in this matter.

Secretary of the Communist Party

The instructions to Dobrynin were specific:

Top Secret
Copy No. 4

Washington
 Soviet ambassador
2054. In connection with the request of D. Rusk to inform him of the reasons for the denial by the Soviet authorities to grant Oswald Soviet citizenship, you may orally convey to Rusk the following:

The Constitution of the USSR and Soviet legislation confer upon Soviet citizens certain rights and place upon them corresponding responsibilities. In examining a petition for Soviet citizenship, the competent organs of the Soviet Union take into consideration first and foremost the degree to which the petitioner can fulfill his responsibilities as a citizen of the USSR and make use of the rights granted him. The motives by which an individual petitions for Soviet citizenship are also taken into consideration.

The competent Soviet organs, which examined Oswald's petition, did not find convincing grounds which would allow them to conclude that he met the demands made by the Constitution and Soviet legislation on Soviet citizens. The motives which caused Oswald to petition were also unclear.

That Oswald expressed himself critically in relation to the government, of which he was a citizen, could not be a determining factor.

For the reasons indicated, Oswald's petition for Soviet citizenship was rejected.

Telegraph execution.

6 December 1963.

Because my attempts to consult with former Soviet ambassador to the United States Anatoly F. Dobrynin in connection with the investigation of the "Oswald and KGB" theme were unsuccessful, I do not know whether he received or executed the Central Committee's instructions. But in the *Warren Commission Report* I did not come across any references to official Soviet explanations for rejecting Oswald's Soviet citizenship. It is possible that such explanations remained the property of the American administration for reasons of their own.

But there were others, in addition to American officials, who showed an interest in having the circumstances related to Oswald's life in the Soviet Union elucidated. His closest relatives approached our embassy in Washington with the exact same goal in mind.

Again, General Z. remembers:

"Now I can't pinpoint the date precisely, but it was sometime rather soon after everything had happened that Oswald's mother and wife visited the embassy. They were concerned with one question: Was Oswald really connected with our intelligence? We calmed them down and assured them that they could be absolutely certain he was not, and to ignore any of the conjectures which appeared from time to time in the mass media.

"In the course of conversation with them, the question of Oswald's health, his state of mind and nervous system was touched upon cautiously. This was done in such a way so as not to hurt their feelings or offend them. We expressed our supposition that his possible shooting at the president's vehicle was the result of some kind of unhealthy condition, or the influence of some factors on his psyche. They agreed with this [view]. They were also very disturbed by the consequences and possible persecution by American authorities. They asked if they could count upon our help in the event this should happen. We explained to them that they had absolutely no reason to be upset. We were in contact with American authorities after the tragedy and we had not heard anything from them about any intentions to harass or persecute the Oswald family. His mother, as I recall, visited the embassy several times, where she was received by the ambassador. Since I had to speak with her during these visits, I can say that she expressed her gratitude for our candor. She also emphasized that she was satisfied we were not trying to involve ourselves in her affairs, or pester her with unnecessary questions."

Early in April 1964, the ambassador telegramed Moscow that Oswald's mother had visited the embassy with the intent of gathering material regarding her son's stay in the Soviet Union. She stated that she intended to prove her son's innocence. She had strong suspicions, not yet proven, that her son was an agent of "a United States agency."

"She tried to familiarize herself with the material we gave to the State Department, with unsatisfactory results. She was told to cease any attempts at her own investigation. However, she remained determined to conclude her investigation and publish the results.

"The embassy informed her that they could not give her any material. She expressed an understanding of the embassy's delicate position but continued to hope that sometime in the future this material would be available to her. She stated that she had made a similar request to Khrushchev but had not received a reply.

"She did not rule out a trip to the Soviet Union to gather the information she needed. The expenses of her investigation would be assumed by a television company, which was currently paying for her trip to Washington in exchange for her appearance on their program.

"Oswald's mother said that Marina and the children were helped by donations from a sympathetic public, her monthly government pension of $148, and the sale of her husband's personal belongings. Information published in the papers said that donations totaled

$40,000. Marina was also paid to appear on radio and television and sold her memoirs to a film company for $300,000.

"In conversations with Oswald's mother, it appeared that she was a reasonable and even-tempered person despite contrary intimations by the press."

The ambassador's telegram to Moscow concluded with the opinion that it was currently inadvisable to release the embassy materials given to the U.S. State Department to Oswald's mother in light of the delicate situation. "There is no reason to completely exclude the possibility of giving her this material in the future, if it is beneficial for our purposes."

The author did not uncover any further requests from the Warren Commission. There is no indication of continuing contact between the Soviet embassy and Oswald's relatives.

Part of the Warren Commission's investigation included the reconstruction of events at the assassination site. Other investigators in America and around the world staged their own simulations of the event. Mossad, the foreign intelligence agency in Israel, carefully recreated the details of Oswald's sniper action and came to the conclusion that he could not have fired such precise shots in so short a period of time. I asked V. E. Semichastny if the KGB staged its own simulation. He replied that the KGB had no interest in such simulations, that the KGB's exclusive concern was to be absolutely certain of its noninvolvement in the assassination.

It is certainly understandable that during this period the KGB's main concern was to prove its noninvolvement. There were also plenty of other concerns.

On April 16, 1964, the director of the Second Chief Directorate, Lt. Gen. O. Gribanov, affirmed the decision that the materials of Oswald's case had important historical value. In the verification section of the document it stated that Oswald was studied for his espionage value, then left for the United States and in November 1963 was arrested as the suspected assassin of President Kennedy. It was further directed "to take *into account the historic value of this material.*"

Decree

The Oswald affair shall be preserved in a special section of the Archival Department of the KGB.

A copy shall be forwarded to the Registry and Archives Department of the Belorussian KGB.

PART TWO

Reflections

If you bump into something unknown, try to explain it as simply as possible. If this doesn't work, advance a more complicated explanation. If that still doesn't suffice, offer a version even more complex. And so on.

—Occam's Razor
William of Occam, 1285–1349,
English philosopher, scholar

Introduction

The purpose of this part of the book is not to sort out the various assassination hypotheses or to prove or disprove the many conspiracy theories. I do not have enough primary information or the multifaceted skills required to do this. I feel that such an endeavor is beyond the scope of one person. I would be extremely satisfied if Part One helps to close one conspiracy theory: if it completely crosses out the former KGB of the former Soviet Union as part of the "cui bono" faction, those who stood to benefit from the attempt on Kennedy.

Simultaneously, while working on my theme, "Oswald and the KGB," I involuntarily turned to events in Dallas as a whole. This is why my sphere of interest widened to include those general questions that have continued to worry not only American society, but the entire world for more than thirty years. The main question being: Was the assassination a conspiracy, and what was Oswald's role in it, sole assassin or scapegoat? In the chapters of Part Two, I'd like to state my thoughts on this matter, supported by the knowledge and experience I accumulated in over thirty-five years of intelligence work.

Insofar as my information is second or third hand—excluding official documents and my own impressions—I do not wish to use this information as the basis for new proof. However, the sum of this information is suitable for the creation of various suggestions and versions. Please bear in mind that all the conclusions in this section are not offered as absolute proof; they are meant to fall within the realm of probability.

8

The Conspiracy That Did
Not Kill Kennedy

It's extremely interesting to search with the author
for the criminal and the circumstances that form
the reasons and consequences of the crime. *Who* is
the spring of intrigue. *Why* is the lifeblood of the
detective.
                              —preface to a detective novel

When a witness is asked to describe what he saw, he
attempts to organize events in a logical chain. He is
extremely disposed to give a rational explanation
mainly based on *why,* in his opinion, it happened.
In truth it is possible that everything happened differently, or didn't happen at all.
                              —Earle Stanley Gardner

How many conspiracies actually occurred in Dallas on November 22–24, 1963? Where did they originate and develop? Did the
conspirators arrive with Kennedy, or were they already in place
along the motorcade's route?

The CIA, the Mafia, and the Cubans had all the necessary elements—people, motives and means—in place for a successful assas-

sination. Evidence shows that these participants could have easily utilized their resources to strengthen their position and solve their problems by liquidating the president.*

Dozens of theories have been proposed in this regard. The list of most frequently mentioned suspects includes:
1. The Mafia
2. Lyndon Johnson and the Secret Service
3. J. Edgar Hoover and the FBI
4. Right-wing extremists in conjunction with wealthy oil companies
5. Cuban anti-Castro immigrants tied into the CIA
6. The military-industrial complex
7. Nikita Khrushchev
8. Fidel Castro†

Ten versions of the murder of the decade: the official version stating that Kennedy was killed by Lee Harvey Oswald. Cuban refugees in the USA organized it, with Oswald in the role of "sitting duck." Castro was responsible in retaliation for the invasion and blockade of Cuba. Oswald's an incidental player, merely deflecting attention. The fourth version states that Hoover and the FBI were responsible. Oswald deflected attention. Theory five points to the Mafia, to avenge Kennedy's threats to its bosses. Oswald is a scapegoat. In theory six, Oswald was a KGB agent, and his eliminator Jack Ruby was also working for Moscow. The seventh version is described in *Mortal Error,* published two years ago in America. Kennedy was accidentally killed by those assigned to protect him.

Finally there are three, in the author's view, more plausible versions. The first is that his assassination was organized by the CIA. Next, Kennedy's death was the result of a conspiracy of right-wing extremists, in which the billionaire E. Howard Hunt played a special role. Oswald, due to his alleged Communist sympathies, was perfect for the killer's role. Finally, the military-industrial complex

---

*Report of the Select Committee on Assassinations, U.S. House of Representatives. March 29, 1979.
†Igor Efimov, *Who Killed President Kennedy?* Documentary historical investigations. (Moscow: "Terra" Publishing House, 1991. Moscow, 1991.

was responsible, since it preferred to have Johnson as president. Oswald was a pawn, used, then eliminated.*

Lyndon Johnson, included in the list of suspects, simultaneously became a conspiracy theorist. Shortly after his predecessor's death, Johnson theorized that "Kennedy might have been killed to avenge South Vietnam's president Diem's death, three weeks earlier."†

An interesting version came from Israel's Mossad. They theorized that members of the Mafia, but not Oswald, wanted to remove the Texas governor, John Connally, who was traveling in the motorcade. Oswald was merely a pawn, and Connally was the real object of gangsters who wanted to muscle in on the oil business. The situation presented the perfect cover. If Connally were killed, it would be assumed that Kennedy was the real target. If Kennedy was the real target, he could have been disposed of anywhere.‡

E. J. Epstein, investigating the events in Dallas, cataloged thirty various theories and published this list in *Esquire*. The basis for these theories revolved around the principle of cui bono, who would benefit from Kennedy's death.††

Even by a very modest count, it is possible that not less than thirty conspiracies existed with the purpose of liquidating Kennedy in November 1963. If it is assumed that each conspiracy required at least one member to complete the task, that means that at least thirty professional killers were in Dallas on November 22, 1963. This kind of oversaturation leads to the conclusion that every available spot for the shooting contained several executioners who vied among themselves for the "opportunity" to shoot the president.

One of the contestants obviously won the competition. Which conspirators were the most clever in securing places and completing their goal? By what means were some able to beat their rivals?

For the past thirty years, conspiracy advocates have gathered every fragment of evidence to support this or that theory. It is impossible to determine how many man-hours and how much paper went into this endeavor.

*Vecherny Klub. Moscow newspaper, November 19, 1992.
†Anthony Summers, *Conspiracy* (New York: Paragon House, 1989), p. 410.
‡Clair Hoy V. Ostrovsky, *By Way of Deception* (New York: St. Martin's Press, 1990), pp. 141–43.
††E. J. Epstein, *The Assassination Chronicles* (New York: Carroll and Graf), p. 14.

The volume of information is enormous, but the degree of proof is insufficient to indict any of the alleged participants in the assassination attempt. However, certain conspiracy theorists are absolutely certain they know who took part in the assassination and proclaim their findings without any trace of doubt. For instance, the English lawyer Michael Eddowes in his book *The Oswald File** made a list: "Soviet citizens involved in the assassination include Oswald's wife, her uncle in Minsk, the head of Minsk OVIR, V. Kostikov and P. Yatskov, both from the Soviet Embassy in Mexico, Consul Reznichenko in Washington," and other, simply mythical figures from his imagination. Due to his stubbornness, Oswald's body was exhumed in October 1981 to prove that he was a "double" sent from the KGB. I don't know if Eddowes was convinced by the results of this examination, which refuted his theory.

It is necessary to take a small step back, since it is apparent that supporters of Eddowes's theory of covert KGB activity still exist. In principle, Eddowes was on the right track but erred about the time and place of the Oswald switch. That is the reason why his hopes for sensational revelations based on the exhumation were dashed.

If any detective-novel authors or scriptwriters of the thriller variety are reading this book in search of a plot, then I will reveal only for them how the "switch" actually occurred.

The KGB in Mexico, in accordance with an already formulated plan, switched the real Oswald with their own Oswald and sent him to the United States on a special mission. The real one stayed in the basement of the embassy in Mexico, where he was politically worked over around the clock. On November 23, 1963, the KGB, in a covert operation, brought the real Oswald to Dallas. That night, in the police station, the Oswalds were switched. Therefore, the remains at the gravesite are the real Lee Harvey Oswald. The KGB double was successfully transported to the Soviet Union, where he still lives and is rumored to be writing his memoirs.

Another conspiracy theorist's work is not too different from the last revelation.

*Michael Eddowes, *The Oswald File* (New York: Clarkson N. Potter, 1977), pp. 209–10.

Oswald would not undertake such a dangerous mission, based only on the assurance of Cuban agents, who manipulated him in New Orleans. He needed assurance from more powerful personages. We already know that in the Soviet embassy Oswald met with the *head of the Western Hemisphere Sabotage and Subversion Division* (author's emphasis), Valery Kostikov."*

I read this revelation to Valery in April 1993. After a long laugh, he asked who awarded him this great position and remarked, "If you see the author, tell him that if I had held such a position when I was thirty, I would have retired as a colonel-general, not as a colonel."

This same investigator recounts the Cuban operatives Oswald allegedly met in Mexico and writes that one of these operatives says, "The Cuban embassy knew about the assassination beforehand."†

This type of disclosure belongs in the curiosities file and is not a part of the serious inquiry, although there are interesting points discussed in his investigation.

What is the sum total of all these conspiracy theorists regarding the death of the thirty-fifth president?

- A list of those who could benefit appeared shortly after the Dallas drama. Within three days three people are killed in front of many witnesses. All this information has remained virtually unchanged for thirty years.
- The sources for the conspiracy theorists have been practically the same group of witnesses for thirty years. It is difficult to even imagine how many times they have answered the same questions posed by official and unofficial investigators. It is possible to assume that the conspiracy theorists asked leading questions for the purpose of fortifying, as opposed to refuting, their views. This is clearly evident in works where the same witnesses are cited to help develop completely contradictory hypotheses. The witnesses

*Igor Efimov, *Who Killed President Kennedy?* (Moscow: "Terra" Publishing House, 1991.
†Ibid.

undoubtedly became used to the process and told the
questioners what they wanted to hear.

• Every attempt to discover a conspiracy must begin with, or
involve, Lee Harvey Oswald. He figures in all the leading
theories. Whether it's the CIA or the KGB, anti- or pro-Castro
forces, the Mafia, or the FBI, there is always a place for
Oswald. Depending on the conspiracy theorist's slant,
Oswald either belongs to the group initiating the conspiracy,
or becomes the killer or the scapegoat, completes an
assignment for an intelligence service, or runs an errand for
the Mafia. He is an all-purpose president liquidator.

Based on the evidence presented, the Stokes Committee believes
that John F. Kennedy was killed as the result of a conspiracy.*

This claim became the manifesto for conspiracy theorists. The
basis for the Stokes Committee's conclusion is built on testimony
of recording experts, who were allegedly able to detect the presence
of a fourth shot. In 1992, E. Epstein's *Assassination Chronicles*
stated that experts at the National Academy of Science established
that the Stokes Commission analyzed a poor copy of the tape
recording made by Dallas police dispatchers through an open mike
on a motorcycle at the scene that was analyzed by acoustics experts
to determine the number and direction of bullets. But when this fact
was revealed in 1982, the commission had already been disbanded,
and its incorrect conclusion became part of the folklore.†

It can therefore be ascertained that thirty years after Dallas, only
one clear suspect in the assassination of JFK remains, and then
there are the numerous *undiscovered* conspiracies.

It is possible that new information exists that does not necessarily
reveal a conspiracy but brings us closer to answering the riddle of
Dallas. I presume that the source of such information will be documents held in the archives of American intelligence. But I would not
want to judge the likelihood of this material becoming available
anytime in the foreseeable future.

---

*Stokes Committee, named after Rep. Louis Stokes, its third chairman. Also known as the
House Select Committee on Assassinations.
†Epstein, *Assassination Chronicles,* p. 24.

As far as witnesses are concerned, its difficult to hope that new people will step forward thirty years after the fact. However, someone's confessions, or safeguarded documents may surface now or in the future. There are various reasons why this material would remain hidden for a lengthy period of time. Take this book as an example. Even five years ago I could not imagine that we would freely reveal the contents of our meetings with Oswald, even though I thought about them all this time. Few were interested in this problem in the Soviet Union, and if someone were, he would wake up in a cold sweat if he even dreamed of turning to the KGB for help. After the KGB leadership informed the Americans of their disinterest in Oswald for operational purposes, the matter was forgotten within that organization. No one returned to it until the 1990s. Even unofficial foreign investigators would probably not have thought of turning to the KGB. Thus, during this entire period, no one asked us anything about the circumstances or details of our conversations with Oswald. In accordance with the inherent secrecy of our operation, we maintained our silence.

Certainly any new information in this area calls special attention to itself. It must be scrutinized for its reliability, since all sorts of falsification and even fantasy are possible. I am certain—and it is understandable—that many will have reservations in regard to this book, and will consider me, as a former colonel in the KGB, an apologist for the organization or Soviet interests. It is very difficult to accept such information considering that the source is not a traitor but a loyal veteran of the KGB. I remain absolutely calm in this regard, since, in the process of writing this book, I have experienced a definite cleansing of the soul. I am also aware of the feelings of my friends and colleagues, who were so instrumental in the book's creation.

I would now like to touch upon the so-called reliable witnesses, who, over the years, either enlivened their testimony with new details or changed them completely to foster up interest in themselves or for commercial goals. Unfortunately this additional testimony recently came from people who were very close to Oswald.

I believe a great deal of information is still buried in the archives, which may contain answers to many of the questions that continue to linger after the assassination, especially those regarding the possibility of a conspiracy. The answer to these questions may lie in a new look at the various conspiracy theories. New approaches in comparative analysis of each, coupled with a supplementary investigation of the unclear or ambiguous moments that occurred and the study of several informational fragments simultaneously from a different perspective, may lead to new answers. Having taken such a position, I would like to offer my thoughts.

To arrive at interesting possibilities, it is necessary to begin with dull theory. It is an indisputable truth that any serious investigation begins with a clear-cut determination of its goal. Reading the works of the conspiracy theorists, I did not find an understanding, which I, attempting to build a conspiracy theory, considered crucial. What is a conspiracy? To these authors the word's meaning was so obvious that it was unnecessary to even discuss it. But it is entirely possible that this is one of their methodological mistakes that leads them to a dead end.

Let us attempt to understand the concept, beginning with its definition:

CONSPIRACY—the secret agreement among several people; joint activities against someone or something in order to obtain certain, definite political goals.*

The main attributes indicating *conspiracy* are the agreement of *several* people and *secrecy*. What follows from this? *Several* means that the minimum number of participants in a *conspiracy* must be two. The maximum number can approach infinity, since *several* is an abstract category. But in this case the number of participants must combine with the secrecy factor. Clearly, secrecy sets a critical limit to the participants; if it is exceeded, it becomes practically impossible to maintain a conspiracy.

In this manner, conspiracy can be conditionally classified on the number of participants into two categories: Maximum number equals a large conspiracy; minimum number, a small conspiracy. The importance of these classifications will become clear as we proceed, but they are absolutely necessary for the analysis of concrete information, which can prove or disprove the existence of various conspiracies.

*Dictionary of the Russian Language, s.v.

The presence of several people, concluding a secret agreement of joint activities, creates the need for a ruling structure to lead these activities and to control the implementation of its responsibilities. In other words, everyone has to pull his own weight.

Secrecy not only influences the makeup of the individuals in the conspiracy, but its internal leadership organization is based on it. These principles are universal and are followed by the intelligence services, the Mafia, and any criminal organization.

Based on this premise, what does the structure of a conspiracy look like?

Framework for a Functioning Model of a Large Conspiracy
Ideologists—Initiators
- setting up the task
- financial arrangements
- Organizers—Directors
- Professionals in operational or criminal activities
- security of information
- determining the place and time
- completion of the big conspiracy
- selection and leadership of the managers
- common scenario of the big conspiracy

Managers
Specialists in various fields of knowledge
- determination of the 'battlefield'
- firming up the plans
- preparing the resources
- selection of the executors
- selection of the cover-up group leaders

Executioner
Professional killers
- primary
- reserve

Cover-up/Support Group
Specialists in other areas

- realization of diversionary tactics, including the creation of a patsy
- getting the executors to the battlefield, their evacuation or liquidation upon completion
- ensuring the scapegoat's discovery or liquidation

At first glance, the model may appear to be too large or overly bureaucratic. But its structure makes a great deal of sense. Any bureaucracy, always strives to minimize responsibility for its own mistakes while carrying out its basic functions. In illegal actions, the cost of "mistakes" or "defects" can be a long prison sentence or even the death penalty. The organization is structured in such a way as to protect its leaders as effectively as possible while dividing responsibility among the "executioners." The structure of the Mafia provides an example of this principle. Intelligence services' operational work is based on the same principles, although there is more accountability.

In speaking of such a sophisticated illegal enterprise as a conspiracy, another principle must be considered: the "Lizard Principle." It is well known that a lizard, confronted with danger, easily gives up its tail to save its head. This principle is fundamental to the structure of the large conspiracy.

This abstract scheme of the large conspiracy is presented in its simplest version. It can be used as an instrument to investigate this or that secret activity pertaining to the conspiracy. How does the instrument work? The abstract scheme gives a possible version of how it can work. Within its framework it is possible to compare and evaluate events and to analyze and form conclusions about the accuracy of the offered version. Applying models enables one to see what positions and versions are necessary to gather additional information and predict where to search for further information.

By no means do I consider this approach a revelation. But I am also certain that applying the abstract model of the large conspiracy can offer interesting results, both positive and negative, in checking the validity of conspiracy theories.

In studying the published works, I came across some investigators who spent enormous energy gathering information, but when they could not make it fit their theories, they would describe the evidence in an emotional fashion so that it would work for them. It is possible that some authors engaged in this practice deliberately to support unsubstantiated conclusions and create uncertainty. It is known that uncertainty sells, and in view of this, it is easier to ask questions than to answer them and to create sensational theories loaded with question marks and exclamation points.

Of all the large-conspiracy theories, I have the greatest interest in Jim Garrison's work. Let me state that I am not interested in his moral and ethical direction or his personal goals. Indeed, what interests me is the technological aspect of his investigation. It seems to me that he worked within the framework of the large-conspiracy model. He may have chosen this approach influenced by his work for the FBI.

Garrison built his investigation within the framework of the following scheme. A priori, he began from the belief that the "ideologists" of the large conspiracy were part of the upper echelon of the American intelligence community. Therefore, the "organizers" came from this group of professionals. Taking into account conditions in New Orleans, including the presence of anti-Castro immigrants, active intelligence employees, and Oswald's stay there, Garrison also includes the possible involvement of "contract agents" of the CIA and FBI. In this way, Garrison searches through the possible "managers" to find the potential "executioner." He was developing a version similar to the Stokes Commission's.

I believe Garrison's work resulted in the Stokes Commission digging deeper into New Orleans than the Warren Commission. In turn, first Garrison and later the Stokes Commission confirmed the connections between Bannister-Ferrie and Oswald.* This information is used in other major conspiracy theories. Unfortunately, even though Garrison was able to uncover some very interesting

---

*The Bannister-Ferrie-Oswald Connection: Guy Bannister was a retired FBI special agent from Chicago who became a private detective in New Orleans and also a "contract agent" for the FBI. David Ferrie was a crack pilot and a CIA contract agent involved in Central American operations. Ferrie and Bannister were connected to the New Orleans anti-Castro community. Oswald was seen in the company of Ferrie and Bannister (presumably) in Clinton, Louisiana. Also, Banister's secretary testified to researchers that Oswald had visited Bannister's office. The Stokes Commission corroborated this connection in 1978. However, I do not believe this association is sufficient evidence to show conspiracy.

peculiarities, he rushed to present them as elements of an exposed conspiracy and tried to instigate a spectacular grand jury investigation without the necessary substantiation. Contact between several people does not yet constitute a criminal conspiracy. For some reason, this skilled lawyer did not want to entertain such an obvious truth. The investigation and its conclusions were compromised, and further investigation in this direction became even more difficult. In effect, Garrison's haste contributed more toward refuting the conspiracy than to its discovery.

In Oliver Stone's sensationalistic *JFK,* based on Garrison's investigation, I saw an attempt to put concrete information into the framework of the large conspiracy. This occurred in the episode when Garrison meets "Mister X" in Washington, D.C. Mr. X's conversation intimates that many factions felt that Kennedy had to be removed. There was a plan, with no paperwork and no traces and no one to blame. Wrapped in secrecy, the plan was created to protect the conspirators against the possibility of detection.

Mister X's monologue sounds as if he had frequently discussed this plan. Since he is a skilled professional from American intelligence, the plan he describes sounds like a standard covert operation. As I have already noted, intelligence services operate very similarly to a large conspiracy, with the exception that their actions are within the law. In this manner, *JFK* hints at a conspiracy, but like its inspiration, Garrison's investigation, there is no substantiation.

At this point I would like to ask and examine two questions that I believe form the basis for any conspiracy theory: (1) If there was a large conspiracy, then to what extent was it developed by November 22, 1963, and (2) was Oswald a part of it.

In examining the first question the following, hypothetical scenario of an ideal, or in the words of journalists, "a broad-based conspiracy," will be utilized.

In April 1963, Vice President Johnson announced President Kennedy's impending visit to Dallas. The idea begins to take concrete shape. The Ideologists formulate the goal, "plot to kill the president in Dallas." Skilled professionals, the organizers, enter into the picture and begin to create the necessary framework. Regardless of who the "Ideologists" are, skilled professionals must exist on the organizational level. If at the organizational level the members share in the belief of the conspiracy, on the lower levels the recruits can be found based on their ideology, or blindly, or even on the basis of financial remuneration. The search for good "managers" leads to the "fertile grounds" where specialists in certain aspects of the conspiratorial action can be found. Then the "executioners" are picked from the same fertile ground.

To ensure the safe "procurement" of the "battlefield," the knowledge of its whereabouts is limited so that counterforces are not aware of it. Retrospective analysis indicates that New Orleans served as the ideal "fertile ground." Miami, also a possibility, was too far away from the site of the action.

The basic preparatory work, done from May to August, entered the completion stage in September. It is important to note that time, like space or distance, is also a factor in the safe development of a major conspiracy. On September 13, Dallas newspapers announced the president's one-day visit, scheduled for November 22 or 23. This can be called the beginning of the countdown in the fulfillment of the big conspiracy.

Information about the visit is collected: schedules, places the president is scheduled to visit, the motorcade route, his security system, and any information about measures to be implemented by the security/intelligence services. Sorting through this information enables the conspirator to pick the optimal spot or the "battlefield." Working our potential scenarios for "Day X," the managers can figure out how to accomplish their goal as well as prepare for additional favorable opportunities. The method for reaching and evacuating the killers from the battlefield is also planned.

The "undercover" group prepares diversions, including the construction of a parallel conspiracy or the establishment of a lone scapegoat. Plans regarding the "executioner" are completed. On November 22, 1963, the large conspiracy's structure goes into a state of high alert.

Why does New Orleans figure as the birthplace of this abstract, hypothetical, major conspiracy? It fits in with the conspirators' basic needs. Their interest was based on the fact that many influential figures with something against Kennedy could be found there.

New Orleans was loaded with operational specialists, experienced conspirators, and professional killers. Moreover, Lee Harvey Oswald spent time there. All this is known, yet after thirty years of diligent effort all that can be said is maybe this conspiracy happened or maybe it did not.

This raises the provocative question What if New Orleans was the parallel conspiracy created to lead investigators to a dead end? Is it not possible that the organizers, situated, say, in Washington or Houston, could have found managers in Chicago or Detroit, the hired killers in San Francisco or even abroad? It turns out that it was impossible to find the black cat in the dark room, since it was not there in the first place.

Up to now, the discussion has centered on the structures and possible scenarios of the large conspiracy. There is also a small-conspiracy category which can be divided into "natural" or "artificial" origins. In the natural case a few like-minded individuals conspire together using any means available, including their own self-destruction. In the artificial scenario, it is a component of the big conspiracy, where someone steps up as the initiator of the small conspiracy and creates a unified group of comrades-in-arms around himself. Subsequently, the initiator directs and controls the group, which becomes an instrument of the large conspiracy, to solve certain problems. (An initiator is the false leader of a small group of conspirators who actually act on behalf of a large conspiracy. The leader works for the large interest but recruits members who are true to the ideology of the small conspiracy. For instance, FBI agents in the sixties created groups of violent antiwar demonstrators in order to discredit all protesters.)

Because a conspiracy is small in scale does not make it less dangerous, and discovering it can prove more complicated than uncovering a large conspiracy. A small conspiracy often consists of people unified in their beliefs, and goal, which they approach not out of fear but as an act of conscience. If the large conspiracy's safety is assured by its complexity, then in a small conspiracy its safety is based on its compact nature and the single-mindedness of its members. Small conspiracies can have their weak spots: the lack of professionals and the need for one person to assume various responsibilities, for instance Organizer and Executioner. This can cause technological mistakes that intelligence services and their sources can detect.

Regardless of the conspiracy, it is always based on activities. The product, or "fingerprint," of these activities, regardless of how secret they are, is information. When illegal activity is involved, then the created information is called "evidence," "traces," or "material proof." Bearers of this information can be objects, documents, and people. No activity can go through space and time and not leave a fingerprint. Therefore, when no evidence can be found, the crime is classified as the *"crimen perfecto."* To my mind, the idea of a perfect crime is irrational.

People involved in an activity turn into "information banks," and those with whom they come in contact, or who observe from the sidelines, are witnesses to the events they see. This theoretical discussion helps us examine the roles of witnesses to the events in Dallas. As is well known, under the guise of theory, a number of witnesses, ranging from ten to more than twenty out of hundreds, disappeared in murky circumstances because they knew something dangerous to someone. Included are witnesses of separate incidents, prominent Mafia figures who were not in Dallas that day, "contract agents" for the intelligence services, and specialists in covert operations.

Since most authors characteristically believe in the infallibility of their own views, I think that by "spinning" concrete versions of events through the large conspiracy model, we can dispense with some of the doubts expressed over the reasons for the deaths of individual witnesses. By placing our witnesses within the context of the model, based on the "critical mass" of their information, it is possible to determine how dangerous that witness was in the view of the big conspiracy and whether he fell under the lizard principle.

The next section will deal more closely with applied analysis of the realities in November 1963. Assuming the role of a "manager" of the large conspiracy, I want to evaluate Dallas, and Dealey Plaza, specifically, the battlefield for the "executive action,"* and consider the placement of the killers.

*CIA terminology.

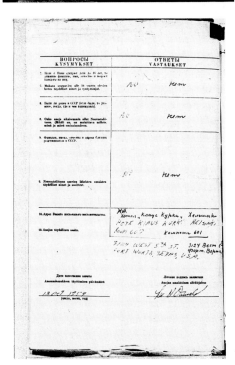

Entry Visa Application: Complete in English (with a Russian translation on the side) written in Lee Harvey Oswald's handwriting with his signature.

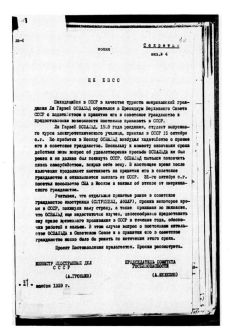

Memorandum to the Central Committee of the Communist Party, November 27, 1959. Signed by Minister of Foreign Affairs Andrei Gromyko and KGB Chairman Shelepin regarding the petition of Oswald to remain in the Soviet Union. Their recommendation is based upon their previous experience with the foreign citizens Sitzinell and Afshar. These individuals were granted Soviet citizenship, lived in the USSR awhile, and then decided to leave. They write that Oswald has not been "sufficiently studied" and therefore should be given temporary residence for one year, provided with a job and housing. The question of permanent residence should be decided at the end of the one-year term. (See Appendix 1 for English translation.)

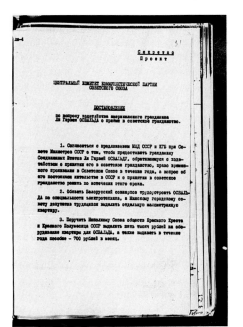

Resolution of the Central Committee of the Communist Party of the Soviet Union regarding the petition of Lee Harvey Oswald. Based on the recommendations of the KGB and the Ministry of Foreign Affairs, the document 1) entrusts the Republic of Byelorussia to provide employment for Oswald as an electrical technician; 2) orders the Minsk City Council (Belorussia) to provide him with a small apartment; 3) and for the Soviet Red Cross to give him five thousand rubles, furnish the apartment and issue him a monthly allowance of 700 rubles for one year.

Residency Permit issued to Lee Harvey Oswald on January 4, 1960, with an expiration of January 4, 1961. Oswald is listed as single, with no occupation.

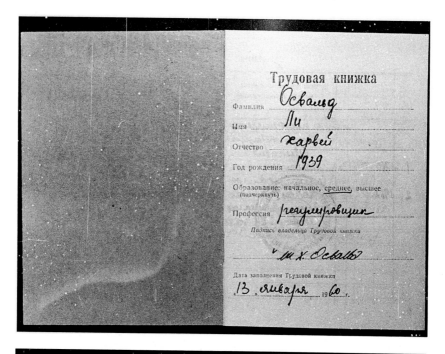

Oswald's employment record. Education: Technical (Vocational) school. Occupation: Maintenance Technician. The first entry states: "Prior to his employment at the Minsk Radio Plant, he had not earned any seniority."

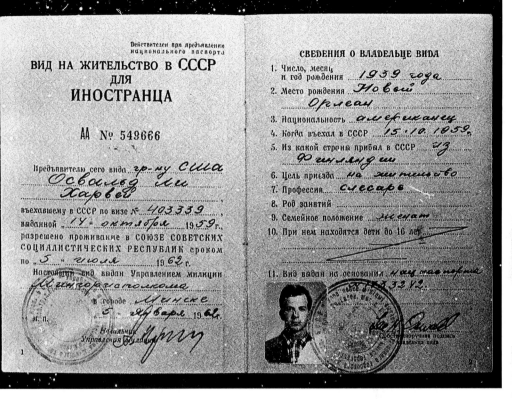

This Residency Permit shows that Oswald is now married with the occupation of a metal lathe operator. It is set to expire June 5, 1962.

Oswald's dossier form the Records and Archives Department of the KGB, USSR Council of Ministers. The cover has stamp indicating that Oswald had not previously been investigated.

Exit visa, dated for departure on June 2, 1962. The document states that Oswald turned in his Residency Permit #549666 on May 29, 1962, to OVIR (The Department of Visas and Registration) in Moscow.

This drawing depicts Lee Harvey Oswald in conversation with KGB counterintelligence agents under cover of consular officers in the Soviet Embassy in Mexico City. The event shown here took place September 28, 1963.

Oswald is sitting with his back to the window at the attached table. Opposite him is Valery Kostikov. Pavel Yatskov is seated at the larger table, under the portrait of Lenin.

Oswald is in a state of extreme agitation while telling the officers about being under constant FBI surveillance. He suddenly draws a revolver from under his jacket, explaining that he carries it for self-defense. Later he announces that, should a life-threatening situation arise, he will use the weapon to protect himself.

The window, in front of which he is sitting, looks out on the Embassy's courtyard. The door behind Yatskov's back leads into the next room of the consular division, where Kostikov and Oleg Nechiporenko sit. The entrance to the consul's office on the right is not shown.

Lee Harvey Oswald in Minsk, 1961, with various friends, actually KGB undercover officers.

I asked my friend Joseph F. Linder, M.D. to help with this aspect of the work. He is the president of the International Counterterrorism Training Association of Eurasia, heads the International Academy for Security Workers. He lives and works in Moscow. He is a world-class expert in, and teacher of, military marksmanship.

It was universally agreed that conditions in Dallas were favorable for the successful conclusion of the large conspiracy. The motorcade route that proceeded through Dallas's business section had five or six clearly visible points suitable for the action. Basically the choices were "breaks" in the route, that is, places where speed had to be reduced, thereby allowing the limousine to become a target for a shooting or the use of explosive devices. There was always the chance that something would go wrong, but there were many points suitable to the "execution" of the big conspiracy along this route. According to the Warren Commission, political wisdom of the time dictated that the Secret Service allow the selection of a route that permitted the president "to see as many people as possible" within the allotted time, giving the assassins a considerable advantage over his guardians because of Kennedy's exposure. If, said the commission, we add that "buildings along the motorcade route were not watched by the police or the administrations of those buildings because the Secret Service routinely *did not demand such measures or instigate them on their own,"* (author's emphasis), then the rest was just a technical matter. On the whole, the Warren Commission was very critical of the president's security.

In choosing spots, Dealey Plaza had to be considered, and it became the battlefield on November 22. There were two breaks or turns here, one of 90 degrees and another which forced the limousine to turn 120 degrees.

The plaza as a battlefield was suitable for several reasons: First, it was open (as opposed to most of the route) and spacious, allowing for shots to be fired from several different directions. Second, it had tall buildings that overlooked the square, and it was flanked by two raised-level parking garages, fences and rather thick vegetation. A railroad viaduct, under which the motorcade passed, and concealed paths made it easy for the executioners to get to and from the site. It is also possible that this spot met the demands of American political murders, where an assassination should not lead to the death of innocent victims near or beside the target.

I asked Dr. Linder the following:

Q. What points in the battlefield would you use for positioning snipers, and what is your overall opinion of each of these points?

A. Considering the situation, there are two appealing spots, the top stories or the roof of the book depository building and the wooded area on the grassy knoll on the west side of Elm Street. The first offers the sniper good cover and the possibility of aiming point-blank, which significantly increases his effectiveness. The angle between the shooter and the target, coupled with the gradient of the street are favorable and make it easy for the shooter. But since the sniper is in a closed space, he effectively becomes a kamikaze, since he has little chance of safe evacuation.

It is necessary to add these facts about the book depository building: November 22 was a workday, and the appearance of an unknown person moving about in the building with an object resembling a rifle might cause the buildings' occupants to become suspicious and notify the police. It would also be known either through recognizance or a participant's information that the sixth floor was being repaired and the workers would not be there but standing at the windows watching the president's motorcade. In sum, there were too many negative and uncontrollable elements to send the executioner here.

This leaves the "grassy knoll." According to Dr. Linder:

The grassy knoll can be considered to be the most suitable battlefield. The trees and vegetation provided the necessary cover. It was easy to get to and to evacuate. The shooting angle was favorable, and there was time to prepare after the motorcade turned on Elm Street. The knoll was elevated in relation to the target. Also, the target was approaching the shooter or shooters, which would increase the likelihood of success. Under these circumstances, even a mediocre marksman could be effective.

According to Oliver Stone's *JFK:* "The conspiracy was destined to succeed. The president would not leave Dallas alive."*

In *Crossfire,* author Jim Marrs asks:

Who did this? With the agreement of many people in the leadership of the American military, bankers, government leaders and the intelligence community, their agents were ordered to send pawns consisting of Mafia members, Cuban immigrants and the CIA to kill the boss.†

There was only one possible result from these "high goals of high people," and that was the physical liquidation of JFK. There was no other choice.

Continuing the conversation with Dr. Linder:

Q. In your opinion, to what extent did the choice of the battlefield guarantee the successful completion of the action?

A. "Guarantees can be secured utilizing the principle of duplication. There are several variants in the duplication, and in two categories; quantity and quality, for example the number and the ability of the shooters. For this event it is necessary to have two focal points, with at least two shooters at each. But naturally what sounds good in theory doesn't necessary happen in reality.

Q. But, say, in light of various circumstances, it was impossible to have other points, and only the grassy knoll was available?

A. Again, you'd have to use quantitative and qualitative duplication. It would be necessary to have not one or two but two or three snipers behind the fence. It would be like hunting a wild boar, elk, or deer. The hunters would spread out, and the beaters would force the animal into the line of fire.

Q. Certain data indicate that there were four foreign professional killers‡ on the battlefield; others claim there were about ten people involved and the situation resembled a 'military ambush.'†† What are your feelings about this?

JFK, directed by Oliver Stone.
†Jim Marrs, *Crossfire* (New York: Carroll and Graf, 1989).
‡Anthony Summers, *Conspiracy* (New York: Paragon House, 1989), p. 403.
††Marrs, *Crossfire*, p. 588.

A. It depends on how much information the conspirators had about the security measures for the visit. Judging the known information, it appears that there were many "holes" in the battlefield. Clearly the Secret Service did not adhere to the practices suggested in *Theories of an All-Encompassing Security System,* proposed by Maj. Victor L. Ott in 1957 after many unsuccessful attempts to kill General de Gaulle? The basis for this theory is that all "critical" points along the route, including anything higher than the motorcade, be "closed." Spectators are not allowed on balconies or near windows during the motorcade, and in addition to the escort convoy, there are massive groups of agents in strategic places. One quick glance at this shows how comfortable the situation was for the executioners on November 22. The police concentrated themselves only on one corner at the entrance to the plaza. There was only one policeman near the book depository and two on the railroad viaduct. The grassy knoll itself was not "secured," if the Secret Service agent who was allegedly there and mysteriously disappeared after the event is not counted. There were enough spectators in all these "critical areas" to allow the participants to blend in with them. Under these conditions it would have been possible to stage a complete military action on the battlefield.

Regarding suspicious characters in the area, every instance must be analyzed separately, but within the framework of the conspiracy. Usually, the executioners enter the place of action without their weapons. These weapons are waiting for them. However, if it was safe enough, it is possible that they carried their weapons. Their arrival had to coincide with the crowd's.

Let's discuss the weapons. When using automatic weapons, there is always the possibility of a cartridge jamming. This can be overcome by having several shooters fire simultaneously or one after the other.

Q. There are discrepancies among the eyewitnesses regarding the direction and number of shots. Some state they definitely came from the book depository; others point to the grassy knoll. Some heard three shots; others, three or more. One

book offers a range of six to nine shots.* The greatest dis-
agreement centers on the shot that struck Kennedy's head:
Did it come from the front or back? Was it the third or fourth
shot? How can these differences in perception be explained?
A. It is known that in a series of shots the first and last are
usually remembered. One of the in-between shots will be
remembered if it is connected with a powerful visual impression. That's why I think that there are differences of opinion
among the eyewitnesses. When they saw the bullet hit
Kennedy's head, they connected it with the sound of the shot
which occurred an instant later and was the last shot. Concerning the possibility of five or six shots, it should be noted
that the elapsed time between the first and third shot was five
or six seconds. If there had been six to nine shots within this
time frame, it would have been impossible to count the shots
or would have sounded like a cannonade.

Putting all the various versions together, it is possible to assume
with a great deal of certainty that by November 1963 the "technological" structure of the big conspiracy existed. It consisted of a
triangle, including the Mafia, anti-Castro immigrants, and American intelligence.

Since the conspirators had full knowledge of the president's security operation, they were able to hypothetically name Dealey Plaza
as the battlefield. They could do so despite a vulnerable aspect of
this location. Dealey Plaza was the last "critical" point on the
motorcade's route through downtown Dallas. Any unforeseen
delay along the route could significantly impact conditions on the
battlefield.

Most likely, executioners and "cover personnel" were in place at
the battlefield, including an executioner at the grassy knoll. He or
they were ready to shoot when the president's motorcade came into
their sector. However, seconds before this moment could occur, a
minimum of two shots rang out, and Kennedy entered this sector
already wounded. The sniper on the knoll had Kennedy's head in

*Ibid., p. 584.

the crosshairs of his sight, and it fell out of his view before he had the chance to fire.

It is my opinion that an independent and unknown sniper at the book depository simultaneously completed and demolished the big conspiracy.

Much has been written in regard to Oswald, including multiple and completely contradictory points of view, but all has been based on the same facts. Since there are so many points of view, I consider it a parallel theme to Oswald's role, and my conclusions are fragmentary and subjective in character. They are based on operational activity I was involved in, both abroad and during my time at KGB Moscow Center, and include trips to Soviet cities to recruit intelligence personnel.

Assuming the existence of a big conspiracy, I will attempt to enter into it and assume various people's responsibilities. I will proceed based on my own criteria, which may not be those of the organizers, or managers, but will probably not differ in any great respect. These criteria relate to the personality of a potential candidate in the big conspiracy and gauge his suitability on a "for" or "against" basis. The candidate is Lee Harvey Oswald, and personality tips the scales toward "against."

For
- Willfulness, even stubbornness in obtaining his goal
- Inclination toward violence
- Secretive character
- Pull toward the "conspiracy"
- availability of arms

Against
- Left-wing political leanings
- Lack of motivation, in this particular case
- Strongly individualistic; conflicts with society
- Psychological, nervous instability
- Inertia when he has no interest in the matter
- Lack of organizing skills
- Lack of any specific professional skills

The characteristics selected and the evaluation method can be debated. It can be suggested that the big conspiracy's personnel did not consider all these facets of his personality in those days. But proceeding on the assumption that the organizers were certain individuals in American intelligence, it is known that they had a dossier on Oswald and that this information would be available to them.

As hard as I tried and as much as I wanted to, I could not find a role for Oswald inside the big conspiracy. But this is based only on his personality within the abstract parameters of the large-conspiracy model. Other parts of the question will be considered in other chapters.

9

"I'm Just a Patsy"

And Aaron shall lay both of his hands upon the head of a live goat, and confess over him all the iniquities of the children of Israel, and all their transgressions in all their sins, putting them upon the head of the goat, and shall send him away by the hand of a fit man into the wilderness: And the goat shall bear upon him all their iniquities unto a land not inhabited: and he shall let go the goat in the wilderness.

—Leviticus 16:21–22

On the morning of November 19, 1963, Lee Harvey Oswald was waiting for the bus that took him to work at the book depository on Elm Street when someone called out his name. He turned and saw a car parked near the bus stop. Inside, a CIA or FBI case officer Lee knew from New Orleans called him over. "Hi, Lee, hop in. I'm going your way. We'll talk a bit."

On the way, his companion turned to Oswald and said, "Listen, Lee, I have to tell you something. Your friends, the Latins from New Orleans you told us about, have a little something brewing. It could have serious consequences not only on the national but on the international level. But we've got everything under control and won't let that happen.

"We have information that they intend to turn to you with a request, which you might think is unusual. They know, just like we know, that you have an unregistered rifle and have decided to borrow it from you for a little while. They'll show up tomorrow.

"We want you to grant their request. Pretend to refuse, and after they pressure you, go along with them. On the day this happens, we'll find you after work and let you know what to do next. Listen to us and don't worry. Everything's under control. Well, see you soon."

After work the next day, someone slapped Oswald on the shoulder. The Latin friends were so pleased with "accidentally" running into Lee that they invited him to a nearby bar. There they told him in confidence that an urgent "little matter" had come up and they needed to frighten someone but found themselves in a tough spot, since they didn't have any serious artillery with them in Dallas. "Someone" told them that he had a rifle, so couldn't they have it just for a few days. Acting according to instructions, Oswald voiced concern, but after repeated assurances that the rifle was only for "demonstration" purposes and would not even be used, he reluctantly agreed. The "friends" suggested that he bring the rifle to work and hide it in an agreed upon place. They would pick it up themselves to ensure "Leon's" safety and to avoid any witnesses.

On November 21, under the guise of needing to get a "curtain rod," Oswald went to Ruth Paine's house. His family lived there, but he did not usually see them during the week. The rifle, manufactured by an Italian concern, Mannlicher-Carcano, was wrapped in a blanket and stored in the garage. After spending the night with his family, on the morning of the November 22 he took the "curtain rod" in a plain paper bag to work and hid it on the sixth floor, among boxes filled with books, as had been agreed.

When co-workers told him that the president's motorcade would pass the building, he reacted in a calm and indifferent manner. Oswald spent the morning processing textbook orders and roamed through the various floors of the Texas School Book Depository where he was employed. When he was on the second floor, he decided to get a Coke from the machine. He took it to the lounge to drink.

When the pale faces of his boss and a policeman unexpectedly appeared in front of him and a gun was jammed into his stomach, Oswald realized that something extraordinary had happened. He remained calm, since he didn't yet connect this incident with his recent actions. The policeman and his boss, after exchanging a few terse phrases, left him alone and ran up the stairs. Then he felt slightly jittery, but countered it with "everything's under control."

On the street, Oswald found himself in the midst of commotion and learned that the president had been wounded and that the shots were fired from his building. Everything became clear; he had been set up. His mind raced feverishly. What am I gonna do? Get home, change, go hide somewhere. See what happens, then decide what's next.

Then he thought, Get home, different shirt, jacket, take the pistol? Yes, take it, they'll start looking for me. Which of them know me in Dallas? Hurry up! They can get here, too. Let's go. Where? Where there's no people. What am I gonna do? What am I gonna do?

Oswald fled the school book depository. On a quiet residential street, in Oakcliff, about a mile from his house, Oswald was approached by a patrol car. The patrolman told Oswald he wanted to question him. Oswald watched as Officer J. D. Tippit stepped out of the car and approached, his hand on his pistol holster. Who is he? Could he be one of them?

The hammer of his gun fell in succession. One, two, three . . . He's down . . . Four . . . okay. That's enough, let's get out of here. Run.

In the dark auditorium of a movie theater, just a couple of people, something flickering on the screen. What am I gonna do? Calm down, think. In a blaze of light, police burst from behind the screen, someone in civilian clothes pointed. "That's him, that's him." Closer, they're getting closer, what'll I do? Shoot. Trigger, click, nothing. Misfire. Slammed in the head, down, handcuffs. Out loud, he said, "Now everything's over."

A long corridor, all sorts of people, movie lights, flashbulbs, microphones, "Wait, soon I'll tell you all who set me up. I didn't do it, I'm telling you, *I'm just a patsy.*"

This is not a film script but a possible version of what Oswald experienced in his last days.

There are countless hypotheses about Oswald's role in the assassination. These theories are based on the same series of facts and interpreted on the basis of the authors' predilections. To this day there is no official or unofficial answer to this question except for Oswald's own undeciphered declaration: *"I'm just a patsy"* (author's emphasis).

The roots of the scapegoat lie in the deep, distant past of human history. A synonym is "patsy," and it is exactly this more colloquial word that Oswald used. He meant that he was set up and blamed by the people who perpetrated the action, for their action.

In the universal language of intelligence, a scapegoat is a phrase that means for purposes of diversion. This is a vital and indispensable part of intelligence practice: A great deal of attention and resources are devoted to diversionary action. Ranging from the biblical goat who carried the sins of the people on his back to subterfuges involving thousands of people, there are two basic reasons for diversion. Responsibility for a completed action is transferred to the scapegoat, or the scapegoat leads adversaries away from an action in preparation. The second type is most commonly used in military operations.

What kind of scapegoat, if any at all, did the large conspiracy of 1963 need? If the conspirators decided to create and utilize such a person, then this candidate had to meet certain criteria:

- Ideally he would be a nonparticipant. Nor would he be part of the structure of the large conspiracy.
- He would have a perceived reason or explainable motives for liquidating the same person as members of the large conspiracy.
- He would have contact with members of the large conspiracy without being aware that they were members. In this case, the scapegoat's time and method of liquidation would be based on the degree that he could endanger the large conspiracy.
- He would be a convenient candidate to divert attention and appear slightly knowledgeable about the big conspiracy's existence and know several of its members. This is a possible variation which greatly increases risks and automatically invokes the "lizard principle." In this case the scapegoat is doomed for liquidation before he can give any information to investigators.

The more I tried to find a "participatory niche" in the big conspiracy for Oswald, the more suitable he became to fill the role of the scapegoat:

- A known adherent of Marxism, an ideology that embraces the use of violent means to achieve its ends.
- His desertion to the Soviet Union, where it can be intimated that he established KGB contact and then returned to America.
- Open praise for the Cuban revolution, recorded in the popular press.
- The large conspiracy's awareness of the availability of Oswald's rifle. The information allegedly came through George DeMohrenschildt, who was a CIA informant. A friend of Oswald's, DeMorenschildt may have been instrumental in getting Oswald a job in 1962 with a graphic arts company that processed photos taken by the U-2 spy planes that flew regular surveillance missions over Soviet territory.
- No knowledge of the big conspiracy's existence but possible contacts with several of its members, without an awareness of their roles.

In sum, all this information enabled the "creation" of a Lee Harvey Oswald who was either a member of a small conspiracy, an agent of a foreign intelligence service, or finally, an unbalanced "fanatic," a lone killer.

Further analysis will be divided into the following three sections:

I. The construction or fashioning of a scapegoat with Oswald's "help" from September–November 1963.

II. The real Lee Harvey Oswald's lifestyle and activities in New Orleans, Mexico City, and Dallas between August and November 1963.

III. The FBI's and the CIA's interest in Oswald from August through November, 1963.

Calendar I: The Imaginary Oswald

September

25   Visit to the military commission in Austin to change
            his marine discharge papers.
25   Three unidentified figures—two Latin and one Ameri-
            can, "Leon Oswald"—are seen at the house in Dallas
            of Silvia Odio, a Cuban immigrant. The characteristics
            of the American: ex-marine, excellent marksman,
            "cranky," a daredevil, anti-Castroite, ready to kill
            Fidel and suggesting that the Cubans take care of
            Kennedy for the Bay of Pigs.

October

First days Three men take target practice in a vacant lot in the
            Dallas suburbs. At least one of them is Latin. Another
            looks like "Oswald." One collects all the fired car-
            tridges. The owner of the lot finds a 6.5-caliber car-
            tridge from a Mannlicher-Carcano. The FBI later
            determined that the bullet was not fired from Oswald's
            rifle.
7–14   A change-of-address form is completed in a New Or-
            leans post office for Lee Harvey Oswald.
13   Someone "identical" to Oswald attends a meeting of
            the Dirección Revolucionaria Estudiantil in Exile
            (DRE), an anti-Castro group. General Edwin A.
            Walker, is present at this meeting. He was active in
            right-wing organizations. According to Marina Os-
            wald, testifying before the Warren Commission, Lee
            Harvey Oswald fired a shot through a window of
            Walker's home, just missing his head.

November

1   A person who looks like Oswald buys rifle cartridges in
            Fort Worth. Oswald was in Dallas on this date.
First days Someone "who looks like Oswald" visits another gun
            store in Fort Worth. He inquires into the possibility of
            attaching an optical scope to a rifle. He was accompa-
            nied by a woman and two small children.

8? "Oswald" applies for a job as a parking-garage attendant at the Southland Hotel in central Dallas. He's interested in the height of the hotel and the field of vision from its top.

8 Oswald goes to a supermarket in Irving to cash a check for $189. Allegedly he was in this supermarket several times, accompanied by two women. This was the neighborhood where Marina lived.

9 Oswald begins to frequent a rifle range in Dallas; he shoots well, but his behavior calls attention to himself.

9 Oswald visits an auto dealership not far from the book depository. He prices an expensive model and test-drives it at high speeds in the surrounding streets. The real Lee Harvey Oswald did not drive a car. "Oswald" tells the salesmen that he'll have a lot of money in two or three weeks. "Oswald" praises life in Russia. Allegedly returned to this dealership a few days before the assassination.

7–14 Sent a telegram through Western Union in Dallas. Several times "Oswald" went to Western Union, where money was wired, accompanied by someone with a "Spanish" face.

16 At a rifle range, "Oswald" deliberately shoots at someone else's target. He uses an Italian-made rifle, firing a 6.5-millimeter cartridge and employing a 4× scope.

18 Pedro Gonzalez, the president of the anti-Castro organization in Abilene, received a note left with his neighbor signed "Lee Oswald." It asked Gonzalez to call him at one of two phone numbers in Dallas. According to the neighbor, he had seen a man resembling Oswald, with other Americans, at Gonzalez's house several times.

23? An informant for the Dallas police states that "Oswald" attended an anti-Castro meeting at an address in Dallas. The same source states that the group abandoned this address several days ago. It is determined that the address belonged to Alpha 66, an extremist anti-Castro group connected to the CIA.

Even a perfunctory glance at these enumerated facts creates a near certainty that they are fragments of a unified performance, directed from a central position. They create the impression that

Oswald's dossier was broken down into component parts for placement of these episodes, which would eventually interweave to create the necessary scapegoat. The completion phase of the big conspiracy began when all these facts were in place.

Each episode, taken singularly, with the exception of one (to be discussed later), do not form the basis for accusing Oswald of any serious wrongdoing. But what if they're interwoven:

A young American, ex-marine, ostensibly married, with two young children, is actively involved with anti-Castro groups operating in Dallas and through the course of his actions maintains his contacts in New Orleans.

From the beginning of October until the second half of November, he displays a heightened interest in rifle shooting. Together with some Latin individuals, he trains with a 6.5-caliber Mannlicher-Carcano, first in a vacant lot, then at a shooting range. He's known for his excellent marksmanship. In the early part of November he buys cartridges and a scope for his rifle.

He has money wired to him periodically, which he picks up at Western Union. He is expecting a large sum of money at the end of November. Knowing this, in the first part of November, he prices an expensive car and shows that he is an excellent driver. During all this he extols life in Russia, where he's already been.

At first glance, everything seems fine, but further examination reveals several peculiarities. Essentially, "creating" the future scapegoat begins with "Oswald's" appearance in late September 1963 at the home of Silvia Odio, who worked for a left-of-center anti-Castro group. His entire "program" is presented, including his full name, while others used only first names. Also publicized were "Oswald's" "crankiness," ex-marine status, excellent marksmanship, his readiness to kill Castro, and his purported comment that he thought the Cubans had no guts, that they should have shot Kennedy after the Bay of Pigs invasion and that killing Kennedy would be "so easy to do."

Leaking this information, for instance, to the FBI, would make it easy to identify the "ex-marine" and to have them label the real Oswald as a "suspected KGB agent" and even "a potential threat to the president's safety." The implications of his visit to Odio border on the absurd. There is a strong probability that this visit would be leaked. Odio was extremely nervous during this period and probably under FBI surveillance, since she belonged to an anti-Castro organization and corresponded with people in Cuba. She mentioned the "Oswald" visit, which even struck her sisters as suspicious, in a letter to her father in a Cuban prison and also to her doctor. If this was set up by professionals, which, based on the integrity of the scenario, it probably was, it is doubtful that they would not have foreseen this chain of events. Evidently they were not concerned about anyone asking who was leading the show. The probability of the existence of the structure of the big conspiracy can be inferred from this visit.

The transformation of Lee Harvey Oswald, who stated on New Orleans television and radio that he was a believer in Marxism and the Cuban revolution, into a "frenzied" anti-Castroite is truly perplexing. If the large conspiracy is investigated within the triangular framework of the U.S. intelligence, the Mafia, and anti-Castroites, then this "fashioning" of the scapegoat does not become a diversion but a way of drawing attention to the members of the conspiracy. Hence, the "scapegoat" becomes "the goat of instigation." But could even this be well thought out by the conspiracy's managers?

All the fragments that went into shaping the scapegoat only "interweave" when the participants or witnesses of individual episodes suddenly see the face, hear the name, or recognize the make of the rifle in conjunction with a shattering event. This occurred in Dallas on November 22, when the face, name, and rifle of Lee Harvey Oswald appeared on television and radio and in the press.

The anonymous witnessing of "Oswald's presence" at an Alpha 66 meeting shortly before November 22 was to become the last act in the scapegoat's construction. This information was meant to lead investigators to assume that the final assassination plan was discussed at this meeting and that Oswald was included in its execution.

Thus, we come back to Oswald's own retort, *"I'm just a patsy."* Who can say now what he meant? Here are several possible meanings to his declaration:

• He did not shoot at the president. During his interrogation, Oswald said this repeatedly.

- He shielded and secured the assassin's safety during the shooting.
- He provided the rifle and assisted in preparation of the "sniper's nest."

In the first case there are three possible variations:
- Oswald had no part in the conspiracy.
- He had some knowledge of the conspiracy's existence and its participants.
- He actually participated in the conspiracies, large or small.

Two of the cases assume an inevitable participation in the conspiracy. Or were these actions performed as the result of duress, blackmail, or someone's recommendations?

The why and how of Oswald's potential for the role of scapegoat, the big conspiracy's related actions, and the possibility of an Oswald "double" have been considered. Now it is necessary to become acquainted with the life and actions of the real Oswald during this period.

Calendar II: The Real Oswald

August 63

9	At a street demonstration in New Orleans, Oswald hands out leaflets *supporting the Cuban revolution.* (All italicization in this section is the author's emphasis.) He's arrested for disturbing the peace after a skirmish with *anti-Castroites.*
10	Speaks, at his own initiation, with an FBI agent at the police station after his arrest. Reiterates his *pro-Cuban revolution position.*
16	Appears on television in New Orleans to promote the upcoming *Fair Play for Cuba demonstration.* The evening news features a clip of him distributing pamphlets.
17	A five-minute interview with Oswald is broadcast on a local radio station in which he praises the Cuban revolution.

21   Radio debates with *anti-Castroites*. Sends letters to
            the Fair Play Committee and the U.S. *Communist
            party* headquarters in New York.

31   Writes to the *Communist* publication the *Daily
            Worker,* in New York inquiring about a job as a pho-
            tographer, saying that he intends to move there
            shortly.

31   Letter to the *Socialist Workers party* headquarters in
            New York stating that he intends to move in October
            to the Washington-Baltimore area, asking how to get
            in touch with party representatives there.

September
1   Writes to the U.S. *Communist party* to state he is
            moving in October and asks how to establish contact
            in Washington-Baltimore.
            Prepares a résumé of his life and political activities
            which he may have taken with him to Mexico.

17   Secures visa to Mexico from Mexican consulate in
            New Orleans.

23   His family move to Dallas to reside with Ruth Paine.
            Oswald's separation from Marina and his family is to
            be permanent, or of indefinite length, based on Lee's
            intention, revealed only to Marina, to leave for *Cuba*
            through Mexico.

25   He leaves New Orleans for Mexico.

27   Visits the *Soviet* and *Cuban* embassies to get the neces-
            sary visas.

28   Second visit to the above-mentioned embassies with
            the same goal.

October
3   Back in Dallas, he looks for work.

15   Begins work at the book depository in Dealey Plaza.

23   Oswald attends a *right*-wing meeting at which General
            Walker speaks. Supposedly Oswald tried to shoot him
            in April 1963.

25   Ruth Paine's husband invites Oswald to a meeting of
            the *liberal* American Civil Liberties Union. Later, Os-
            wald paid dues and joined the group. Spoke at a meet-

ing and commented on anti-Semitism within the John Birch Society. Speaking with people after the meeting, Oswald stressed that Kennedy was engaged in "really useful work" in the civil liberties field.

November

1   Sent a letter to the U.S. Communist party "lecturing" about the "left"- and "right"-wing meeting he attended. Asked for advice: How can *"we raise"* progressive tendencies in the ACLU.

9   Wrote a letter to the *Soviet* embassy in Washington about his visit to Mexico and mailed it on the twelfth.

12   Went to the FBI in Dallas and left a note addressed to Special Agent James Hosty, the contents of which expressed Oswald's "irritation" for FBI harassment directed against his wife.

21   Unexpectedly went to the Paines' residence, spent the night there, and drove to work in a neighbor's car on the twenty-second.

The chronology and content of Oswald's life in these last months has been broken down into practically hourly increments. There was no room or time in his life from the middle of July until November for participating in a conspiracy. Here are eyewitness accounts of his life during this period:

The occupants of the house where he rented a room noted his reticence. He regularly came back at 5:30 [P.M.], used the telephone and spoke in a foreign language (to Marina). During the course of the week he spent evenings in his room alone, and in this five or six week period, no one visited him. In the words of the house's owner, he spent ninety-five percent of the time in his room alone and five percent in front of the TV. At work, his boss was pleased with Oswald. During lunch, he stayed in the building and ate a sandwich along with the other workers.*

*Priscilla McMillian, *Marina and Lee* (New York: Harper and Row, 1977), p. 479.

This is the period when "Oswald" was very active at anti-Castro meetings and engaged in shooting practice.

Judging by "Calendar II," Oswald's "isolationist" behavior, especially during the last two months, precluded the possibility of his involvement in any left- or right-wing groups. It is very unlikely that he had any inkling of a "parallel Oswald" playing his role at anti-Castro activities.

During this period the actual Oswald persistently "demonstrated" his completely opposite views. Upon his return to America in 1962, until November 1963, Oswald sent and received about fifty to seventy pieces of correspondence. The main parties involved were the Soviet embassy in Washington, headquarters of the Communist and Socialist Workers' parties, and left-wing book and magazine publications. He had to know that the FBI would be aware of the contents of this correspondence.

Within the context of this correspondence, Oswald presented himself as a left-wing activist, which, except for a brief period, does not jibe with reality. In New Orleans, Oswald established a chapter of the Fair Play for Cuba Committee, a pro-Castro organization. He described himself as the president. In fact, he was the only member. Some believe Oswald created a paper organization to make it appear he was a pro-Castro sympathizer.

His last letter to the Soviet embassy merits further discussion. The history of this letter is a graphic example of how the same fact can be interpreted in different ways. According to the Warren Commission:

> When the differences between the draft and the final document are studied, and especially when crossed-out words are taken into account, it becomes apparent that Oswald was intentionally beclouding the true state of affairs in order to make his trip to Mexico sound as mysterious and important as possible. . . . In the opinion of the Commission, based upon its knowledge of Oswald, the letter constitutes no more than a clumsy effort to ingratiate himself with the Soviet embassy* (author's emphasis).

*Warren Commission Report, p. 307.

Michael Eddowes, obsessed with the idea of a KGB conspiracy against Kennedy, breaks the letter down, line by line, and comes to a single conclusion: Oswald used the mail to inform the KGB of the assassination plot's development and that "the letter *is meant more for Moscow than for the embassy in Washington"** (author's emphasis).

I have the following comments in regard to this letter. It consists of two basic parts. The first part presents itself as the continuation of an ongoing "business" relationship between the embassy and the correspondent. In a very veiled manner, the author hinted at facts the embassy was supposed to have "known" and "accounts for" his "previously planned actions." The second part informs the embassy of the FBI's actions and Oswald's reaction to them.

Within the framework of correspondence between the Oswald family and the embassy, the first part of the letter would appear senseless to the person reading it. The second part was of limited informational interest, since it mentioned the family's relocation, the attention of the FBI, and the birth of a second child.

What can further analysis of the letter offer? I believe that even though it was addressed to the Soviet embassy in Washington, it was primarily *intended for the FBI* (author's emphasis). This conclusion can be substantiated by the following:

- FBI special agent Hosty's visits to Ruth Paine's house on November first and fifth strongly irritated Oswald.
- On the weekend of November ninth through the eleventh, Oswald labored over the composition of this letter. He probably mailed it on the twelfth.
- On the twelfth he left the note for Agent Hosty at the local branch of the FBI. It can be suggested that he wrote this note at the same time he wrote the letter.
- Fully aware that mail sent to the Soviet embassy in Washington would end up at the FBI, Oswald counted on the contents of the letter to call attention to itself. Then an inquiry would be sent to Dallas, and possibly those

*Michael Eddowes, *The Oswald Files* (New York: Clarkson N. Potter Publishers, 1977), pp. 79–83.

responsible for the clumsy way in which Oswald was handled would be reprimanded.

- It appears that Oswald suspected Ruth Paine of having some kind of relationship with the local FBI branch, so he left a copy of the letter where she could easily find it. He could simultaneously confirm this suspicion and double the chances of having his letter reach the "intended" address.

If these were Oswald's calculations, then they were correct. A copy of the letter reached Dallas from Washington on the morning of November 22 and lay on Hosty's desk, unopened, until the twenty-third. Ruth Paine was indeed interested in the letter, copied it, and was ready to give it to the FBI.

By introducing two more facts, the contents of Calendar II illustrate one of the "paradoxes of Oswald" contained in chapter 3. Despite his enmity and fear of the FBI, Oswald knowingly and steadily waved a "red cape" at the bureau. This in the form of his letters and other actions of a "left-wing activist." He seemed to derive some kind of satisfaction from taunting this agency and calling attention to himself. Does the explanation for this behavior lie within the realm of conspiratorial activities or psychoanalysis? Whatever the answer is, judging by "Calendar III," he achieved his "goals."

Calendar III: The FBI and Lee Harvey Oswald

August

10   Oswald, at his own initiative, is questioned by FBI agent John Kelly after a street brawl with anti-Castroites.

22   The New Orleans FBI, hearing Oswald's radio interview, learns that he is a Marxist and "Cuba is the most revolutionary country."

23   FBI headquarters asks the New Orleans branch for results of its investigation of Oswald.

September

10   The New Orleans FBI is in charge of monitoring Os-

wald. FBI headquarters asks the Dallas branch for information on Oswald.

24 The New Orleans branch informs headquarters that the investigation is continuing and will inform them of any further developments.

October

2 New Orleans determines that the Oswalds have moved. Dallas continues the investigation.

10 FBI headquarters is informed of Oswald's contact with the Soviet embassy in Mexico by the CIA.

18 FBI headquarters receives this same information from its representative in Mexico.

22 FBI agent Hosty receives analogous information from the Immigration and Naturalization Service and forwards it to New Orleans.

26 New Orleans informs Dallas that the Oswalds have deserted the Irving address and asks them to determine the new address.

30 Agent Hosty informs New Orleans that the Oswalds live with Ruth Paine but that Lee does not live there.

31 New Orleans sends the results of its investigation to FBI headquarters.

FBI headquarters informs the CIA of Oswald's activities in New Orleans.

November

1 FBI agent Hosty visits the Paine residence and speaks with Mrs. Paine and Marina. He learns that Lee works at the book depository and lives alone, address unknown.

5 Hosty revisits the Paine residence.

12–15 Hosty picks up Oswald's note from the receptionist. It lay on his desk, unread, until the twenty-second.

8 The CIA gets the FBI information on Oswald from October 31.

15 The CIA directs the FBI's Oswald information to its counterintelligence branch, Special Services Division, Special Affairs Staff in charge of all Cuban operations.

22   This same document is transferred to counterintelligence; whether before or after the assassination is undetermined.

18   The FBI in Washington receives a copy of Oswald's letter to the Soviet embassy and directs it to Dallas.

22! This document arrives in Dallas, but Hosty only acquaints himself with its contents after the assassination.

While I compiled this calendar, it struck me that in mentioning the different cities and divisions, it could be taken for a record of KGB activities. The bureaucratic principles of intelligence operations are so similar, even though they're on different sides of the ocean. It would be hasty to conclude that the material, consisting only of documents within Calendar III, can lead to any conclusions. But a few crumbs can be "scratched out" from this scant material and used for suggestions. What can be read into this calendar?

The FBI "woke up" to Oswald after the culmination of August's events (the arrest of Oswald and his talk with an FBI agent). The Washington, New Orleans, and Dallas FBI found out what New York knew about him. By way of reminder, beginning in March 1963, he was investigated by the Dallas FBI while he actively fought for "fair play" for Cuba in New Orleans. In the middle of the summer, when it was learned that he not only lived in New Orleans but was very politically active, the investigation was transferred to the New Orleans branch. During this time, he moved to Dallas. Then information about his Mexican visit came from the CIA. With this development, further communication between the four FBI offices—Dallas, New Orleans, New York, and Washington—resembled a careening Ping-Pong ball. The CIA becomes interested, and information about him in New Orleans went from the intelligence division handling Cuban affairs to the counterintelligence division. New "gifts" come from Oswald, consisting of the letter to the Soviet embassy in Washington and the note to Hosty in Dallas. The FBI reacted to them after November 22.

It brings to mind an involuntary analogy, that of Lee Harvey Oswald in the Soviet Union and his relationship with the KGB. There he began his "stunts," and the KGB was forced to deal with him carefully. Right from his first days in the Soviet Union he became a political hot potato.

Leaving this analogy, I feel that it is possible to explain the contradictions in Oswald's behavior toward the FBI. What strikes us as a contradiction—his fearful and simultaneous attention-seeking behavior—may not have been a contradiction to Oswald. Certainly his "strange" behavior makes it possible to "see" it as the realization of someone else's schemes or manipulation. But it could be his natural behavior based on the peculiar, individualistic characteristics of his psyche.

It is difficult to agree with the assessment, found among some KGB work, that Oswald's behavior was "unpredictable." Possibly this appraisal was made without enough study. Examining his life story, one might conclude that he seemed to have existed in two worlds. He dealt with grounded domestic questions in a rational and enviably persistent manner. Only when he tried to realize his political fantasies did he become irrational and his "plans" take on an illusory character. Bystanders could view them as bizarre or even suggest that the behavior was coerced. But this was his individual "logic," the logic of the world he sometimes entered, and based on this, his behavior could be considered predictable.

Regarding his relationship with the FBI, I find it difficult to believe that Oswald's pro-Cuban stance was not documented by the FBI and CIA. It is extremely doubtful that what Jim Garrison found out a few years later did not reach U.S. intelligence during this period of complete control over Cuban immigration into the United States. If Oswald's activity wasn't documented, it's strange; if it was documented and hidden in a secret service national archive, that is even stranger. It's difficult to accept that this material was "banished" based on the need to protect the methods and sources of obtaining it. These can be encoded to fully "sanitize" the document. If these documents were to appear, it would remove the basis for uncertainty, speculation, and the proliferation of so many rumors. But, as they say, that's an "in house" matter.

I would like to touch upon the question of Oswald's trip to Mexico in September. There are so many suggestions and versions regarding it that their number may even exceed the number of conspiracy theories. I'll only name three "positions": the "Oswald" who went to the Soviet and Cuban embassies was not really Lee Harvey Oswald; Oswald was in Mexico to receive KGB instructions for killing Kennedy; Oswald was sent south of the border within the cunning framework of the big conspiracy.

The factual, detailed accounting of Oswald's trip encompasses two chapters in Part One. I hope that these chapters disperse many of the "KGB training" notions, and I'm sure that they raise further questions. Certain moments call for additional clarification. This is why I'd like to continue my commentary on this episode, still worrisome to many.

First of all, the main question: Was our visitor the Dallas Oswald? I consider that this question has been answered in the previous chapters, but I'll try to add some more details. The grammatical mistakes and phonetic distortions in our visitor's Russian pronunciation were very similar to those found in the letter Lee wrote to Marina as he set off to "hunt" for General Walker in April. Soviet documents presented by the visitor appeared to be genuine and not counterfeit. The question of validity also applied to the U.S. passport bearing the name Lee Harvey Oswald and the photograph which resembled the visitor's appearance. Of course, there can still be doubt. The documents could have been stolen and skillfully forged, presented by their owner voluntarily or under duress, and so on.

Then there is the question of height. My impression was that he was slightly taller than my five feet eight inches. Pavel Yatskov felt they were approximately the same height, five feet nine. Valery Kostkikov remembers Oswald being shorter than his own five eleven.

This question is closely related to the next point: Was the visitor to the Soviet and the Cuban embassies one and the same? This became a contentious issue after the Cuban consul, Ensebio Azcue, and a co-worker, Silvia Duran, "suddenly" announced that the "September Oswald" differed in appearance from the Dallas Oswald.

After the second Saturday conversation on September 28 with Oswald, Yatskov tried to telephone Azcue, who was out of the office. Yatskov and Azcue had been friends since 1959. They met a little later, and Azcue initiated the following conversation:

"Pablo, why'd you send me this schizo for a visa?"

"How could I have sent him, I don't handle your visas. I told him this when he asked me to solicit you," "Pablo" Yatskov replied. During the course of their conversation neither person expressed any doubt as to whether both embassies were visited by the same person, the authentic Oswald.

The photograph of the undetermined person (*Warren Commission Report,* exhibit no. 132) engendered a great deal of controversy. This photograph, which the CIA gave to the commission after the assassination, showed a person calling himself "Oswald" at the Cuban embassy.

When I first saw the photograph, which did not resemble Oswald in the slightest, it produced some vague associations but nothing concrete. Later, looking at three blowups of the individual,* dressed in similar and different clothing, something began to stir in my memory. The person in the photograph was a former American serviceman, discharged for reasons of health. I cannot remember the date and purpose of his first visit to our embassy, but in my conversations with him, it became clear that he was psychologically disturbed. Subsequently, he came to see us several times, and the intervals between each visit increased. I remember that during each visit something was explained to him in connection with his requests, and he listened calmly and left fully satisfied.

In his book *The Night Watch,* then head of the Western Hemisphere Division of the Directorate of Plans of the CIA, David A. Phillips, detailed how these photographs become "connected" with the recordings of Oswald's telephone conversation with the Soviet embassy and how this led to the "photographed" person becoming "Oswald."† There are investigators who react skeptically to this explanation and feel it is an attempt to "cover up" secret operations linked to Oswald or his double. Even taking into account Phillips's specialty, covert operations, his story strikes me as completely realistic. Such "bungling" within the bureaucracy of intelligence operations is not unusual.

I'm certain that the fact that Oswald was armed when he visited our embassy the second time raises many questions. This may be new information for some, but I have grappled with it since the fall of 1964, when I first read the *Warren Commission Report.* Material evidence included the photograph of Oswald's gun, with which he

*Ibid.
†D. A. Phillips, *The Night Watch* (New York: Atheneum, 1977), pp. 139–43.

allegedly shot Officer Tippit. Since it resembled the one that lay in front of us, I showed the photograph to Valery and Pavel. Valery held the pistol in his hand, and Pavel even disarmed it. Both said that the pistol in the photograph indeed looked like the one Oswald carried with him in September. I began to think about whether there were any witnesses to the fact that Oswald carried a gun before or after his return from Mexico. In 1992, studying Jim Garrison's *On the Trail of the Assassins,* I literally jumped out of my seat after I read the following:

> Some of the scenes ("Oswald" appearances) were so preposterous that only the most gullible could swallow them. One of these tableaux occurred in the Mexican Consulate in New Orleans. It was the early afternoon of a mid-September day in 1963. A young man, accompanied by a woman with a scarf tied around her head, appeared at the consulate. On this occasion, Mrs. Fenella Farrington happened to be there to see about getting her family automobile returned from Mexico. It had been left there on a recent visit with her husband.
>
> The young man asked the clerk at the desk, "What is the weather like in Mexico City?"
>
> "It's very hot," she replied. "Just like it is here today."
>
> He then asked her—now striking the sinister theme repeated throughout these pages—*"What do you have to do to take firearms or a gun into Mexico?"* This was a question that would catch almost anyone's ear. The lady at the consulate asked why he wanted to take a gun, and Fenella Farrington, standing nearby, volunteered that 'the hunting's wonderful.' "
>
> The man, whom Mrs. Farrington described as "tall and very thin," seemed resentful of her contribution, making no effort to show any signs of appreciation. Mrs. Farrington also recalled that he appeared ill-at-ease and not relaxed as were the other tourists seeking visas.*

In advancing his conspiracy theory, Garrison presents this episode as incontrovertible proof of the existence of a double Oswald,

---

*Jim Garrison, *On the Trail of the Assassins* (New York: Penguin Books, 1992), pp. 65–67.

the same "Oswald" who appeared in Mexico at the Cuban and Soviet embassies. I believe that this example involves the real Oswald and that a week prior to his departure he was preparing to go to Mexico, armed. It's possible that Garrison would have reevaluated his conclusions if he knew the circumstances of our meeting with Oswald in the embassy on September 28.

But what's even more interesting are the consequences of this episode:

Four days after the President's murder, Mrs. Farrington was visiting relatives in Washington, D.C., when the FBI hunted her down. The FBI agent who called her from the Washington office gave her the phone number so that she could call back for confirmation of his identity. This done, he informed her that the Bureau had located her because of the scene in the Mexican Consulate in New Orleans. The scene had been photographed, he informed her, by an invisible camera. It had been set in operation when the young man mentioned firearms and, insomuch as she was present, the Bureau had traced her from the photograph. The young man, he added, was *Lee Harvey Oswald* [author's emphasis], whose picture had been taken at the same time."*

In the book, the agent tells Farrington "that the Bureau has a photograph of the young man who wanted to take a rifle to Mexico, and that this was *Oswald*" (author's emphasis). However, she was never shown this photograph. According to Mrs. Farrington, the FBI suggested that she had met Oswald previously in Mexico, despite her insistent denial. Later, the investigators requestioned Mrs. Farrington and her sister, who was also present at the Mexican consulate, and showed them pictures of Jack Ruby and insisted that he was also at the consulate on the same day. Mrs. Farrington and her sister said that the photograph of Ruby did not resemble anyone they saw at the consulate.

Garrison writes that Mort Sahl and Mark Lane [his investigators]

*Ibid., p. 67.

showed Mrs. Farrington seventeen photographs and asked if
any of them appeared to be the young man in the New Orleans
Mexican Consulate. She replied that two of the pictures could
have been the man. She picked out a picture of Lee Harvey
Oswald. And she picked out a picture of Kerry Thornley—
Oswald's friend from Marine days back at El Toro, who had
later moved to New Orleans.*

The similarity of Thornley's and Oswald's appearances is well documented.

In regard to this photograph mentioned by the FBI agent, Garrison asked if it was a picture of Oswald, why wasn't it published by
the government. What were they afraid of that this photograph was
never made public? The answer to this question must consist of
answers to many other questions. The main parts of these questions
include:

- When did the photograph become property of the FBI?
- When and through what means was it determined that it
  was a likeness of Oswald?
- When and what operational measures were implemented in
  connection with this?

These are key questions assuming the likelihood of the episode
continuing along three basic paths:

- The photograph came into the bureau's possession and was
  determined to be Oswald before his trip to Mexico.
- The FBI "stumbled onto" unknown related materials as a
  result of following the "Mexican trail," after receiving
  information that Oswald had contacted the Soviet embassy
  in Mexico.
- Same as above, but after Kennedy's assassination.

Depending on the variable, a different version can be constructed
for each. In the first example, it can be inferred that Oswald's trip
was controlled by the intelligence interests. In version two, Oswald
was intentionally not included in the category of potentially dangerous persons, and this material was used to construct a scapegoat.

*Ibid.

But based on the dates of correspondence between the various FBI branches in Calendar III, it is unlikely that any branch began operational steps of checking the second version until after November's events.

If the third version occurred, it could be viewed by many as serious bungling by the FBI, with many unpleasant consequences for the bureau. Taking this into account, the questioning of Mrs. Farrington can look like natural bureau activity within the tumultuous context of the first stage of the investigation and the suppression of it an attempt to "save face."

There is an interesting question nestled within the "Mexican consulate in New Orleans" story. Could the woman in the scarf with Oswald be his cousin Marilyn Murret, recently returned from Mexico and accompanying Oswald at his request?

In my opinion, Oswald's Mexican episode is worthy of reinvestigation based on the material presented in Jim Garrison's *On the Trail of the Assassins,* in which he describes Oswald's visit to the Mexican consulate in New Orleans. It is interesting to note that of Oswald's known contacts in Mexico—with the Soviet and Cuban embassies and a group of university students*—he only complained about the FBI's pursuit twice and in similar terms. Eusebio Azcue and Silvia Duran do not mention any such complaints.

What role could an "armed Oswald double" have in visiting the Soviet embassy? The revolver was produced in a way that made it easy to disarm him, and this information was forwarded to Mexican authorities through their foreign affairs ministry. It may have been subsequently forwarded by the Mexicans to the U.S. embassy. I cannot see how this incident could be of any purpose to the big conspiracy.

Based on the pistol brandishing, Oswald could be viewed as temporarily insane or affecting temporary insanity as a last-ditch attempt to get what he wanted, which was to exert psychological pressure on us, by showing that his position was so desperate that he had to be armed and should therefore be allowed to immigrate. It is clear that Oswald was not concerned about the negative reac-

*Jean Davison, *Oswald's Game* (New York: W. W. Norton, 1983), p. 210.

tion and the consequences of displaying the gun. This behavior fits in with his character, of doing whatever was necessary to accomplish his immediate goal.

The CIA is alleged to have received information regarding Oswald's contact with the Soviet embassy from "confidential sources." What can we assume from this claim? That this information came from one or several elements of the entire CIA arsenal, including: agents within the Soviet embassy, stationary and mobile surveillance outside the embassy, and microphones within the confines of the embassy or consulate for wiretapping internal and external telephone conversations. It's only possible to try to ascertain the information's source when the internal reports of the special service are available. For instance, in Michael Eddowe's *The Oswald File*, it is clearly stated that "the FBI's confidential informant, implanted in the Soviet embassy in Washington received a copy of the letter* (Oswald's letter of November 9). Not excluding this possibility, I lean toward the view that the FBI must have received the aforementioned copy in a more roundabout way, through the routine, "gentlemanly" surveillance of the embassy's incoming and outgoing mail. Back then the intelligence services were more chaste, and it was considered impolite to mention this form of surveillance even though it was an open secret.

As far as the information procured by the CIA in Mexico is concerned, I can only speculate that this "confidential source" was another routine and "gentlemanly" method—eavesdropping on embassy conversations. The CIA also utilized material gleaned from another "confidential source," external surveillance situated near the Soviet embassy. Combining all this information resulted in the Warren Commission's material evidence, the photograph of the undetermined, mythical "Oswald."

I have more concrete information as to how the embassy telephone lines were tapped and how the FBI worked with Mexican special services on the Oswald case. I learned this from a member of el Dirección Federal de Seguridad (DFS) whom I'll call "José."

---

*Michael Eddowes, *The Oswald File*, (New York: Clarkson N. Potter, Publishers, 1977), p. 80.

Surveillance photo of Marina Prusakova Oswald with friends.

Valery Kostikov, a KGB officer involved in the meeting with Oswald in Mexico City, standing by a car that he and author used for official business the first three years of their posting in Mexico, early 1960s. It was in this car on November 22, 1963, that Valery heard over the radio news of President Kennedy's death.

Pavel Yatskov in the courtyard of the Soviet Embassy
in Mexico City, 1963.

Yuri Mostinsky, who worked in
foreign counterintelligence in
the KGB's First Chief
Directorate, handled the
Oswalds' request to return to
the Soviet Union in autumn
1963. It was dated
November 22, 1963.

Valery Kostikov and family before leaving for vacation in the USSR, 1964. Pavel Yatskov is in background between Lydia Nechiporenko and Roza Kostikova. Standing behind Sabena employee, in the right-hand side of the photo, is Ivan Obyedkov (looking at his watch), embassy commandant, whose telephone conversation with Oswald on October 1, 1963, was recorded by the CIA. In discussion with author, June 9, 1993, Obyedkov could not remember having such a conversation. Author learned of it for first time from Edward Jay Epstein's book *Legend: The Secret World of Lee Harvey Oswald*.

After fishing, the author in Balle de Bravo, one day after Pavel Yatskov's trip with "Pes" to a lake near Cuernavaca, 1964.

The Soviet Embassy soccer team in Mexico, before a game against a combined team from other socialist countries, 1963. Valery Kostikov seated second from right, author standing second from left.

March 21. 1971. Final steps on Mexican soil. Oleg Nechiporenko before boarding the plane back home after being declared *persona non grata* by the Mexican government, along with five other Soviet diplomats. To the author's left in light sport coat is Valery Kostikov. (Photo from newspaper *El Sol de México*, March 22, 1971.)

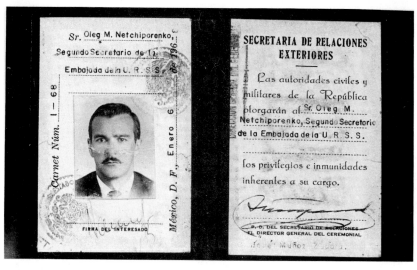

(Top and lower left) Diplomatic identification card for foreign diplomats accredited in Mexico. It was such a document that Valery Kostikov presented to Lee Harvey Oswald during his first visit to the Soviet embassy when Oswald expressed doubt that Kostikov was a Soviet consul. The author retained his card after being declared *persona non grata* by Mexican authorities and ordered to leave the country immediately. In theory, this card was to be returned to the Mexican Ministry of Foreign Affairs when a diplomat completed his tour of duty.

(Lower right) At a cocktail party in the American Club in Mexico City on the occasion of reelections of the Association of Foreign Consuls. The author was elected for a second term as vice president, November 1970. In photo with author is Dr. Rafael Fusoni, Argentine consul and director of journal *Monitor*. Fusoni has also been described in Phillip Agee's *CIA Diary* as a CIA agent. (Photo from *El Sol de México*, November 29, 1970.)

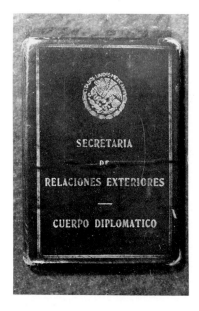

Sección D — Página 4

Oleg M. Netchiporenko y Rafael Fusoui.

Russians visit city school

A party of 23 students from all parts of the Soviet Union, who are over here to find out about Scottish education, toured Edinburgh yesterday. One of the high spots of their tour was a visit to the new Gracemount Secondary School—and above they have a cup of tea and talk things over, through an interpreter, with head master Mr Hugh Tannahill. BELOW—The Russian students, cameras and notebooks at the ready, were greatly impressed by the school's indoor swimming pool.

Two M.P.s agree over

Oleg Nechiporenko's visit to city school during "tourist" mission to Scotland. Author, then a young KGB agent, is standing, first from left. (Photo from newspaper *Evening Dispatch*, Edinburgh. November 24, 1959.)

Oleg Nechiporenko. Mexico, 1963.

The author and his wife, Lydia, at a reception in the Soviet embassy. Late 1960s.

Colonel Nechiporenko with a submachine gun during a break from his lectures given at the International Counter-Terrorism Training Association. The lectures occurred in February 1993, near Moscow.

He was part of the group that protected the Soviet cosmonauts, and we were friends for several years.

The CIA and FBI conducted a very thorough investigation of Oswald's stay in Mexico, without the assistance of the Mexican special secret service. The DFS was very interested in clarifying individual moments pertaining to Oswald in their country, and all the information that they gathered was presented to representatives of the "legal attaché" of the U.S. embassy. This division of the embassy represented the FBI in Mexico, and its employees maintained close contact with Mexican law enforcement. During this period the legal attaché was Joseph Garcia, who had long served in this capacity. Traditionally, the FBI had plenty of its own resources in Mexico and, like the CIA, solved problems without the knowledge or participation of Mexican police.

Shortly after the assassination, José said that many in the DFS felt that Lyndon Johnson was responsible. José was very interested in pursuing the investigation. He traveled to Guadalajara to investigate a conspiracy lead involving Oswald. The lead turned out to be a letter from a lunatic who had engaged in this type of activity before.

Shortly after the *Warren Commission Report* was published, I feigned ignorance and asked José how he was able to obtain the last name of one of the Soviet embassy personnel who spoke to Oswald on the telephone. Oswald never met with this person, but his name was mentioned in a phone conversation with a woman who worked at the Cuban embassy. He assured me that due to instructions from the country's leaders, their "office" did not monitor the telephone conversations between embassies but the "gringos" had great resources for eavesdropping and did it themselves.

Later, in 1968, preparing for the Olympic Games, we became aware of what these resources were. Beginning in March 1968, at Telefonos de México, a woman began to work as an operator handling international calls for Soviet businesses in Mexico. She was born in Sonora, held dual Mexican-American citizenship, and spoke Spanish, English, and *Russian* (author's emphasis). Her name is listed in the US embassy internal phone directory of January 1968. She went to work for Telefonos de México at a lower rate of pay but was able to maintain her lifestyle. Probably after beginning to work for the phone company, she had a new job description, that of "confidential informant."

Members of the DFS viewed the *Warren Commission Report* with skepticism but tried to use it for their own advantage. Special emphasis was placed on the section recommending more stringent security precautions in protecting the Mexican president.

I told José's story and debriefed him for one purpose. At the end of the 1960s, he became very ill and underwent a serious operation. Then, as his health started to improve, we resumed our friendly relationship. During one of our meetings he told me that during the course of his recuperation he went through a deep depression and in this state went to the American embassy and told my adversaries about our conversations. They suggested that he inform them of our meetings beforehand and report back with what was said. I saw no purpose in continuing to socialize with him.

The scapegoat theme is closely related to the question of possible collaboration between Oswald and the special services. Depending on the author, these services can be the KGB, CIA, FBI, and Cuban intelligence. With regard to the KGB, I hope an exhaustive answer was given in the first part of this book. The "general theoretical" point of view on this subject is presented in Chapter 3. Concerning other intelligence services, I feel that those actively involved in them should comment. But bear in mind that protecting its agents is a sacred trust for clandestine services.

There are many ways to achieve this goal. In American intelligence during these years "contract agents" were widely used. Clandestine services made an agreement with these people to collaborate for a certain period or until an operation is completed. Depending on the needs of the operation, these contract agents can range from professional killers to outer-space surveillance developers. They are compensated for their services based on their professional abilities. Contract agents often assume the role of "recruiters" and "group leaders"; in other words, they create and lead their own agent networks. This simple method enables the clandestine services to completely hide people once their tasks are completed. The subsources of the contract agents exist, but there is no record or proof. They can spend years working on an assignment and not know who it's for and during the course of this period never meet with an operations officer. In the event of failure, this is very convenient for both sides. The intelligence service can easily and officially disavow any knowledge of those involved in the failed attempt.

It is considered an established fact that there were two contract agents among Oswald's contacts in New Orleans during the spring-summer of 1963. They were private detective and ex-FBI agent Guy Bannister and professional pilot David Ferrie. It would be most helpful to establish the regular FBI and CIA personnel who directed Bannister and Ferrie during this period. These intelligence personnel knew the basis for the relationship between the contract agents and Oswald and the time and reason for their cessation. I think Bannister and Ferrie severed their relationship with Oswald no later than September 1963.*

Having studied the various aspects of the scapegoat theme, I have come to the following conclusions:

- There is a high probability that all of Oswald's pro-Castro activity in New Orleans, in the spring-summer of 1963, was *constantly* (author's emphasis) monitored by units of the American intelligence apparatus. Contract agents were involved in this process without direct contact with the intelligence personnel responsible for this decision.

- Insofar as there was no formal investigation or operation centering on Oswald during this period, it is possible that the material gathered on him accumulated or settled in other related files.

- Evidently, after Oswald's publicized, public pro-Marxist and pro-Castro statements, the FBI's and CIA's views of him underwent a change.

- Beginning in September, a scenario was staged, episode by episode, and featured an "Oswald" who was aggressive, "ready for anything," an active anti-Castroite and an expert marksman. There is no conclusive proof that Lee Harvey Oswald participated in these episodes. It can be said that these episodes were "performed" without him and without his knowledge. Therefore, it is extremely doubtful that he

*Garrison, *On the Trail of the Assassins*, pp. 105–6.

was set up on the firing line on November 22 as the scapegoat, within the framework of this scenario.

- Oswald's behavior from September to November provides no basis for believing that he regularly participated in any organized group activities or even had any regular contacts. His "political" activism was of a distinctly individualistic character and consisted of correspondence with left-wing organizations and attendance at two political meetings.

All this causes me to truly doubt that Oswald was *set up* on the firing line on November 22 in the role of scapegoat within the framework of someone's scenario.

10

Political Terrorist Or . . . ?

... If someone really wanted to shoot the President
of the United States, it would not be very difficult:
all one would have to do is find a tall building and
a rifle with a telescopic sight, and no one would be
able to do anything to protect him.
    —John F. Kennedy, Texas, November 22, 1963

"Find the motive and you've found the killer," said
Pat.
    —Mickey Spillane, *My Gun Is Quick*

During the course of three days in November 1963, three prominent murders took place in Dallas. The motives for two of them
remain unclear, and the proposed motive for the third has raised
grave doubts. Now it is possible to offer endless interpretations of
the motives for all three murders, since those responsible for them
are no longer alive. Only Oswald died "accused" without discovering the motives for Kennedy's assassination.

Before discussing the motives and other aspects of these murders,
beginning with the assassination of President Kennedy, I would like
to offer a "sociopsychological" portrait of the "accused," Lee Harvey Oswald, within the rubric of the following:

The Paradoxes of Oswald

1. Although Oswald became world famous after November 22, he was no longer just an ex-marine but a figure of international prominence. During the preceding four years, his fate concerned dozens of government agencies in three countries: The United States, Soviet Union, and Cuba. In the Soviet Union, the Central Committee of the Communist party, Supreme Soviet, and the Council of Ministers dealt with his case. Among other agencies, the U.S. State Department and the Immigration and Naturalization Service were involved. In Cuba his documents passed through the Foreign Ministry. Due to Oswald's persistence, his personal and family problems assumed a political character. This in turn influenced the way decisions concerning him were made. For instance, the question of allowing him to leave the Soviet Union and to return to the United States became a bureaucratic nightmare for both countries. Each side was concerned that a delay would engender the propagandistic outcry of "violating the civil rights of an American citizen." To avoid this possibility, the agencies involved deviated from established procedure in these matters. (The more skeptical conspiracy theorists argue that Oswald was under the guardianship of the United States and the Soviet Union for some important future purpose.)

2. During this four-year period Oswald was simultaneously watched by the intelligence services of the two countries. (The Cubans got information on him only after his visit to Mexico City.) In the United States, this surveillance probably began while he still served in the marines. The KGB and the FBI and CIA had ultimately gathered enough information to determine their operational positions regarding Oswald. In theory, he may have been considered for operational work either in a "blind" capacity or even for the scapegoat role, since he possessed some suitable characteristics, including his secrecy and tenacity. But overall, he was not a "desirable" candidate for use as an agent.

3. During his stay in the Soviet Union and after his return to the United States, each country's intelligence services viewed Oswald as someone presenting a definite threat to "state" and "national" security but not potentially dangerous as a terrorist. This percep-

tion can be confirmed by the KGB's reaction to his last "hobby" in Minsk—constructing bombs. However, it is entirely possible that the KGB's relatively calm reaction was based on his imminent departure from the Soviet Union.

Oswald's involvement with firearms was known to those who had him under surveillance in the United States. George DeMohrenschildt, with his CIA contacts, knew that Oswald with whom he had formed a close friendship, had a rifle with a telescopic sight. The reaction of the FBI and the CIA is not clearly known. When Oswald brandished his pistol in the Soviet embassy, it was not viewed by his KGB interviewers as a terrorist tactic but the action of a person who would resort to arms in an extreme situation.

4. The interrelationship of the Soviet and American intelligence services with Oswald is based on the principle of first, then second. He acts; they react. Oswald's behavior and individual actions were almost impossible to predict. They were the result of his personal goals and fundamental idealism. Both intelligence services reacted to his actions as they perceived their responsibilities, but always leniently and carefully. There is a remarkable "solidarity" in the tactics of the opposing services pertaining to Oswald. This can be explained by their concurring view of him as an idiosyncratic person, unworthy of more serious measures. In all probability there was a political factor involved, based on the peculiar status that Oswald and his family had developed over the last four years. Oswald skillfully utilized this status. As soon as he objected to the actions of one government, he quickly and tempestuously asked for protection from the other. In Minsk, Oswald complained in letters to the American embassy and Sen. John Tower of Texas about the oppression of his wife and the delay in permitting a "U.S. citizen" and his family to leave the Soviet Union. In Mexico City, he complained to the Soviet embassy about his pursuit by the FBI and even distorted facts. Since Oswald knew that the other side would also read his letters, he utilized the same method in both situations, more to "blackmail" the affected intelligence service than to obtain any support from the side receiving the letter.

5. Oswald was essentially "worthless" to both American and Soviet

clandestine services while he was alive, but after his death his name provided an "appealing" tool. During the long years of the Cold War, the three intelligence services of the United States, the USSR, and Cuba alternately used his name for propagandistic purposes against one another (U.S.↔USSR + Cuba). Numerous publications, some directly accusing, others merely hinting, saw him in the role of agent-killer or scapegoat. These publications were issued for the general reader, especially during periods of official or unofficial investigations of the assassination. Within these publications, "notes" in different languages would suddenly appear. They were addressed to, or allegedly originated from, Oswald. This so-called proof served to strengthen certain theories while refuting others. As a result of all this "informational activity," events in Dallas became so muddied that today it is extremely difficult to distinguish between sincere attempts to understand what happened and the "work" of the various intelligence services. The former opponents could now assist in clarifying all this information, probably without any great detriment to themselves, if they wished to do so.

6. The last two stages of Oswald's life, in the Soviet Union and the United States, were filled with attempts at realizing his Marxist ideals of constructing a Communist society and the practical problems stemming from this quest. A hiatus occurred in the last months, possibly precipitated by a crisis in his worldview. It appears that real, everyday problems took the place of his political dreams. There are a variety of signs that he was interested in establishing a stable family life, but this wish was impeded by irreconcilable differences with his wife.

7. Since he was an introvert, during this period Oswald acted in an aloof and guarded manner, within the context of any social group. This behavior contrasts with his Minsk period, when those he associated with noted his relaxed manner and readiness to establish contact. There were periods when Oswald leaned toward establishing trusting relationships with friendly people, specifically Kerry Thornley and Nelson Delgado in the marine corps, Pavel Golovachev, a co-worker in the radio plant, and Erick Titouyets, both in Minsk, George DeMohrenschildt, Os-

wald's and Marina's older friend in the Russian colony in Dallas and Marilyn Murret, Oswald's cousin in New Orleans.

In October, Michael Paine, Ruth Paine's husband, attempted to befriend Oswald but was unsuccessful. Oswald's family resided in the Paines' home in Irving from September until November of 1963. Judging by all the available data from August to November 1963, Oswald did not enter into any trusting relationships, with the exception of his wife.

Despite the antagonistic nature of their relationship, there were moments when Lee entrusted Marina with his most secret thoughts, including his plans to hijack an airplane, enter Castro's revolutionary army, his trip to Mexico, and his attempt to kill General Walker. In conversations with her during October and November of 1963, he spoke of his plans to settle down with the family without tying this desire with any political fantasy or goal.

8. During the course of his short life, Oswald's behavior alternated between aggressive manifestations and periods of deep depression. A detailed analysis of his biography leads to the conclusion that Oswald had a pronounced sadomasochistic personality and was capable of destructive and violent action toward others as well as toward himself. Although the doctors at the Botkin Hospital considered his wounds non–life threatening, they came to the conclusion that he was capable, under the right circumstances, of attempting suicide in the future. This belief could be a factor in the KGB's treatment of him.

Examples of Oswald's sadomasochistic tendencies would include the wrist-slashing incident and several others. In one incident, Richard Nixon demanded, in a public speech given in April 1963 in Washington, that the Russians be forced out of Cuba. He also accused Kennedy of being too soft on Castro. When Oswald read the speech and knew that Nixon was coming to Dallas, he took his gun to "see him" on his arrival. Then, on about the third week in August, Oswald told Marina that he decided to go to Cuba, but since there was no legal way to get there, he was going to hijack an American commercial airplane.

In his "Historical Diary," he described his state after the suicide attempt:

> I think when Rima [Shirokova, Oswald's Intourist guide] comes at eight to find me dead it will be a great shock [causing pain to a person he cares for]. Somewhere a violin is playing as I watch my life whirl away. I think to myself, How easy to die a sweet death [enjoying the act or the dramatization of his self-destruction].*

In the incident involving his attempt to kill General Walker, a violent action against another person, Oswald also mentally paints a picture of what will happen to him post factum. His martyrlike preparations are detailed in his letter with "instructions" for his wife. He expresses superficial concern for his family, but the satisfaction of his own needs assumes paramount importance. He does not seem overly concerned with the damage his actions and their consequences will cause his wife.

This collection of "paradoxes" serves as a background for discussing the purported motives of the two murders—President Kennedy and police officer J. D. Tippit—that Oswald is suspected of committing.

An analysis of his last two months, including his behavior, psychological state, and relations with his family, leads me to conclude that he did not join others in any capacity in the preparation of a terrorist action. It is unlikely that any outside influences motivated either his individual actions or overall behavior.

This means that Oswald's behavior was based on internal, individualistic motives, influenced by processes developing in his external environment. While it is extremely difficult to delve into the secret consciousness of a nonexistent person, the investigative process permits one to at least form an hypothesis.

I will attempt to present how the layers of Oswald's conscious or

*Michael Eddowes, *The Oswald File* (New York: Potter, 1977), pp.192–93.

subconscious mind formed the motives for the actions he allegedly committed within the course of an hour in Dallas, on November 22, 1963.

Ideological-Political

Oswald's attempt to assassinate General Walker and to meet Vice President Nixon while armed and his intention to hijack an airplane are ideological and political in nature. Successful or not, they were motivated by, and occurred during, his period of ideological "arousal" and political activity. All of these acts manifested themselves in various ways. They included the long and careful preparation to kill General Walker and, as a result, the nervous state in which Oswald found himself; a demonstrated euphoria before his armed meeting with Nixon; and an elaborate scenario that involved hijacking the airplane, with definite roles assigned to himself and Marina. All three examples fit the framework of Oswald's ideological aspirations.

Thus, Oswald, who considered himself "Marxist" and "Communist," attempted to kill General Walker, who was reactionary, anti-Communist and pro-Fascist. Richard Nixon practically called for a new invasion of Cuba that would force the Russians out of that country and by doing so earned Oswald's enmity. His intention in hijacking an airplane was to go to Cuba to build the new "Just Society" and to help the Cuban revolution.

During this period there are no accounts of John F. Kennedy's being included in Oswald's list of potential political enemies; more likely, Oswald viewed him favorably.

During October and November of 1963, his ideological-political activity abates, while all external signs point to his interest now focusing on domestic concerns and projects. But the ideological-political ideas remained, stored in the "bank" of his subconscious, and were still combustible, capable of being easily ignited under the right circumstances.

Elements in this volatile mixture included the feeling that all his political ideals were in ruins after his own observation of, and disappointment in, the system: A Cuban official in Mexico City refused to accept him with open arms as a revolutionary, and the

American Left failed to see him as a useful political activist. Other elements concerned his own reevaluation and probable regrouping of ideological illusions and his self-doubt regarding his political self-realization.

The spark which could ignite this mixture appears with FBI agent James Hosty's visits to the Paine residence and conversations with Marina. Hosty was an agent in the bureau's Dallas office. On November 1 and 5, 1963, he visited the home of Ruth Paine, where Marina Oswald was living with her children. He wanted to speak with Oswald. He was then given his work address at the Texas School Book Depository. When Oswald learned of the visits, he slipped into a dark mood and sought out Hosty at the FBI office.

But there wasn't enough critical volume to cause the explosion; more supplementary mass was needed.

Moral-Psychological

Oswald's irrational political fantasies were replaced with a concrete concern: the creation of a separate home for his family. This new concern occupied his thoughts, and, with his inherent persistence, Oswald tried to make it a reality. He ran into a serious impediment, since Marina would not leave the Paine residence.

Ruth Paine had met Oswald and Marina at a social gathering in February 1963. Two months later, Oswald decided to go to New Orleans to seek work, and Ruth, who spoke some Russian, invited Marina, with her small daughter, to stay with her in her home in Irving, Texas, a Dallas suburb. In May 1963, Marina rejoined Oswald, who had found work in New Orleans. In September 1963, Ruth took Marina back to Irving, where they again lived until after the assassination. This served not only as an irritant, but began to threaten the disruption of Oswald's domestic plans, and when this occurred, he showed signs of violence. Even his "hobby" in Minsk of constructing bombs was precipitated by his perception that his emigration had been unfairly delayed.

The combustible mixture begins to approach the critical limit. New instances added more fuel: In discussing the FBI agent's visit, Marina, who was aware of her husband's feeling toward the bureau, described the agent to Oswald in a sympathetic light. Shortly thereafter, she discovered the apartment Oswald had rented and was hiding in to escape FBI surveillance. Marina then tried to reach him by telephone. This attempt to contact him provoked an angry reaction on his part. All these events occurred as more and more information of the president's impending trip to Dallas were made available—the same president in whom Marina had been interested for some time and whose portrait hung in her room. She saw a resemblance between Kennedy and Anatoly Shpanko, a medical student in Minsk with whom she was in love before she met Oswald on March 17, 1961. But Marina did not share this "discovery" with her husband. Why couldn't Oswald, who knew Anatoly was jealous of him, make the same discovery that Anatoly and Kennedy resembled each other?

Having examined what might have percolated in Oswald's consciousness, it is necessary to review the chronological sequence of the events shortly before the November 22.

November 18: Oswald finds out about the November 17 telephone call made by Marina and Ruth Paine to his apartment and becomes indignant, afraid that the FBI will discover where he is hiding. In the ensuing days he breaks the established pattern of telephoning Marina by not calling her at all.

November 19: The Dallas newspapers announce the president's motorcade route. It is entirely possible that Lee heard his co-workers discuss, or even read in the papers, that the motorcade would pass the textbook depository.

November 20: Oswald is present in his boss's office when a co-worker shows what he, the co-worker, purchased—a small-caliber rifle and a Mauser.

November 21: Without forewarning, Lee appeared after work at the Paine residence. He justified the unusual visit by saying that he missed "his girls." He had not been able to visit the preceding weekend, when the Paines had had a birthday party for one of their children. He explained to his co-worker and the Paines' neighbor, with whom he got a ride from the depository to the Paine's home, that he had to pick up a "curtain rod." During this visit, Lee tried to reconcile with his wife and insisted that the family live together. He suggested renting an apartment and stressed that he was tired of living alone. Marina would not be persuaded and refused his request.

During the day's conversation, the president's visit was mentioned. Marina expressed her interest and asked, "I'd like to see him *in person* [author's emphasis]. Do you know where and when I could go?"

"No," he said.*

There was an earlier episode involving a heightened interest in the Kennedy family:

Once Marina said casually: "He's very attractive. I can't say what he is as President, but, I mean, as a man." Lee's response was the usual: "You mustn't like any other man but me."†

On the evening of the twenty-first, Lee was especially tender with the children and went to bed earlier than usual. Before going to bed, he spent some time in the garage, where his rifle was stored in a blanket. Nobody knew what he did there.

November 22:   Based on his wife's observations, on the night of November 21–22, Lee only fell asleep shortly before dawn, although he pretended to be asleep. In the morning he did not react to the alarm clock, which was unusual for him. He went out for breakfast, then went into the bedroom and said good-bye to his wife, without kissing her, which was their routine. At this time, Marina did not know that he took off and left his wedding ring, which he had never done under any circumstances, even before his attempt to kill General Walker.

*Priscilla McMillan, *Marina and Lee* (New York: Harper and Row, 1977), p. 522.
†Ibid, p. 413.

The details of these days are taken from Priscilla McMillan's *Marina and Lee,* which to my mind is a valuable source of information concerning the Oswalds' domestic problems. This work is important for two reasons. The author met and talked to Oswald in Moscow in 1959 during a stressful period for him, and this information certainly helped her to more deeply understand the information she received from Marina and others. Also, the information was still fresh and unique and only known by Oswald's wife when she was interviewed by McMillan. Marina had not yet been exposed to a variety of factors, which influenced her over the course of the following decades.

I fully share Priscilla McMillan's conclusions concerning Oswald's mixed character and the individual motivations which brought him to the sixth-floor window. But I differ in the emphasis placed on these motivations. Ms. McMillan stresses the prevalence of ideological political moments strengthened by elements of delusions of grandeur and daily irritants. I lean toward the view that the growing family conflicts, suddenly blocking the path to realizing his domestic goals, brought out his sadomasochistic tendencies, which he projected on three objects: himself, his wife, and President Kennedy. Probably the deadly reaction would not have occurred had the family "detonator" not worked within the context of his political frustrations.

This is how Oswald's complex motives merge to explode into the fatal moment:

- *Catalyst:* The confirmation of attention from the FBI, Marina's positive reaction to the bureau's representative, increased indignation at the FBI's "pursuit," and the growing fear for the safety of the family.
  Reaction: Taking protective measures—the note to the local FBI and the November 8 letter to the Soviet embassy complaining about the pursuit.
- *Catalyst:* Anguished state due to the impossibility of seeing his family due to the Paines' birthday party; indignation caused by Marina's telephoning him, which could call the FBI's attention to his "hideout," which in turn strengthened his thoughts of creating his own "fortress" and unifying the family; the flow of information regarding the president's

Dallas trip; remembering that the president's brother
Robert, as attorney general, is head of the FBI, which is
persecuting him.
Reaction: Showing Marina how displeased he is by cutting
off telephone contact.

- *Catalyst:* The impending passing of the president near his
place of work, the demonstration of firearms inside the
book depository, thoughts of emotionally blackmailing his
wife by threatening Kennedy in the event that she refused to
live with him.
Reaction: Visiting the family with the goal of making peace
and forming concrete reunification plans.

Priscilla McMillan felt that Oswald came to the Paine residence
on November 21, having made the decision to go after Kennedy. I
also differ with her on this point. I believe that the final decision
took shape during the sleepless night, when feelings sharply inten-
sify and even the craziest thoughts become hypertrophic. It was at
this point that Oswald added the final building block to his motives:

- His wife's categorical refusal to accept his conditions for
living together.
- New signs of Marina's interest in Kennedy.
- Feeling rejected by everyone, experiencing diminished
self-worth, questioning even his manhood.

It's possible that en route to Dallas from the Paines' residence,
Oswald had these thoughts: Well, well, so you want to see what he
looks like in "person," Come on, I'll show you. And those FBI
punks, they'll find out that they're nothing. I know how to take care
of myself. I've got nothing to lose. I'll show you, I'll show all of you.

The complex of motives becomes a plan of action.

It is doubtful that Oswald, seeing Kennedy in the cross hairs of
his sight, aimed at him because he was the president of the United
States and realized the scale of his crime. He probably saw a smiling
Marina in his mind's eye, happily waving at the passing motorcade,
and was fully concentrating on this vision, maybe even muttering,
"Look, take a look, now you'll see him. Then you'll find out which
of us is stronger."

Pulling the trigger, again and again, he shot not at the president but at his rival, and this helped him to be exceptionally accurate.

I would like to interrupt this discussion of motives and return to the question of technology, only this time not as part of a conspiracy but to describe Oswald's actions as a lone person involved in the events at Dealey Plaza. Comments regarding the scenario of the big conspiracy will also be included.

Delivery of the Rifle

If Oswald was involved in the large-conspiracy scenario and was assigned the extremely important scapegoat role, then during the final stages the conspirators had to guard him "with their lives" and keep him under constant surveillance.

If Oswald's role played out without his knowledge and the plan was to "connect" him just at the final stage by compelling him to bring the rifle, then his surveillance had to be extremely secret so that he wouldn't think that it was the FBI and start complaining and in this manner prematurely become a "potentially dangerous" person to the president.

If Oswald participated in a conspiracy and was in full possession of his senses but did not realize the extent of his role (in his hypothetical assignment of bringing the rifle to the "battlefield") he would be extremely valuable, since any misunderstanding with him would threaten the entire action. This could have dire consequences for someone.

If this is how events were scheduled to unfold, then on the appointed day someone would have to meet with Oswald for transmitting last-minute instructions, and this would have a psychological influence on him. The extent of the influence and his reaction would depend on his mood. He would also be warned that he would be under constant surveillance to ensure that nothing went wrong. He would be told not to worry if he noticed that he was "accompanied" by someone.

Such a meeting could have occurred on the twenty-first, in the interval between his leaving the apartment and arriving at work. During this interval Oswald could have been prompted to drive to work with the Paines' neighbor, which would have created a witness to his delivering something to the book depository and thereby "strengthened" the scapegoat role.

Unfortunately, since there is no information about this period, it is impossible to judge if there is the slightest indication that Oswald was under someone's control or surveillance. It is untenable to speak of a big conspiracy without this kind of control to ensure the delivery of Oswald's rifle to the appointed spot.

However, within the realm of realizing his own intentions, his actions are perfectly natural. Most likely the intentions were improvised, possibly finally formulated, as already stated, the night before and not thought out in detail beforehand.

Comparing these actions with his preparation to assassinate General Walker, the act in Dallas lacks the long, careful planning of the previous one. Then there is the question of the rifle's condition. Since his move from New Orleans two months previously, there are no reports that Oswald touched it. As far as is known, it lay in the garage. Within the realm of the big conspiracy, is it possible to undertake such a serious mission without first checking the readiness of the chosen rifle?

There are analogies here with his armed trip to Mexico and the demonstration with the pistol in the Soviet embassy. In both instances Oswald did not consider the possible intervening complications. He just plunged ahead.

The Shooting

Two deeply rooted questions are still passionately debated in this regard: Did Oswald shoot the president, and was he a sufficiently competent marksman to hit a moving target three times during a short interval?

I'll begin by answering the second question first and address the other question at the end of the chapter. The last two to four months of Oswald's life are the basis for analysis in this chapter. Therefore, many well-known aspects will not be presented now in the "Oswald and the Rifle" section, but only events from this period. Referring back to *Marina and Lee:*

One evening during the last week in August . . . (Marina) found Lee on the porch, perched on one knee, pointing his rifle toward the street. It was the first time she had seen him with his rifle in months—and she was horrified.

. . . A few evenings later, she again found him on the porch with his rifle.

Playing with your gun again, are you?" she said, sarcastically.

Fidel Castro needs defenders. I'm going to join his army of volunteers. I'm going to be a revolutionary."

. . . After this Marina often frequently heard a clicking sound out on the porch while he was sitting there at dusk. She heard it three times a week, maybe more often, until the middle of September. . . . Often she saw him clean the rifle. . . . She knew that he had never taken it out of the house to practice.

. . . She exacted a promise from him that he would not use his rifle against anybody in the United States. . . . "I won't," he promised her in a quiet voice.*

It is worth noting that conditions during these "dry runs" or training exercises were similar to those in November. In both instances there was a building and a street below.

I'd like to bring in some experts in this area. First Dr. Joseph Borisovich Linder, president of the International Counter Terror Training Association, from Chapter 1, will answer some questions:

Q. Using a rifle with a 4 × scope, what are the chances of hitting a moving target at a distance of 265.3 feet twice within 4.8 to 5.6 seconds without practicing beforehand?

A. It would not be particularly difficult for an average marksman who is familiar with using the rifle and in a stationary position. As far as I can judge, the positioning of the shooter in the book depository in relation to the moving target was favorable for successful execution.

Q. Does it make sense to invoke the "lottery principle" when

*McMillan, *Marina and Lee*, p. 452.

evaluating the number of times the shooter will hit from the book depository window? (I'll clarify the lottery principle. A poor marksman will hit the target three to five times out of 100 shots in a series. But he won't be able to achieve this result in the next series. An average marksman will hit the target 55–65 times out of 100; an expert marksman, 95–97 times out of 100.)

A. Yes, it does. The aim is also affected by the psychological makeup of the shooter and his ability to rise to the occasion. A weak shooter can significantly improve his results due to psychological readiness or preparedness, and a good shooter might not match his usual score based on this factor.

For instance, in 1972, in Munich during the Olympic Games, the snipers who were trained to combat terrorists, at the first encounter with a live target, lost their heads, and this affected their accuracy.

By November 22, Oswald had already practiced on a live target, General Walker, although "unsuccessfully." It is possible, to the good fortune of General Walker, that Oswald's accuracy may have been affected by worrying about shooting at a human target.

Here is what the authoritative expert, the distinguished coach of Soviet sport shooting, Lev M. Weinstein, has to say in this regard:

Having read the article by *Izvestia*'s U.S. correspondent, Aleksandr Chalnev entitled "America Argues About the Crime of the Century, Again" and having seen Stone's JFK, I decided to offer my opinion on a certain aspect of the question. I have a great deal of experience in the field of sports shooting, and I reiterate that it is *fully possible for an elementary-level shooter-sportsman* [author's emphasis] to successfully hit a target three times within 5.6 seconds, using a rifle with a scope. Based on previously published material, it is known that Oswald had engaged in sports shooting.

Time allotted for the shooting. This was established by counting the frames of the Zapruder film. But in aimed shooting, time is not spent on the shooting itself but in the preparation, positioning the rifle, aiming, and squeezing the trigger.

Since time was marked by the first shot, it does not count. Therefore, the 5.6 seconds involved two, and not three, shots.

Optics. It is known that the fatal shots came from a rifle with an optical scope. This fact creates heightened demands on the shooter's preparation:

- It is necessary to fix the position of the head with the level of the rifle. This takes time.
- The recoil after can put a shooter off his aim. The solution to this problem occurs when the rifleman uses a stationary rest position. By being at rest, even an insufficiently practiced shooter can ensure higher accuracy by quickly reestablishing his aim following a shot.
- *Rest position.* During the quickly flashing frames of *JFK* someone "kneeled" at the school depository window ready to shoot. But it is extremely difficult to achieve a rest position shooting from a "kneeling position," especially with an optical sight. Taking into account the tempo and high accuracy rate, the firing occurred during a *prone or rest position* [author's emphasis]. It is also possible that the shooter knelt and rested his upper body on the windowsill, which would approximate a prone position.
- *Experiment.* Citing Aleksandr Chalnev's article, "Neither the FBI, nor those who Stone hired were able to approach Oswald's amazing shooting record, and he was, based on unified opinion, a horrible shot." But judging from the film, these experiments were conducted in the kneeling position and therefore destined for failure. If the shooting was conducted from the prone position, then Stone would have seen that there *was nothing unusual* [author's emphasis] in Oswald's results.
- *Lee Harvey Oswald* was characterized as a "horrible shot." This description comes for those who went duck hunting with him. But shooting a gun at a flying duck is completely different from firing a rifle at a "moving target." The shooter is not psychologically ready until he has aimed. Hunting is shooting at something flying about, at a direction. It is possible that Oswald, with his acquired target-shooting habits, could not conform to the

requirements of hunting and thereby earned his terrible
reputation.* During a telephone conversation with the
author in the summer of 1992 Lev M. Weinstein confirmed
these opinions as published in *Izvestia.*

It is important to note that none of the experts quoted was
familiar with the *Warren Commission Report.* They are unaware of
the experiments conducted using Oswald's rifle and firing from the
book depository building and the results which state: *A person
would not have to be an expert sniper to kill with this rifle* [author's
emphasis].

I forwarded the conclusions of the firearms experts from the
Warren Commission Report and a copy of the Zapruder film to the
corresponding experts at the Ballistics Laboratory of the Moscow
Division of the Ministry of Internal Affairs and asked them to
evaluate this material. The experts employed special methods to
analyze frame 313 of the Zapruder film and concluded that the fatal
shot was made from above and from the rear. Their conclusion
appears in the appendix.

Oswald's Behavior After the Shooting, Up to the Time of His Arrest

This interval is also the subject of discussion and interpretation.
Any version that seeks to establish the truth should be examined.

Those who maintain Oswald's innocence base it on witnesses'
accounts and assert that he was not on the sixth floor at the time
of the assassination. If he had been, he would have inevitably
bumped into a co-worker as he descended from that floor after the
shooting.

But based on these assumptions, it is probable that Oswald, just
like anyone else, would not be able to leave without attracting
attention, so this leads to the conclusion that no one shot from the
sixth floor. Anyone who knows anything about the day's events
would find this difficult to believe.

*Izvestia, March 3, 1992.
Warren Commission Report, p. 190.

Others who maintain his innocence point to his calmness when he met officer Marrion Baker and his boss, Roy S. Truly, and insist that he could not be in a calm state if he had just committed the crime of the century.

Marrion Baker was one of several motorcycle officers escorting the presidential motorcade through Dallas. After the last shot, he raced into the book depository building. Baker saw a man through the glass window in the door of a second-floor lunchroom. With Roy Truly, superintendent of the book depository, close behind him, Baker flung open the door and challenged the man, with gun drawn. When Truly identified the man as a book depository employee, Officer Baker continued up the stairs to the roof.

The conspiracy theorists explain all his actions within the framework of the large conspiracy: that Oswald acted in accordance with a plan, either as the possible killer or the nonshooting scapegoat. For example, he was only the rifle's courier.

By connecting different points of view to the chapter's theme, I would like to offer my explanation of events during this time frame:

After shooting President Kennedy, Oswald entered into an autopilot state. Along the way, he hid the rifle among the book boxes and descended quickly to the second floor. While still in this other "world," his "calmness" reflected his indifference. He was ready for anything that might happen to him, including being shot by the president's security force or the police.

Meeting Baker and Truly "woke him up" by returning him to reality. The feeling of indifference to his fate and doom was replaced by an awakened instinct of self-preservation.

After he left the Texas School Book Depository, Oswald found himself surrounded by panic and confusion. Gradually, the awareness of the implications of his actions grew on him. The importance of his personal motives dissolved. Fear and guilt became the driving forces of what he did next.

It is widely known how fear can destroy a person's logical behavior, disrupt the understanding of cause and effect, and bring about temporary insanity. During these moments a person reverts back to his animal instincts, and it is no wonder that the phrase "seized with an animal fear" exists.

That Oswald had been gripped by fear before is shown by his condition after his attempt to assassinate Walker. In *Marina and Lee,* Priscilla MacMillan writes:

> That night, twenty fours after his attempt on Walker's life, Lee suffered anxiety attacks in his sleep. He shook all over from head to toe four times at intervals of a half hour or so, but without waking up. . . . The next night he again suffered convulsive anxiety attacks in his sleep.

After the Walker incident, Oswald only imagined the consequences. Now, in every fiber of his body, he must have felt the danger, which could come from anyone.

I feel that all of Oswald's actions after he stopped at his apartment were based on this growing fear. At his apartment and already confused, he feverishly changed, later explaining "that his clothes were dirty." He grabbed a pistol and headed toward that part of Dallas where there were few people. This struck him as safe. He did not think that if his picture had been broadcast on television that people could spot him even from the windows of the nearby houses. Unexpectedly, a patrol car caught up with him, and a policeman approached. Oswald realized this was a real threat, which, combined with his temporary insanity, caused him to shoot the officer. What other explanation can one offer for the fact that Tippit was shot four times and witnesses say the last shot was fired when he was already down?

I recall something Oswald said in passing in Mexico—"But if they don't get off my back, I'm going to defend myself"—meaning that he would fire in self-defense if someone threatened his life. Considering his state when he met Tippit, this was a life-threatening situation. Spectators say that after he shot Tippit, he reloaded his pistol; that is, he prepared for new attacks. Oswald also tried to use the gun against his pursuers in the movie theater while police detained him.

After Oswald shoots Tippit only one thing is left for him to do—find a hiding place. But first another "costume change." He throws his jacket into the bushes, which again changes the appearance of the shooter. His first reaction to the sound of approaching sirens is to duck into a shoe store, then into a movie theater, a dark place that created the feeling of temporary safety.

When the police appeared in the movie theater and rushed toward him, Oswald reacted in a terrified fashion, which explains his panicked resistance and even the attempt to use the pistol again. Given all that happened, his "everything's finished" remark is a reasonable and appropriate response.

Oswald's actions and comment raise the question Who could convincingly explain why someone acted like this if he wasn't feeling guilty?

Often the imagined punishment is worse than the actual punishment. Based on this theory, one can assume that if the police had come a little later, Oswald could have, without leaving the theater, used his gun on himself.

Oswald's Behavior After His Arrest Until His Death

In the Police and Courts Building, Oswald's first phrases to the gathered press were shouts of "I'm innocent" and "I'm just a patsy." These proclamations could indicate that he immediately tried to acquit himself of the death of the president. They can also serve to indicate that while he was shooting at Kennedy, he was not trying to change the course of world history.

From the moment of his arrest until Jack Ruby shot him, Oswald did not make any public political statements. He did not avail himself of the opportunity to announce his ideological and political views to the world, as a political terrorist would do. In similar circumstances, a political terrorist would not only admit his participation, he would underline his sense of pride in his action and certainly not feel any guilt.

While under arrest Oswald may have realized the nonproportionality of his motives with the consequences of his actions for America and the rest of humanity.

What did the person to whom he was closest, his wife, Marina, notice about him during their only meeting at the Police and Courts building:

He looked pitiful, his eyes were full of trouble.

His words were the old Lee, full of bravado, but Marina could tell by the pitch of his voice that he was frightened. She saw fear in his eyes. . . .

He was saying goodbye with his eyes *as she was leaving* [author's emphasis].

Marina was now certain that Lee was guilty. She saw his guilt in his eyes.*

Even more than that, she felt that if he were innocent, he would start screaming about his rights and unfair treatment and demand to meet with the highest officials, just as he had always done. His admission that he was treated "normally" signaled to Marina that he was guilty.

Marina saw that Lee's expression simultaneously indicated satisfaction and remorse. She did not feel that he discarded the weight he always carried around with him.

He looked at her, altogether uncharacteristically, with supplication in his eyes. He was pleading with her not to desert him. He was begging for her love, her support, and above all, her silence. He knew that this was the end.†

Marina noticed that he soothed her and gave her advice "in words almost identical to the ones he had written in the 'Walker note.' "‡ He had written to Marina then: "You have friends. They'll help you. If it comes to that, you can ask the Red Cross for help. You mustn't worry about me. Kiss Junie and Rachel for me."

If all the pathetic elements and the literary style of *Marina and Lee* are discarded, then the essence of Marina's then fresh recollections lead to the following: *Marina was convinced of her husband's guilt in Kennedy's assassination* (author's emphasis).

I'd like to comment on three moments during her last meeting with Lee:

- The feeling of guilt, which Marina noticed in Lee's eyes, probably, and primarily, consisted of his guilt toward her.

*McMillan, *Marina and Lee*, p. 547.
†Ibid., p. 548.
‡Ibid., p. 547.

This leads to the sadomasochistic motivation of the assassination. Therefore, it is doubtful that if Oswald had remained alive and been convicted of killing the president he would acknowledge the real reason for his action. This would mean taking into account his inflated self-esteem, combined with the worthlessness he felt in the eyes of those who surrounded him, as the reasons for his actions.

- Advice to Marina in the spirit of the "Walker note" attests to his understanding of the inevitable, approaching punishment and is an oblique admission of his guilt.
- In speaking of Oswald's habit of loudly demanding his rights, Marina did not understand the conditions surrounding his interrogation and was unaware that he had already banged his fists on the table during this period.

Did he do this because he was innocent? Based on material from the first interrogation on November 22,* Lee reacted with great animosity toward the appearance and participation of special agents of the FBI, especially Hosty. It's possible that the bureau members' appearance played a "stimulating role" and became the turning point in Oswald's behavior. This "constant irritant" helped Oswald strengthen his righteous stance and reduce his feelings of culpability. As a result, Oswald's confusion and guilt were gradually replaced by his inherent self-assurance, and even in this instance his relationship with the authorities returned to the first-second, or action-reaction, principle.

From the meager notes available on this interrogation, it is evident that Oswald "gathered" himself and became a stereotypical version of himself. He shamelessly and deliberately lied and denied or distorted the facts. He issued his "own" scapegoat statement when he said that he had seen another co-worker bring a rifle to work the day before the assassination. He created his own alibi— that he was eating on the first floor—and named co-workers as table mates, who were clearly documented to be at the fifth-story windows, watching the motorcade.

What could a person be thinking, weaving these "fairy tales," knowing that they would fall apart at first verification? It's possible

*Warren Commission Report, Appendix XI, typewritten page 3.

that Oswald had not had enough time alone to come up with some kind of story and stubbornly stick to it.

By combining all the elements examined in this chapter—the motives, his behavior on the eve and day of the assassination, and the delivery of the rifle and the shooting—it is possible to come to the conclusion that it was Oswald who assassinated the president.

Most probably the act was committed alone, based on his own motives, which reached a critical point during the night of November 21. Led by these motives, Oswald chose to shoot the president as a form of suicide.

In regard to the third killing, of Oswald by Jack Ruby, without fully rejecting the elements of personal motivation but with a great deal of certainty, it can be assumed that the reasons for this murder came from the outside, since Oswald somehow, most probably in New Orleans in 1963, came into contact with members of the big conspiracy and therefore fell under the lizard principle.

In examining the theme of the last chapter, Marina Oswald's unique observations were widely used. Anyone who is familiar with her story cannot help but feel an enormous human compassion for all she has lived through for the past thirty years, since her first meeting with her husband-to-be on March 17, 1961. Maybe if all the adversity she experienced was spread out among dozens of people, there would still be enough left to physically and morally destroy many of their lives. Therefore, her emotional strength is to be commended.

But in the summer of 1992 I came across a disturbing fact that put me on my guard. I was in Minsk when I read the following interview, published in the *People's Newspaper* on August 6 of that year:

"My husband could not have shot President John Kennedy," Marina Porter née Oswald told her interviewer from TASS. She was the Russian wife of Lee Harvey Oswald, the man who was officially found guilty of killing President Kennedy.

"I *consider* [author's emphasis] that Oswald could not shoot the President," Marina Porter repeated. "He was in the book depository building because he worked there and was supposed to be *there* [author's emphasis].

During the same interview, Marina proclaims that "shortly after the birth of our second daughter, "they" had a chance to live in his brother's house in Dallas" and "it was there, during a news bulletin" that she "first heard of the assassination." She added, "The police arrived shortly thereafter and clarified that her husband was suspected in the assassination."

Someone should ask Marina Oswald who lived at the Paine residence between September 24 and November 22. Where did Oswald spend the night of November 21–22? In whose garage, seemingly in Marina's presence, did the police search for a rifle belonging to Oswald after the assassination?

At her meeting with Lee at the Police and Courts Building she was accompanied by Oswald's mother, and not his brother, as she says in the same interview. In this regard the *Warren Commission Report* clearly states, "From 1:10 to 1:30 P.M., Oswald's *wife and mother* [author's emphasis] visited him in the fourth-floor visiting area." The report also mentioned that Oswald's *brother* met with him for ten minutes on the same day, but later than Marina and Mrs. Oswald.

There is a thirty-year difference between Marina's quotes in *Marina and Lee* and those in the interview. I hope that Marina Oswald understands when I ask these questions:

Which of her views are to be believed?

What was the author of *Marina and Lee*'s position?

What other "amendments" can we expect from her in the future?

Naturally Marina has the right to change her views on Oswald's role in the assassination. But in doing so her explanation of such a dramatic turnaround from her prior stance is necessary.

PART THREE

Fates

I have lived, I have run to the finish the course
which fortune gave me.

—Virgil, *The Aeneid*

Introduction

Part Three examines the fates of certain individuals whose lives, at one point or another, intersected with Lee Harvey Oswald's and the consequences this had for them.

The three chapters of Part Three describe the fates of three former KGB officers: one who voluntarily became a traitor to his side; one whom the opposing side tried to make a traitor; and one whom the enemy "neutralized" by publicly exposing his activities.

With all three the events related here took place within the parameters of the skirmishes carried out by the opposing intelligence services of the two superpowers during the Cold War of the 1960s and 1970s.

Specific examples also show how, in a number of cases, paranoid suspicion and insufficient knowledge caused huge expenditures of effort and money to be directed against the enemy. Ironically, it often produced the opposite result.

11

Paranoia Versus Common Sense (Pro and Con)

I believe that Nosenko should be recognized as a genuine defector.

—Adm. Rufus Taylor,
Deputy Director CIA,
October 4, 1968

Nosenko was a plant, is a plant, and will always be one.

—Tenneat Harrington "Pete" Bagley,
Deputy Chief of the Soviet Division
of the Directorate of Plans, CIA

On February 5, 1964, a game of "telegraphic Ping-Pong" was begun between KGB headquarters in Moscow and the rezidentura in Geneva. Over the next several days coded telegrams flew back and forth between the two cities. The exchange of telegrams with other rezidenturas in Europe and the United States also increased. All were marked "Top Priority" or "Urgent." After being decoded, they were rushed to the desk of the head of the First Chief Directorate, from where they were immediately sent on to the office of the chairman of the KGB at 2 Dzerzhinsky Square.

Since nothing out of the ordinary was taking place in international politics, it might have been assumed that some kind of major operation was taking place or that an emergency had occurred. Everything became clear one week later.

On February 12, at 5:05 P.M., a Russian-language broadcast from Rome reported the following sensational item:

According to sources in Geneva, Yuri Nosenko, who has asked for political asylum in the United States, handed over [to the Americans] information of great importance, including that related to the production of nuclear weapons.

The day before, Lt. Gen. Oleg Gribanov, head of the SCD had informed the KGB leadership that, based on foreign news reports, Yuri Ivanovich Nosenko had defected to the American side. He was in Geneva at the time attending a conference when he was listed as an "expert" in the Soviet delegation. "The reasons," Gribanov reported, "which caused him to do this, and the circumstances, are not known."

Nosenko, born in 1927, had been a member of the Communist party since 1957 and an employee of the KGB since 1953. He held the rank of captain (contrary to previously published reports). As deputy head of the Seventh Department of the Second Chief Directorate, he had been sent to Geneva to carry out counterintelligence activities.

According to data provided by the rezidentura in Geneva, Nosenko had gone into the city shortly after twelve noon on February 4 to have lunch, after which he disappeared. A six-day search for his whereabouts had proved unsuccessful. There was no evidence that Nosenko had been preparing to "commit a crime" while abroad.

Gribanov concluded his report by stating that Nosenko, in accordance with the nature of his work and position, was "highly informed" about the KGB's counterintelligence activities against foreigners.

An employee of the Soviet Ministry of Foreign Affairs, who was also a member of that delegation and who is mentioned only as "T," gave the following testimony in 1964:

I met Nosenko on the airplane January 19 while on the way to Geneva via Paris. In Paris everyone left their baggage at the Soviet embassy and went sightseeing. Nosenko was with us the whole time. He constantly had in his possession a stamped leatherette brown folder with a zipper on top.

While we were filling out customs declarations for Geneva, he let me hold the folder. It was heavy and felt like it was crammed full with papers.

Nosenko liked to wear dark glasses in Geneva. He exhibited a tendency to prefer being by himself; he ate alone. I personally never had occasion to see him drunk. However, several members of the delegation told me that toward the end of his stay in Geneva he had obtained some bottles of alcohol and had become extremely intoxicated.

During the times I saw him Nosenko never said anything about himself, and our conversations were general in nature.

For the first two or three days Nosenko apparently was experiencing financial difficulties and asked me to loan him twenty to twenty-five francs, which he later returned. He subsequently showed no interest in receiving his allotted per diem of 259 Swiss francs. I do not remember now whether he had the folder with him in Geneva.

Another member of the delegation, "R," lived with Nosenko in the same hotel room and remembered him as being "an unpleasant roommate who snored very loudly." He also recalled seeing him on February 3, that is, the day before his defection, and that he was very drunk. The next day, R returned to the hotel room at eleven in the evening, but Nosenko was not there. This did not cause him any concern, since Nosenko, as a rule, came back late. In the morning when he awoke, he noticed that Nosenko had not spent the night in their room. Now R became worried, because on February 5 the delegation was to move from the hotel to a newly renovated villa.

On the morning of the fifth, a car was sent to the hotel to pick them up. R reported Nosenko's absence to another member of their delegation, who in turn told him there was no need to worry, as Nosenko had probably stayed with one of the women in the delegation. Another delegation leader also said there was no reason for alarm, but R was concerned for another reason: He would have to pay for another night's lodging if Nosenko's luggage remained in the room, and he did not have enough allowance to cover it.

At eight in the morning R again told the delegation head there was no sign of Nosenko and that he was now going to gather his roommate's belongings and take them to the villa. While packing Nosenko's bags, R noticed that he had left his razor behind, but his shirts and the brown leatherette briefcase were missing. R seemed to recall that Nosenko had not weighed this briefcase at Sheremetyevo Airport in Moscow. In addition, he had not handed his passport to the general secretary of the delegation upon their arrival in Geneva, which constituted a gross procedural violation.

As Gribanov had clearly stated in his memorandum to the KGB leadership that Nosenko had been dispatched to Geneva to carry out "counterintelligence activities." This meant he was assigned to look out for the Soviet delegation and guarantee its safety. The rezidentura of a country, to which a Soviet delegation or tourist group was sent, would receive a message from the Center informing it of the arrival of an operative and instructing its employees to give him all the assistance needed to carry out his mission. One of the employees working in counterintelligence would have to establish contact with the arriving operative. If he were unknown to the rezidentura, contact would be made using a password thought up by Moscow. After contact was made, the operative would be brought up to speed on the conditions in the country and city, the actions of the enemy intelligence services and their agents against Soviet citizens, and the conditions for transmitting messages back to the Center. In turn, the operative would periodically report to the rezidentura on the circumstances in and around the delegation and, if necessary, would ask the rezidentura for additional help in fulfilling his assignment.

Nosenko also maintained contact with the Geneva rezidentura, which knew beforehand that they were not dealing with just any operative but a rather high ranking staff member. Because of his position, no attempt was made to search for him on February 4, the date of his disappearance. It was assumed that he had his own affairs to attend to. Only on the following day, when the head of the delegation reported Nosenko's absence to the Soviet representation to the United Nations in Geneva, did the local rezidentura actively seek him out. Members of the "Soviet colony" were questioned, but to no avail. They inspected his belongings left behind in the hotel room. Among the items missing were two new nylon shirts, purchased in Geneva, a woolen shirt, which he wore every day, pajamas, and an expensive briefcase.

On the eve of his defection, Nosenko had reported to the rezidentura on his work and his contacts while categorically refusing the rezidentura's offer to participate jointly in a number of actions. He said that he would join them only with permission from the Center. According to an employee of the rezidentura, Nosenko's behavior during the report did not cause any suspicion of him.

Swiss citizens were questioned as well, but they were able to tell the Soviet agents nothing about Nosenko's disappearance. One Swiss police officer said that Nosenko had supposedly visited his hotel on February 4 at around five in the afternoon, but the hotel's porter could not confirm this. Still, the Soviet investigators could not believe the Swiss police, since it could just as easily have been disinformation they were handing out. On the other hand, the Swiss authorities complied with the Soviets' request not to make public for several days the fact that one of their members was missing. On Saturday, February 4, 1964, a French journalist caught wind of Nosenko's defection and phoned the Soviet representatives for details. Now the cat was out of the bag, and newspapers around the world began to report the news. One paper even printed a photograph that was allegedly Nosenko; in fact, it was another member of the Soviet delegation.

The first foreign newspaper reports about Nosenko's defection were extremely vague, more conjecture than anything else. But after the announcement by Semyon K. Tsarapkin, the head of the Soviet delegation in Geneva, reports appeared in the papers that Nosenko had betrayed his country and that he was of great value to American intelligence. The press also reported that Nosenko was a KGB employee who knew a great deal about the inner workings of that organization and that "the Americans had never had anyone like him before."

Until the reports of his voluntary defection were confirmed, the rezidentura tried to allay their worst fears by supposing that Nosenko had been abducted by American intelligence, but there was no information to support this supposition.

On January 20, 1964, a long-awaited telegram arrived from Geneva at one of the CIA's safe houses in New York. Within a few hours two employees of American intelligence, who both knew Russian, caught two different flights to Switzerland to meet their "old friend."

In June 1962, KGB officer Yuri Ivanovich Nosenko, in Geneva operating under cover of the Soviet delegation for disarmament, made contact on his own with American representatives and offered his services to the United States. He claimed his offer was motivated by the fact that he had spent all the money officially allotted to him and he agreed to sell secret information for three hundred dollars. He subsequently announced that this was a cover story, so that he would not be perceived as a KGB provocateur.

During his meetings in 1962 with CIA officers, Nosenko handed over information about several KGB intelligence and counterintelligence operations, which led to their failure and the arrest of foreign agents, and reported on the presence and position of eavesdropping devices in the American embassy in Moscow and about many other aspects of KGB counterintelligence activities. He also informed American intelligence that a secret agent had been exposed by Moscow who had made use of the CIA station in the embassy and was being held. That agent was Col. Oleg Penkovsky, a GRU military intelligence officer who spied for the Britons and Americans between 1960 and 1962 and who was then exposed and executed.*

The value of the information was so great for the American side that the two officers who had been working with Nosenko, "Peter" Bagley and K. Kiselvater, known as "Teddy Bear," flew back to Washington on different flights in order to guarantee its safe delivery. One carried tape recordings with him; the other was entrusted with Nosenko's handwritten notes.

Nosenko agreed to continue his cooperation with American in-

The Penkovsky Papers detailed much of the data Penkovsky revealed and became a best-seller in the United States in 1965.

telligence under two conditions: (1) Contact with him was forbidden while he was in the Soviet Union, and (2) he should not be expected to defect immediately, for he did not intend to leave his family behind. Future contacts would be made only during his subsequent trips abroad. He was given an address in New York where he was to send a letter, postcard, or telegram describing everyday life using a false name as soon as he found himself abroad.

Bagley and Kiselvater had absolutely no doubt as to the bona fides of their contact and in the authenticity of his information. CIA headquarters at Langley, Virginia, and the Soviet Russian Division of the Directorate of Plans also had a high estimation of it. In CIA terminology, they had received a "defector in place," one who professes loyalty to another government, usually hostile to his own, but who remains at his post and thereby becomes a so-called penetration agent.

But not everyone at Langley who knew about the case felt the same euphoria. First and foremost, the legendary "mole hunter" James J. Angleton, CIA director of counterintelligence had doubts concerning Nosenko's legitimacy.

When Bagley, the younger of the two officers, flew back to Washington, barely able to contain his excitement about the big fish they had just landed, Angleton, an inveterate fisherman, patiently heard him out and then acquainted Bagley with the materials relating to another defector, Anatoly Golitsyn, who had deserted from the KGB's ranks six months before Nosenko.

During testimony given at a congressional hearing into the investigation of President Kennedy's death, Bagley stated,

> Nosenko had seemed genuine to me. But after becoming acquainted with Golitsyn's case, whose reports I had not seen before returning to headquarters after my meetings in 1962 with Nosenko, he began to look rather strange.

Thus, under the impression of what he had read and Angleton's influence, Bagley became a staunch supporter of only one point of view—Nosenko was a KGB plant.

I can well imagine the impatience the two specialists in "Soviet affairs" must have felt as they flew to Geneva to meet their "defector in place." On the eve of his impending meeting with a valuable source, a case officer lapses into a condition which I would call the "informational thirst syndrome." All other cares are put on the back burner. His thoughts are focused on how to obtain the maximum amount of information in limited time, quickly evaluate its significance, report back to his superiors, and give the source new assignments while exerting a tutorial influence over him.

I do not know what Bagley and Kiselvater felt when Nosenko told them, during their first meeting in January 1964, that he had personally handled Lee Harvey Oswald's case during his Soviet period. Such information at such a time could easily have induced shock.

A little more than a year and a half had passed since Oswald had returned to the United States. Four months before, he had visited the Soviet and Cuban embassies in Mexico City. Two months earlier he had been arrested as the alleged assassin of President Kennedy. Two days later Oswald himself had been killed by Jack Ruby. For two months now the Warren Commission had been trying to get to the bottom of the assassination. Suppositions of KGB involvement in the murder hung in the air.

Nosenko later declared firmly that the KGB had expressed no interest in Oswald in an intelligence sense and stubbornly insisted that the KGB had nothing to do with the events in Dallas. Because of his position and unofficial contacts in the espionage milieu, Nosenko truly was an extremely informed person who was able to provide the enemy with very valuable information. For example, he unmasked an American serviceman in Paris who had been handing over to the KGB extremely valuable strategic NATO information about NATO military scenarios and its war mobilization plans in Europe. Both this source, Robert Johnson, and his contact were later arrested by the FBI and sentenced to twenty-five years each. In addition to information about specific operations, Nosenko helped the CIA draw up a detailed organizational chart of the KGB and identified all the employees he could remember.

During those first meetings in Geneva, Nosenko hinted that he was considering remaining in the West. He announced that a telegram had arrived from the Center on February 4 calling him back to Moscow. This could have meant that the KGB was getting suspicious. Therefore, he was afraid to return, since he could be arrested, tortured, and eventually shot. Nosenko sought CIA protection and asked that his defection be organized no later than the following day. He later confessed that he had made up the story about the telegram in order to pressure the CIA. But since Nosenko was informed on the Oswald case, immediate approval was granted to the suggestion made by the Geneva station to transfer him to the United States in spite of the doubts already existing at CIA headquarters as to his bona fides.

On that day, February 4, Nosenko, who by now was a "defector" instead of a "defector in place," found himself in an American vehicle with falsified American documents and dressed in street clothes (according to other sources, in an American army officer's uniform), heading across the Swiss border into Germany. He was detained there for a week in a safe house on the outskirts of Frankfurt am Main. It was also there that David Murphy, head of the Soviet unit of the CIA responsible for collecting information as well as implementing clandestine operations against the USSR throughout the world, met with him to discuss the question of Nosenko's further cooperation. Murphy confirmed that Nosenko would be recompensed for his previously conveyed information and that he would receive the annual stipend of $25,000. At the same time he warned him of the need to verify his bona fides by taking a lie-detector test. Murphy belonged to that group within the CIA which did not believe in the authenticity of Nosenko's information, at least as far as the KGB's relationship with Oswald was concerned.

While in Germany, Nosenko, at the suggestion of his "handler," signed several papers placed before him. He was told that they constituted his "official request for political asylum." On February 11, accompanied by CIA employees, Nosenko was flown to Andrews Air Force Base, outside Washington, D.C. From there he was whisked away to a safe house in the northern part of Virginia and assigned the code name AEFOXTROT. For its code names, the CIA used combinations of two letters, known as digraphs, to indicate geographic or other subjects. Soviet defectors or agents-in-place were given the diagraph AE.

On February 14, a letter from the U.S. State Department was express-delivered to the Soviet embassy in Washington. It read:

The State Department, in reference to Embassy Note No. 3 dated February 11, 1964 concerning Nosenko, Y. I., has the duty to inform you of the following.

As is known to the Embassy, the State Department on February 14 of this year organized a meeting between Nosenko, Y. I. and two representatives of the Soviet Embassy. At this meeting Nosenko informed the representatives of the Embassy that he had requested of his own free will asylum in the United States of America. This request was granted.

What follows is a recap of a recording of the conversation by one of the Soviet embassy representatives who spoke with Nosenko:

The meeting took place in an office of the American Immigration and Naturalization Service [INS]. On the American side was Robert Owen from the U.S. State Department, a representative from INS, and a third person, who did not introduce himself but was no doubt an employee of an intelligence agency.

Entering the room where Nosenko sat and confirming his identity, I asked him how he had come to be in the hands of the American authorities. Nosenko answered with a statement that had obviously been prepared beforehand: "The decision to leave the Soviet Union was made by myself not suddenly and not in the last few days. This decision had been ripening for a long time. My job gave me the chance to see deeper and more than what is written in Soviet newspapers. As a result I made the decision to remain in the West in sound mind and without any outside pressure. On the night of February 4–5, I left Switzerland and turned to the corresponding American authorities with a request for political asylum. I made the decision firmly, taking into account all the circumstances."

To the question of how his family should understand his decision and what we should tell his children about where his father had gone and what he had become, Nosenko answered, "This is the most painful question, but there is nothing I can say about it at this time. Let's not talk about it anymore."

Nosenko also confirmed that he was renouncing his Soviet citizenship. In conclusion, the Soviet embassy employee stated that he could not detect any signs of psychological or other pressure being exerted on Nosenko during their conversation and that Nosenko had indeed conscientiously and on his own defected to the West, although, as a disclaimer, he added that it was impossible to be certain this was so on the basis of just one conversation.

Nosenko's desertion was now an open fact; henceforward, he would be referred to in all internal KGB documents as "Idol," meaning idolatrous.

As a result of his defection, Nosenko turned into an isosceles triangle, with him at the base and the two powerful intelligence agencies of the two superpowers representing the opposite sides. The triangle was fluid, with each side living and acting in accordance with its own interests and way of thinking. What was unique about this triangle was that not one of the sides, as a rule, knew what the other two were doing at any given moment.

Having "chosen freedom," as it was said about defectors from East to West then, Nosenko could assume, but not know for certain, what measures the KGB would adopt after his betrayal. The plans of his hosts, in whose hands his fate now wholly depended, were equally unknown to him.

At that time the KGB still had no idea that Nosenko had betrayed them back in 1962 and that his defection was his second act of treachery. The KGB also did not know the exact volume of secret information that had been handed over to the enemy or how the CIA planned to make use of it, nor did it know the CIA's attitude toward its defector, how much it trusted him, and how it was going to use him in the future—as a consultant, a recruiter, or an active operative.

The CIA, in turn, faced a dilemma. Did they have a genuine defector or "a defector on assignment," that is, a KGB plant? If a plant, then what was the goal of such an operation, and how much of the information offered by Nosenko was real and how much disinformation?

Probably the KGB leadership had the easiest task of sorting out what to do in light of the situation. That one of their counterintelligence officers had defected was undeniable. Therefore, the main concern was to localize the incident and to minimize as much as possible the damage to Soviet intelligence.

I asked Vladimir Semichastny, KGB chairman at the time, the following question: What was the reaction in the KGB and in the government to Nosenko's defection?

He answered: "The initial reports concerning the circumstances of his defection led to the conclusion that Nosenko was working with some woman as an object of study and possible recruitment. But it turned out that she was studying him. Supposedly, that evening, after making calls to Moscow, Nosenko left with her for a restaurant beyond the Swiss border and then turned up on an American air force base located on West German territory.

"It was like a thunderbolt out of the sky for us. This was a very serious matter. We were more than simply upset—we were shocked. The mood at the First Chief Directorate and Second Chief Directorate was not a happy one. I did not rush to make an immediate report to the Central Committee until I had received the rezidentura's answers to our own questions. Then I phoned [Soviet premier] Nikita Khrushchev and said that there was the possibility of serious damage having been done by Nosenko's defection since he had worked in the KGB eleven years and knew a great deal. Khrushchev told us to do what it took to get to the bottom of the case, and then he added, 'You're letting the country down. He didn't leave simply as one of yours but as an employee under the roof of our external affairs organization [Ministry of Foreign Affairs].'

"All this time Aleksandr Sakharovsky, chief of KGB foreign intelligence, and I were discussing how to keep the damage to a minimum and figuring out how many operatives Nosenko could compromise, which ones to recall from their rezidenturas, and other measures. During these discussions we came up with the idea of having Khrushchev send a personally signed letter to President Johnson requesting him to return Nosenko. We would cite the fact that he had an elderly mother and a highly decorated father in the Communist party.

"This period of tense days for us coincided with a session of the Supreme Soviet. I resolved to approach Khrushchev with our plan during one of the session's intermissions. The entire Politburo was relaxing in a room behind the stage. Khrushchev was standing there, next to Anastus Mikoyan. I went up to him and proposed to him our idea of sending a letter to President Johnson. After a pause, his face turned crimson, and the muscles of his entire body tensed. 'You fucked up,' he said. 'Clean up your own mess. I'm not going to take up any more of my time with this shit. You let the country down. We sent you to the KGB to clean house.' But this statement of his had also hit a nerve, and I couldn't hold myself back. 'Nikita Sergeevich, I can't begin my job by purging the sons of ministers. . . .' Mikoyan, who overheard this exchange, made some suggestion, to which Khrushchev yelled back at him, 'What are you doing sticking your nose into everyone else's business!' Khrushchev had made it perfectly clear that he had no intention of getting involved in this matter and that we had to deal with it ourselves.

"About twenty or thirty minutes later, I was summoned to Khrushchev's office in the Kremlin. He was alone and had obviously calmed down. I told him, 'Nikita Sergeevich, we're conducting a secret war. There will be successes, and there will be losses, including some from our own staff. As a result of this affair we will have to take approximately four hundred people out of battle.' In a quiet voice he answered, 'Well, all right. You made a stupid proposal, and I got excited. Take care of this matter, but try to do it in such a way that our losses are kept to a minimum.'

"I told him about all the measures we were employing, and then the conversation turned to Nosenko's family. It was rather unusual, to say the least. His father, a minister of shipbuilding, played billiards with his adolescent son for money, and his mother had a general for a lover, which was no secret to her son. He was expelled from every academic institution he attended despite intervention by his father. His father, with the help of protection from former KGB chairman Ivan Serov, helped him get into the KGB. It's clear how he rose to such a high position in counterintelligence."

We also heard about Nosenko's defection from the Mexican newspapers. In our rezidentura there was only one employee who knew him well from his former work in internal counterintelligence. When this employee read the reports in the Western press about Nosenko, he became very worried and began to pack his bags, for we all knew how similar "acquaintances" with defectors ended.

True, his spirits picked up when he saw the photograph that was supposedly Nosenko but was, in actuality, someone else. We even assumed that this was a provocation by the American special services—that another person had deserted and that an active campaign was being waged against Nosenko to compromise him.

But soon, after all our doubts disappeared when a coded telegram arrived from Moscow Center confirming that Idol had indeed betrayed his country. Moscow was aware that one of our employees had worked in the past with the traitor, but at the time, our colleague's surname had been different, and Idol did not know to which country he had been posted. After several days of anxious waiting, he unpacked his bags and went back to work at our rezidentura for another year.

While our side was licking its wounds and preparing criminal action against the traitor, the newly anointed "political refugee," now living in "freedom," gave in to his persistent habit of many years and began to drink. According to Richard Helms, who at the time was deputy director of plans for the CIA, Nosenko "did not want to do anything except carouse and binge." At one of his "stops" Nosenko drank himself into such a state that he began banging plates at the bar. He had no interest in the country in which he now found himself. He began to display a lack of interest in discussing the details of KGB operations and to improvise his answers to the questions posed to him. He would break off a conversation by saying, "Let's go have a drink." The CIA decided to "soften him up" and organized a "vacation" to Hawaii but was disappointed with the results when they saw that Nosenko's habits had not changed upon his return.

John Hart, a CIA veteran who analyzed the Nosenko affair in the second half of the 1970s, explained the defector's state of mind at that time: "He was very worried that after he had been 'milked' of his information, he would be discarded and the KGB would attempt to apprehend or kill him. Nevertheless, he was compliant and continued to cooperate, although in the last few weeks he had become more difficult. He had suffered a serious personal crisis which led to his heavy drinking."

I will allow myself to add that even though the CIA had already become convinced of the defector's predilection for alcohol, they had no idea back in 1964, or at the end of the 1970s, or perhaps not even to this day, that Nosenko began drinking at the age of thirteen and by nineteen was a total alcoholic. Therefore, Mr. Hart could have genuinely been misled when he concluded that Nosenko's "personal crisis" led him to "heavy drinking." More likely, the opposite is true: Alcoholism led him to this profound crisis and to his own moral bankruptcy.

Having received their "gift" of Nosenko, the CIA simultaneously had a hot potato on their hands: his confession that he directly handled the KGB materials on Oswald both prior to the assassination and after. In the days when the Warren Commission was conducting an intensive investigation of the tragedy, such a confession could neither be ignored nor obfuscated for fear of getting burned.

I can well imagine the difficult situation in which the CIA leadership and Nosenko's direct handlers found themselves during that time. On the one hand, they had to evaluate immediately this most sensitive information concerning the blank spot in the life of the president's alleged assassin, that is, his Soviet period, and to determine whether this information was real or disinformation. On the other, the "fifty-fifty" principle of working with defectors was activated: Was he a genuine traitor or an enemy plant? One had to answer the second question, in order to unambiguously resolve the first. It was practically a closed circle. But time was slipping by. Nosenko had already spent a month in the hands of intelligence, and yet nothing had been made clear.

At the end of February, the FBI, as the lead organization assigned to carry out the investigation of the president's death, was allowed access to AEFOXTROT for the first time. On February 26 and 27, two employees interrogated him about Oswald. On March 1, the first official document, signed by J. Edgar Hoover and containing information offered by Nosenko about Oswald and the KGB's relationship with him, was sent to the Warren Commission. This information perfectly suited the FBI, for it justified their official position as to why Oswald was not considered a "dangerous element" prior to the assassination.

During this time, the CIA drew up a list of questions about

Oswald to send to the Soviet government through diplomatic chan-nels. More likely it was one of the first steps in the plan to discern AEFOXTROT's authenticity. The thinking was clear: to try to obtain additional information from the Soviets for use in analysis of the KGB-Nosenko-CIA triangle. But the State Department de-clined to use this list, fearing that it might lead to undesirable diplomatic complications. In particular, one of the questions al-luded to the Americans' suspicion that Oswald was a Soviet agent, followed by a request to the Russian government to confirm this suspicion with documentation.

On March 3 Soviet Russia Division of the Directorate of Plans of the CIA responsible for Nosenko, compiled a list of forty-four questions and subquestions for the FBI to ask Nosenko in connec-tion with Oswald. Hoover, though, refused to approve the list, and once again the FBI interrogated Nosenko on March 3, 4, and 6 with their own questions. Nosenko expressed a readiness to give testi-mony to the Warren Commission about Oswald, but no positive response followed. On March 9, the Soviet division of the CIA protested in writing the FBI's refusal to use their forty-four ques-tions and expressed their doubt that the FBI was capable of extract-ing the information about Oswald's Soviet period. It also stated the impossibility of working on the Oswald affair without the necessary information.

Another side had been added to the triangle, turning it for a while into a quadrangle. The new player was the FBI, which now became the CIA's opponent in evaluating the defector's loyalty to Ameri-can intelligence. There was no single opinion within intelligence as to who had the "right of first night" with AEFOXTROT, who, in the course of two months, had turned into a major headache for his masters.

Then a brilliant idea was hatched by one of the heads in the CIA's Soviet division, supported by someone from the CIA's internal counterintelligence service: Subject the defector to total isolation and "strict interrogations." In 1978, at a congressional session into the latest investigation of the death of President Kennedy, John Hart explained that since it was impossible to obtain Nosenko's confession in a friendly atmosphere, it was decided to put him in more Spartan surroundings for interrogation. The goal was to create psychological discomfort, frighten him, and shake out the hidden secrets.

The idea was taken to the leadership of the Justice Department. Richard Helms, deputy director of the CIA, who considered the Nosenko affair "a bone in the throat," met with the deputy attorney general to discuss such an unprecedented suggestion and then got the support of U.S. attorney general Robert Kennedy.

On April 4, Nosenko, the political refugee, a.k.a. CIA secret source AEFOXTROT, a.k.a. KGB traitor Idol, "submitted" to a polygraph test and found himself in solitary confinement for more than three years and in isolation in general for four years and eight months without trial.

In 1978 Nosenko shared his recollections of his isolation, beginning with his first lie-detector test and his further contacts with his handlers, to whom he had voluntarily entrusted his fate in 1964:

The CIA employee began to shout that I was lying, and several guards immediately rushed into the room. They ordered me to stand against the wall, undress, and submit to a body search. After this they led me up into one of the rooms in the attic. The only thing in there was a metal bed attached to the floor. No one told me anything—how long I would be there or what they were going to do with me. A couple of days later two CIA employees began their interrogation. I tried to cooperate, and in the evenings I even wrote for them everything that I could remember about the KGB. They interrogated me for two months. The tone of the interrogations was rude and hostile. Then they stopped coming. They held me in this room until the end of 1964 or beginning of 1965. They forced me to get up every day at six A.M. and did not allow me to lie down until ten P.M. The conditions were very bad. I could take a shower only once a week and shave once a week. They did not give me a toothbrush and toothpaste and fed me very poorly. I was hungry the whole time. I wasn't allowed to speak with anyone or to read. I wasn't even allowed to go outside or look out the window. The only window in the room was tightly sealed by a grate and blinds. The door into the room was steel plated, and on the other side of the door two guards watched me around the clock. The only furniture in the room was a narrow bed and a lamp. In the summer it was very hot.

How can the CIA's actions toward its voluntary helper be evaluated? It all depends on what criteria are used to make the judgment. From a human point of view, it was inhumane. From a professional point of view, it was the only correct move in that specific situation. This is my reading of it as a former intelligence officer. Even though thirty years have passed since the incident, I do not see an alternative to the measures taken by our adversaries. I shall attempt to explain my reasoning.

While the defector remained free and constantly in the grip of the "demons in the bottle," it was useless to work with him. Moreover, he could have quickly succumbed altogether to the d.t.'s. Therefore, the argument for the therapeutic effect provided through isolation made a great deal of sense.

The contrast exhibited by his handlers, from benevolence to sharply hostile, plus the conditions of confinement that unequivocally put an end to his drinking binge, could break down his story as a suspected KGB plant.

The information accumulated over the course of systematic interrogations by repeating the same questions over and over on the same theme would allow the CIA to check the validity of his version of events.

The isolation broke the connection between the participants (Moscow Center and the plant) of the alleged KGB operation and excluded their possibility of being able to correct or further develop the operation.

It negated the possibility of his defecting back the other way, whether as a plant or a genuine, but disgruntled, traitor. The defector became inaccessible for possible hostile KGB actions (if he were a genuine traitor) as well as to nosy reporters eager to learn the truth.

More than two months of isolation and intense questioning did not produce the desired effect. Nosenko did not "confess." Instead, he stubbornly continued his insistence that the KGB had no interest in Oswald during the latter's stay in the USSR. At the same time, though, he tripped up in the details of his own biography and contradicted himself in specific answers to the Oswald case, which was supposedly under his charge. The correct tactical decision had not worked, for it was carried out via a strategy that was wrong from the start. I shall explain what I mean by that a bit further on in this chapter.

It was now the second half of June, and time was passing quickly. The Warren Commission had to wrap up its investigation by September, before the presidential elections in November. Such were the orders of President Johnson. Yet one of the central questions concerning the participation of foreign governments in the assassination was far from being resolved. Equally murky were Oswald's actions in the Soviet Union and the reasons for his visits to the Soviet and Cuban embassies in Mexico two months before the assassination. To complicate matters further, the commission now had in its hands the most important witness, the one who supposedly held the answers to such questions, but was he real or a disinformer?

The difficult task of sorting out the answers fell upon the shoulders of Richard Helms, deputy director of the CIA. On June 24 he met in private with Chief Justice Earl Warren, chairman of the president's commission, and warned him that the subject of their conversation constituted a state secret and that no transcripts or other witnesses would therefore be allowed.

Helms explained that two schools of thought existed within the intelligence community in regard to Nosenko. One school held that he was a bona fide defector and that his information on Oswald was accurate. The other maintained that he was still a KGB operative and was acting upon instructions to mislead the commission about Oswald's activities in the Soviet Union. From here on I shall refer to the followers of each school as "believers" and "skeptics," respectively. Helms also stated that the CIA could not say for certain which of these two points of view was the correct one (though it was precisely within the CIA that this difference of opinion existed; so far, access to Nosenko had only been granted to the FBI, whose employees—including Hoover—were believers, that is the first school of thought) and could not resolve this question before the scheduled publication of the *Warren Commission Report*. When Warren asked him what to make of the FBI memorandum, in which such concerns are not mentioned, Helms calmly answered that he could only speak for the CIA and repeated his contention that he could not unequivocally state whether Nosenko was genuine or a KGB plant.

Later that day a dispirited and perplexed Justice Warren convened a working session of the commission in which the Nosenko question was discussed in confidentiality. The outcome of the meeting was that the commission made its first cardinal decision about Nosenko. He would not be called to testify, and he would not be interviewed by any of the commission's members. The FBI memorandum would not be published in the report; instead, it would be sent to the National Archives for safekeeping.

During these same days, on the far side of the triangle in his former country, the traitor and deserter was also the object of close scrutiny. The preliminary investigation into his criminal act, begun in February, had concluded. On June 15, 1964, Yuri Ivanovich Nosenko was indicted by a military board at a closed-door session under Article 64, paragraph A of the Russian Criminal Code for betrayal of the Motherland.

Looking back at it from today's vantage point, the situation seems tragicomic. One government was preparing to convict a former officer of its intelligence organs for defecting to the enemy. The other, to which he had voluntarily offered his services, was holding him in solitary confinement on the mere suspicion that he had been sent by his former employers on a mission of disinformation. I am certain that all my colleagues, who suffered as a result of Nosenko's betrayal, probably rubbed their hands in glee when they learned of the conditions in which he was detained by the CIA and thought to themselves, Render unto Caesar what is Caesar's.

I have no idea how Richard Helms would have reacted had he read the KGB indictment of Nosenko. More likely than not he would have put off his meeting with Earl Warren, or perhaps he would have called a meeting of the CIA's believers and skeptics. Both groups, though, probably would have viewed the document as additional confirmation of their positions. "What, you still have doubts about the defector's bona fides?" the first group would have asked. To which the second would probably have retorted, "It's just another KGB trap to support the legend of the plant!" But the status quo of the triangle was maintained. Not one of its sides still had any idea what the other two were doing and thinking.

On July 27, a second meeting was held. In view of the decision rendered as a result, it can also be considered historic. At the meeting were the members of the Warren Commission, Allen Dulles, former director of the CIA, and representatives of the CIA under Helms. According to a CIA memorandum, the idea of releasing Nosenko into society "for a certain period after the publication of the *Warren Commission* Report" was discussed. But if the commission were to refer to him in its report without mentioning the CIA's doubts in the matter, there would exist the "danger that his information would be read in mirror image by the press and society and lead to the conclusion that the USSR directed the murder." Therefore, the commission decided to render its pronouncements on Oswald and the Soviet Union *without* citing Nosenko.

The events connected with this individual virtually coincided in Moscow and Washington. The investigation into the criminal matter of the former KGB employee had come to a close, and the materials were handed over to the Military Board of the Supreme Soviet. On July 23 in Moscow, four days before the meeting described above took place in Washington, the Military Board, after reviewing the particulars of the case in camera, pronounced Nosenko guilty of treason to the Motherland and sentenced him to death by firing squad.

Once again, I find it seductive to play the "if then" game:

If the Soviets had published the Military Board's sentence on Idol, then would the meeting in Washington on July 27 have been held? What decision would have been taken?

If the Americans had made public the information given them by Nosenko about Oswald, then what would have been the reaction of the Soviets?

If the release of such reports had coincided with one another, then what steps would both sides have taken?

As in the other round of "if then" questions, I realized that such a list could drag on for a long time and their answers could have many variants. Therefore, let us return to the factual chronology of events.

By sentencing Nosenko to death, the KGB had at least received some kind of moral compensation for the colossal damage his actions had caused it. Various directors and co-workers were severely punished for their "irresponsible attitude in their estimation of the moral, political, and business qualities of Nosenko and for giving nonobjective recommendations of him." Three were sacked from the KGB and stripped of their military rank. Three others were simply fired, and still ten more faced stiff disciplinary sanctions. The head of the Second Chief Directorate, Lt. Gen. Oleg Gribanov, was removed from his post. In April 1964, Gribanov had approved sending the materials on Oswald to the KGB special archive for their "historical value." Several hundred operatives were recalled from their foreign assignments or transferred to other subdivisions. Those employees of the First Chief Directorate who had been working in Moscow at the time of his desertion and whom Nosenko either knew or could conceivably have known became "housebound," that is, their careers in intelligence were over.

At the end of September 1964 the *Warren Commission Report* was published. Neither the name of Nosenko nor the information he reported on Oswald's stay in the Soviet Union and his relationship with the KGB was mentioned. Instead, everything written in the report about the alleged assassin's time in the USSR was based on his "Historic Diary," the testimony of Marina Oswald, materials from the American Embassy in Moscow, and documents handed over by the Soviet government where Anastas Mikoyan, head of the Council of Ministers, attended President Kennedy's funeral.

The interrogation of AEFOXTROT continued under the same conditions and with the same results. Little did he know that in just one year from now he would be moving into a "well-equipped" bunker, "a very expensive structure made of special steel and concrete construction," especially prepared for him on the territory of the CIA's training grounds, Camp Perry, or as it was called by CIA employees, "the Farm." On August 14, 1965, the "housewarming" was held. As far as the details of that joyous day in his life are concerned, AEFOXTROT testified to the Stokes Committee in 1978:

> My eyes were bound, and I was handcuffed. I was taken by car to the airport and put on a plane. I was flown to another place, where I was put in a concrete chamber with bars on the door. There was only a metal bed and mattress without a pillow, sheets, or blankets. In the winter it was very cold. I asked for a blanket which they gave me only after a few days. Day and night I was watched by a television camera.

A year later, Richard Helms became CIA director. In his new capacity, he clearly began to find the "bone in the throat" even more troublesome. He gave the team of "skeptics"—the Soviet Division and Foreign Counterintelligence—sixty days to resolve, once and for all, the AEFOXTROT case.

But the quarrels between the believers and skeptics dragged on for more than two years. The Soviet Russia Division again sat the defector down to a lie-detector test and again obtained conflicting results. This was followed by a nine hundred-page conclusion of the case. Its compiler was Peter Bagley, AEFOXTROT's "godfather," who from enthusiastic trailblazer of the case had turned into the obstinate inquisitor of his own offspring. The conclusion could be considered dumbfounding. The defector was not at all who he claimed he was; moreover, he had never worked where he said he did. After this, discord broke out in even the ranks of the skeptics.

Ten years after these events, the indefatigable John C. Hart, a twenty-four-year intelligence veteran, searched for CIA documents that corroborated the deep crisis felt among the skeptics in the Soviet Division and, most of all, by Bagley himself. He found a letter Bagley had sent to James J. Angleton, head of the CIA's foreign counterintelligence, warning of the "destructive consequences" if Nosenko were to be freed. Then, in his own handwriting, Bagley had jotted down a list of possible ways to handle the Nosenko problem:

5. Liquidate subject.
6. Render him incapable of giving a coherent story (special dose of drug etc., and possibly commitment to an asylum).

7. Commitment to a mental institution *without* making him insane.

This would truly be an amusing situation if each side had known then the position of the two others. But what is most curious of all, in my opinion, is that when one side had already sentenced him to death, the other, to whom he had defected, was figuring out the best way to liquidate him physically since it could not get to the bottom of whether he was a plant or genuine.

After Bagley's "jottings" were revealed, he became extremely irritated and announced that these thoughts, which he had never shown to anyone, were his own. But there is one detail here that I personally find bothersome. If these "thoughts" were attached to the case, then, obviously, they had been consigned to some category of official documents with a corresponding registration number and stamp of secrecy. This means that they were "alive," independent of their creator. Someone had access to them, and sooner or later, the recommendations could have been carried out. But this is just speculation.

Meanwhile, someone in the Soviet division made the wise decision to "send AEFOXTROT and all his rich baggage to the CIA's Security Service." The ceremonial transfer occurred in September 1967, and by the end of October, AEFOXTROT had been moved out of his bunker into a safe apartment outside Washington, D.C. Now the "believers" subjected him to their own polygraph tests. The results were positive. The new findings, also set forth in several hundred pages and known as the Solie Report, after its author Bruce Solie, concluded just the opposite from the Bagley report: The authenticity of the defector was beyond doubt.

As soon as the AEFOXTROT case slipped out of the hands of the Soviet Russia Division, everyone who had been directly involved with him, including Murphy, Solie, head of the division, and Bagley, his deputy in counterintelligence and expert on the KGB, were sent on overseas assignments, primarily to Europe. At the same time, other specialists in Soviet affairs, whom CIA insiders called "the Slavs" and who had a certain degree of familiarity with the case, were transferred from the Soviet division to other subdivisions. They were replaced by personnel from various geographic divisions who did not know the Soviet line and did not even have command of Russian. One CIA employee would later call this the "great purging of the Slavs." Just as in Moscow with the Idol case, in Washington, with the AEFOXTROT affair, there were those who suffered.

Finally, one year later, in October 1968, the inspector general of the CIA convened everyone who had an interest in the AEFOX-TROT case. Director Helms, his deputy Admiral Taylor, Solie, and other employees of the Security Service, the new head of the Division of Soviet Russia, and representatives from foreign counterintelligence were in attendance. Angleton that day was in the hospital. The inspector general told all present that the case against Nosenko had been without basis and improperly resolved. He then proposed that Nosenko be freed and settled somewhere in the United States and that the government treat him as it does any other Soviet defector who chose to live in the United States. It would not cost the CIA much, and it might help to avoid negative consequences.

Practically everyone there nodded their heads in agreement, with the exception of the representatives from foreign counterintelligence. Even though the ranks of skeptics had diminished following the purge, those that remained clung steadfastly to their views. They explained that they were nonetheless convinced that Nosenko was a KGB agent and disinformer. Therefore, in agreeing to his freedom, they insisted that all information received from him in the past as well as any he might give in the future be marked: "From a source who most likely had access but whose reliability has not been established."

Soon after, the Security Service helped Nosenko buy a home in North Carolina. He was given the promised yearly stipend of $30,-000 a year and applied for American citizenship. In exchange, he had to keep his mouth shut concerning his three years of incarceration, the accusation that he was an "envoy from Moscow," and his subsequent acquittal by American intelligence. Now the CIA was assiduously licking its wounds.

In the following winter of 1969, AEFOXTROT, under a new name, began a new life and shortly thereafter married for the fourth time. Everything had come off just as he had suggested when he announced to Soviet diplomats on February 14, 1964, in Washington that he planned to settle in the United States and take American citizenship.

A few more years would pass, and the services of the "most contradictory FBI defector in the history of America" would begin to be used by both believers and skeptics within the CIA. He became a consultant to foreign counterintelligence, but without his nemesis of many years, James Angleton, the unsuccessful "mole hunter," who had been led into retirement.

To the uninitiated, this all might seem like a paradox or nonsense. Quite the contrary. It was not so much his services as it was Nosenko himself who was needed, for this made it easier to keep tabs on him, a very important consideration after such a long, "friendly" dialogue. Moreover, information about specific cases could be thrown to the defector from time to time, under the pretext of "consultations," to see how the third side of the triangle would react. It should be kept in mind that it was foreign counterintelligence which stuck to its guns about the bona fides of AEFOX-TROT.

Was this a manifestation of common sense or paranoia? Before answering concretely, I will allow myself to philosophize somewhat. After more than thirty years working in intelligence, of which almost a quarter century were spent in foreign counterintelligence, I came to the conclusion that, as applied to operatives, the differentiation has to be made between "professional" and "clinical" paranoia. All my thoughts and definitions are the result of direct observation.

When I hear the comment that an operative is a professional, I immediately link it to a whole set of qualities: broadly general and profoundly specific knowledge, mastery of the methods of formal logic combined with a simultaneous ability to develop his activities illogically and to read this type of response in the thoughts and actions of his opponent, a high degree of intuition, and the capacity to adapt quickly to a changing environment. When all these qualities collectively reach a high level after many years of experience, the operative attains an extrasensory "perception of the enemy," along with a reflexive preparedness for deflecting the enemy's anticipated threat. However, this is not maniacal suspicion but that condition which I call "professional paranoia." Counterintelligence

employees suffer from it to a greater degree than intelligence operatives, which is conditioned by the diversity of their responsibilities.
If an intelligence operative is concerned primarily with the safety of
his own activity, then a counteroperative, besides his own, is accountable for the safety of a certain subject and all the personnel
surrounding that subject.

At the same time, there are people, predisposed to paranoia or to
an initial stage of its development, who enter the special services.
These individuals, finding themselves in "favorable" surroundings,
experience constant nervous stress and physical overloads, after
which the disease progresses and gradually becomes irreversible in
nature. In the process of trying to substantiate their *idée fixes,* they
construct elaborate diagrams, which are so convincing that their
colleagues fall under their sway. It is not readily noticeable that
such individuals, in making their deductions, discard everything
else that could refute their obsession. This inexorably gives rise to
groupings of like-minded confederates who passionately defend the
righteousness of their "ideology." In this aspect I would say that
paranoia bears the symptoms of an infectious disease.

It frequently happens that as they ascend the professional ladder,
such "ideologues" add the authority of bureaucratic power to their
mania, crushing all those who disagree. I consider this phenomenon
a form of "clinical" paranoia. In my opinion, James Angleton
could be called a striking example of this variety. Obsessed by the
idea of the presence of a Soviet agent in the highest echelons of the
CIA, he hunted for the "mole" with maniacal obstinacy for more
than twenty years. During this time he broke the careers of several
capable and qualified operatives, which to a significant degree low-
ered the effectiveness of the Soviet Division against its main rival,
the USSR. *Although he never caught anyone, he continued at the
same time to maintain friendly relations with KGB agent Kim Philby,
the famous British turncoat* (author's emphasis).

Returning to the services of Nosenko, the new CIA and FBI
consultant in Soviet affairs, it seems to me that this was a tactically
correct continuation of a fundamentally incorrect strategy.

A few years after the tumult surrounding the AEFOXTROT
affair had died down, the CIA and FBI again took up Nosenko's
case. On May 11, 1977, both agencies jointly concluded, based on

a reevaluation of all the information he had offered, that he was a genuine defector. It is possible that the results of his activities as a consultant were also taken into account.

Almost a decade and a half had passed since the first appearance of the defector, whom Richard Helms had labeled an "evil spirit" and whose case, which had "caused [Helms] more anxiety in his life," was closed. The skeptics finally surrendered. But life is filled with surprises.

In the second half of the 1970s another congressional commission, chaired by Sen. Louis Stokes, reinvestigated the Dallas assassination. This time the former defector was called before the commission to testify as an official witness, and his information about Oswald, beginning with 1964, was painstakingly analyzed. The *Stokes Commission Report* was published March 29, 1979. The following is an excerpt:

> *Yuri Nosenko*—Of all the questions investigated by the Commission in connection with the possible Soviet involvement in the murder, none of them offers as much promise as the study of statements made by officers of the KGB who have gone over to the side of the United States. To determine how the KGB regards American defectors, its former employee may present significant interest. In this sphere the Commission had access to three such individuals; one of whom, Yuri Nosenko, announced that he had significantly more than just basic information about American defectors at his disposal.
>
> Ultimately, the Commission was also not in a position to resolve the Nosenko matter. The method employed by the CIA in regard to Nosenko—its questioning and findings— virtually disabled him as a valuable source of information relating to the assassination. Nevertheless, the commission is convinced that Nosenko lied about the KGB's noninvolvement with Oswald, whether to the FBI or CIA in 1964, to the Commission in 1978, or to both. The reasons for his lies about Oswald vary from the possibility that he simply wanted to increase his own significance to disinformational hypothesis with its harmful consequences.
>
> Due to a lack of sufficient evidence for analyzing the various

alternatives, the Commission has chosen to limit its conclusion to the description of Nosenko as *a doubtful source* [au-
thor's emphasis] of information about the murder or more
precisely as to whether the KGB made contact with Oswald
and kept him under observation.

Thus, the worm of doubt had now burrowed into the minds of
the American legislators. Again the skeptics appeared, but this time
they were from outside the intelligence community. But, judging by
Peter Bagley's statement, which serves as this chapter's epigraph,
there is still suspicion about the authenticity of the defector among
CIA employees to this day.

And with that I had originally intended to close the chapter. The
comparative chronological exposition of events, accompanied by
several commentaries on the course of their development, had run
its course. I could have limited myself to nothing more than this
since the fate of Idol is not the subject of my book. But as I said
earlier, it is inextricably bound to the fate of the alleged murderer
of President Kennedy, who is the main figure of my investigation.
Moreover, the American side (a small but influential part) lost its
way, as we say in Russian, "in three pine trees" (KGB-Oswald-
Nosenko). In other words, it could not see the forest for the trees.
As a result, the doubts about as to the KGB's role in Dallas have
not been cleared up to this day.

All this compels me to express my own, deeply personal, opinion
as to why Idol became the "evil spirit" and not the key to unlocking
the most "mysterious" period of Oswald's life. These deductions
are based on factual information culled from books by Western
authors on the subject, separate official American documents, materials from the KGB's criminal case against its defector, personal
recollections of those days, as well as the memories of my colleagues
who were directly involved in the investigation of Idol's flight.

Thus, why did experienced CIA specialists in Soviet affairs, who
were occupied with the Nosenko case, stumble into a dead end?

I shall try to name and examine three reasons or three fallacious
approaches to the case which I see as being the most important:

1. At the end of December 1961 a "fresh" defector, an employee
of the KGB's rezidentura in Helsinki, turned up at CIAs. This was

a great gift for James Angleton, who had just marked his seventh anniversary as head of CIA foreign counterintelligence. By a strange coincidence, he had been named to the post on December 20, the same day as the "Day of the Chekist," that is, the annual professional holiday of the KGB.

Anatoly Golitsyn, who was assigned the code name AELADLE and "John Stone" by American intelligence, "KAGO" by British intelligence, and "Hunchback" by the KGB, gave the Americans information about a high-ranking Soviet agent who had infiltrated the CIA. This immediately made him a favorite of Angleton's, who had been motivated by the same idea in his seven-year search to ferret out the "mole" in the organization, right up to the highest levels.

Stone also presented the CIA with the KGB's "model" for future KGB infiltrators. In this model, "support" people would be sent "from within" the KGB posing as defectors or double agents who, by handing over bits of disinformation, would strengthen the credibility of the mole. In turn, the mole would reaffirm the authenticity of the new "defectors." If the CIA really understood how the KGB worked, the model's flimsiness would have been obvious. Each additional person trained for the operation does not guarantee the mole's safety but creates additional weak links and a greater risk of failure. But Stone clearly looked out for himself. In discussing the "model," he added that future KGB "defectors" would also be assigned to compromise and discredit his information. Having occupied the place of favorite, he sequestered himself from possible future rivals.

Judging by everything that followed, "Hunchback's model" was not subjected to rigorous critical analysis by the CIA but accepted at face value, perhaps with self-congratulatory cheers, and became a trap for the expected "defectors." It was not long before one fell into it, along with Peter Bagley, who had triumphantly returned to Washington from Geneva with his prize catch. The "prognosis" had proved correct; the model had worked.

In 1964 a new defector, Yuri Nosenko, appeared with "sensational" information about Oswald. But under questioning Nosenko's answers were contradictory behavior which simply supported the model's proponents. I have the impression that in all the hubbub of the first few months, those individuals who were working with the defector simply failed to take one circumstance into account. How could a serious, multipurpose, and long-term plant, especially a professional, high-ranking operative, deliver himself into the hands of the enemy, thereby depriving himself of any control over his actions and making an absurdity of the whole operation? That is why I believe it was a tactically correct move to isolate Idol, since it severed his umbilical cord to the Center. According to the model, Nosenko had to be a plant; therefore, all actions taken in regard to his case were based on this premise, at least until the publication of the *Warren Commission Report*.

Gradually, the model's inaccuracies would become more noticeable, but bureaucratic inertia refused to acknowledge it. To admit to the basic flaws of the model would mean to admit to one's own incompetence (with all the attendant consequences). Responsibilities are feverishly abdicated. Bagley's "thoughts" about getting rid of the source of the headache appear, followed by the brilliant bureaucratic decision to hand over the case to other employees unconnected with it. In order to get rid of the spirit of the model more quickly, its adherents are removed from the scene. Incidentally, the "great purge of the Slavs" is also a consequence of the scheme, because, according to "Hunchback," that same mole in the CIA, on whose account all the fuss was made, was himself of Slavic origin.

Such, in my opinion, was the first operative mistake made in the AEFOXTROT case, along with the attempts to rectify it.

2. Within the framework of the model, the main question concerning the central figure was decided: Was he a plant or not? But not a single one of the publications I have read questions the suitability of the suspect for such a role. Essentially, whether the answer to it was positive or negative depended in general on the idea behind the first question and the reality of the whole model in this specific case. If such a question was not even examined, then it was the second serious mistake in resolving the Nosenko affair. It is difficult to believe that no one raised it.

Perhaps it does figure into closed CIA documents. I am aware of how much American intelligence accords importance to accumulating biographical and characteristic information on persons it is interested in. I also admit to making use of their wonderfully elaborated questionnaires in my own operative activity. Again, judging by the available publications, great effort was given to obtaining detailed information on Nosenko's biography and data on his unusually rapid professional ascent. But then, considering the dead-end situation that later arose in the case, the answer to the aforementioned question was not found.

The reasons could have been insufficient information or inability to evaluate it by the yardstick of the values of Soviet society and the "canons" of the KGB. Possibly both played a role.

3. If I attribute the previous mistakes to be operative ones, then the third error is one of methodology insofar as it affects the analytic work in the case. I am talking about the use by "curators" of the laws and methods of formal logic. As is known, "logic is the art of being mistaken with the certainty of its correctness."

In 1978, Bagley wrote a letter to the Stokes Commission announcing the conclusion he had made concerning Nosenko's "mission."

If Nosenko is a KGB plant, *of which I am convinced* [author's emphasis], then there can be no doubt that the story he has told us about Oswald in the USSR is a KGB message. The message, in an exaggerated and unlikely form, says that Oswald had nothing in common with the KGB. By sending such a message, the KGB is virtually indicating that it has something to hide. This "something" might be the fact that Oswald was a KGB agent.

Bagley's conclusion may have seemed concise and "very convincing," but it was just the opposite. In this specific case we are dealing with reasoning which in logic is called *proof,* that is, "having as its goal to establish the truth (or falsehood) on some conviction, which is called the thesis of proof. Judgments, on which proofs are based and from which the thesis logically follows, are called arguments. In all proofs, all arguments must be *proved.* An unproved argument, from a logical point of view, is not an argument, and a proof, based on such an argument, is a *false proof.*" But this is how Bagley arrives at his conclusion:

1. "Nosenko is a plant" is an *unproven* subjective opinion. From 1977 on, the contrary finding exists.

2. "The information about Oswald is a KGB message" is unproved.

3. "By sending the message, the KGB is trying to hide something" is unproved.

Thus, he commits a logical error in his proof, called *petitio principii* (begging the question), which implies that the conclusion is made from a position which itself has yet to be proven.

On November 16, 1978, Bagley was called to testify before the Stokes Commission. After repeating the basic tenets of his letter, he related a case which illustrated the falsity of Nosenko's information. He told about the fate of a Finnish couple who, having fallen for Communist propaganda, illegally crossed the border into the USSR in 1953 and asked the police for Soviet citizenship. They were interrogated for eleven months by the KGB before being sent off to a concentration camp. Bagley related this incident to the case of Oswald. On the one hand, we have a former U.S. Marine; on the other, a simple Finnish man and wife. They both want to live in Russia. But the Finns are questioned for eleven months and then exiled to a camp as suspected enemy agents, while the KGB does not even bother to speak with Oswald. The experience of the Finns confirms everything "that we know about the real Soviet Union from Solzhenitsyn and many others." After this, he concluded that "Oswald's experience, as Nosenko tells it, cannot be true."

Here Bagley resorts to indirect refutation, which is also a kind of proof in logic. The thesis, which he refutes, is that "Oswald was not interrogated by the KGB." But the condition of such a refutation "is proof of the truth of the contradiction." From the truth of such a position on the basis of the law of contradiction the falsehood of the refuted thesis follows. Unfortunately, Bagley again errs or gets confused and falls into a trap of logic. He demonstrates the "truth" of the contradictory position with only one example and references to Solzhenitsyn and "many others." From this he concludes:

1. All defectors to the USSR are interrogated by the KGB.

2. Oswald is a defector to the USSR.

3. Therefore, Oswald was interrogated by the KGB.*

Generally speaking, one must carefully employ logical methods when analyzing the operative activities of others. Many intelligence operations are similar in their basic methods, but *each* is unique in its goals, the combination of methods, the participants, place, and time. Is it possible to reduce, as Bagley does, the story of a Finnish couple illegally crossing the border and the case of the American tourist who expressed a desire to remain in the country to a common denominator, events which, moreover, occurred ten years apart from one another? They can be compared by one or two similarities, that is, by analogy, but in no way can they be considered identical to offer them as proof.

Of course, I do not deny the usefulness of the methods of formal logic in operative analysis. One example will suffice. Angleton's "mole" hunting within the CIA led to him becoming a suspected Soviet agent. Perhaps one of his colleagues made the connection based on the following deduction:

1. December 20 is "Day of the Chekists."†
2. Angleton was appointed head of CIA foreign counterintelligence on December 20.
3. Therefore, Angleton is a chekist!

Having reproached the skeptics for failing to answer Nosenko's suitability for the role of plant and emphasizing the importance of this circumstance, I realized I had not expressed my own opinion on that score.

Let us assume that someone in the KGB took it into his head to justify Golitsyn's model with a plant. Now a search is conducted for the right candidate. Let us also hypothetically imagine that, as an operative, I am given the assignment to review the possible plants.

Before defining the criteria for evaluating the candidates, the first

---

*Nosenko was interrogated by the CIA and the FBI. Oswald was never interrogated by the KGB, only debriefed by KGB officers who appeared to him as employees of other organizations. There is a great difference.

†The Cheka, the ancestor of the former KGB, was founded on December 20, 1917, by V. I. Lenin to protect the Bolshevik Revolution against counterrevolutionary elements and their plots. The KGB, established in 1954, adopted the Cheka emblems: the shield to defend the Revolution, the sword to smite its enemies. KGB officers named themselves "Chekisty." December 20 of each year was Chekists Day, in honor of the Cheka's birthday.

question arises: Will the game be played only on the territory of the Soviet Union, or will the plant cross the border? It turns out that it will take place abroad and for a prolonged period. Therefore, the decision is made to select a reliable and experienced professional. Now look at the biography of the candidate.

During the difficult first years of the Great Patriotic War (World War II), the highest echelons of Soviet power and state apparatus were evacuated to Kuybyshev. There Yuri, son of an old Bolshevik, an honored people's commissar in the Soviet shipbuilding industry, completed the eighth grade of a special naval academy in 1943. It is possible that his father dreamed of someday seeing his son at the helm of one of his ships and sent him to that academy. It is also possible that this is the desire of a son taken by the romanticism of plying the high seas on distant journeys.

In 1943, Yuri was a student in the Naval Preparatory Academy in the city of Baku. But his stay there did not last long and ended rather unexpectedly. On January 18, 1944, Nosenko deserted the school several days before the beginning of vacation and fled to Moscow using falsified documents. The matter was handed over to the Military Registration and Enlistment Office in Moscow.

Judging by future events, this little incident caused no adverse consequences for Nosenko. On August 18 of the same year, he enrolled in the Leningrad Naval Preparatory Academy, but he would be expelled within two months for "lack of discipline." While playing around with pistols, he accidentally shot himself in the left hand.

Fortunately, the wound was not serious. On October 16, he was discharged from the hospital and sent the same day to continue his studies at the Leningrad Shipbuilding Technical Secondary School. In 1945 he completed the tenth grade. The following year, he changed direction and enrolled in Moscow's prestigious Institute of International Relations to become a career diplomat. But Nosenko was not a good student. One report card after another noted his frivolous attitude toward his studies and unpreparedness for examinations. His studies at the institute had ended, but still ahead were the state examinations. But on May 19, 1950, a letter was sent to the institute's director, signed by the deputy minister of higher education, which said that Nosenko had been allowed to take the state examinations *without presenting his high school diploma* (author's emphasis).

This meant that he could take the entrance examinations and remain in the institute without the basic document that gives a student the right to enroll in an institute of higher education. This alone is quite revealing.

Still Nosenko received his diploma from the institute, with a specialization in international law and American studies. I can imagine the level of his knowledge in international law, area studies, and English language. From March 1951 until April 1953, Nosenko served as senior translator to the head of intelligence of the Seventh Naval Fleet in the city of Sovgavan and then as translator of the Seventh Naval Intelligence Post of the Fourth Naval Fleet.

The vocation seems to have defined itself. It is time to serve in intelligence. But an obstacle has to be overcome. Only strong and healthy fellows have a chance to become professionals; while in the navy, Nosenko had undergone a prolonged treatment at the TB sanatorium of the Central Outpatient Department at the Kremlin Medical Administration (he suffered from both tuberculosis and emphysema of the right lung).

Such a diagnosis should prevent him from entering the security service. According to the strict regulations, a candidate's application can only be started after he had been examined by the Central Military Medical Expert Commission with the conclusion that the applicant's health answered the operational requirements. However, any obstacle can be overcome if you have a nomenklatura father who was a minister and a member of the Central Committee of the CPSU. (Nomenklatura refers to those in the "power elite" of the Soviet Union.)

On April 7, 1953, upon the personal instruction of the Deputy Minister of Internal Affairs, a lieutenant general, Nosenko Junior was quickly made a case officer of Department 1, First Chief Directorate of the Ministry of Internal Affairs (MVD) of the USSR—without undergoing the routine procedures and without the approval of the Central Military Medical Commission.

The justification ran as follows "Taking into consideration that Nosenko J. I. has obtained a higher education, has a good command of English and his professional reputation is positive, it is considered possible to take him into the services of the Ministry of Internal Affairs *in accordance with the existing regulations*" [the author's emphasis]. In doing so, the deputy minister violated his own strict regulations.

In May, 1953, Nosenko became a counterintelligence officer once he was an "expert on the USA." Obviously, he was made a case officer of the first (American) department of the Second Chief Directorate. Nine years later he had earned enough commendations to be promoted deputy chief of the Seventh Department (foreign tourist). This happened on July 31, 1962. I deliberately emphasize the date. For in giving Nosenko this promotion, the authorities didn't take into account his *new* "American" experience—his treachery in Geneva in June and the beginning of his collaboration with the CIA.

Thus, one layer of the candidate's biography provides his overall education and professional experience from which he can be judged. Although the picture it presents is rather colorful, it is still somewhat early in the decision-making process to formulate a general conclusion. It remains to be seen how he is viewed by others around him—his close friends and relatives, neighbors, and co-workers.

The first person to whom the question should be posed is his mother, Tamara Georgievna. The following is an excerpt from her testimony given in 1964, after her son's defection:

Q: What do you know about the circumstances of how Yuri got a job in the organs of state security?

A: I don't know. I didn't have any conversations about this question with my husband. I remember my husband saying that *our Yuri drinks* [author's emphasis], and he doesn't have the right to work in the organs of state security. The people who work there have to be squeaky clean. Judging by my husband's words, I'm certain that he did not assist Yuri in getting a job in state security, just as I did not.

She's a sly one, this Tamara Georgievna, but who can blame a mother for covering for her son? A little earlier in her testimony she admitted to *knowing of certain isolated incidents* (author's emphasis) of her son's dubious behavior at their dacha, where he drank excessively and partied with his friend and their girlfriends.

Nosenko's lawyer at his trial, who had the chance to become intimately familiar with the defendant's life as well as with the materials of the criminal case, said in a statement, part of which is excerpted here:

> From the age of fifteen Nosenko was undeservedly rewarded by his mother, and even at times by his father, and was brought up in a spirit of leniency. Thanks to his father's high position—minister of shipbuilding—Nosenko easily got ahead in life. It's puzzling how he was hired by the KGB.

The answer is to be found in the first part of the sentence: "Thanks to his father's high position . . ."

In May 1961, when Nosenko had moved up another rung of the job ladder to become deputy chief of the Seventh, or Tourist, Department of the Second Chief Directorate, he was given nothing but negative character assessments by his neighbors, who called him a degenerate and alcoholic. This comes from an official document of the Directorate.

In 1961 one of his colleagues described Nosenko as "a spoiled person, who conducts himself arrogantly and rudely on the job, ignores the head of the division, and is given to drink."

A KGB employee who spent time with Nosenko in Geneva in 1962 at the disarmament conference had this to say about him:

"Nosenko was not very busy at work. He explained his absence in the evening by meetings with agents. He arrived back at the hotel usually around ten or eleven. In the daytime he rarely went into the city. He was either at the Soviet Mission to the United Nations in Geneva or at meetings. He didn't show any interest in me as an employee of the First Chief Directorate."

Another of his colleagues testified at his trial,

> Beginning from approximately the summer of 1962, I observed that something was bothering Nosenko. It later became clear that it was caused by the fact that he was counting on

getting the vacant position of deputy chief of the department. He was often unbalanced and sometimes screamed at operatives for no reason.

It can be assumed that it was not only the thirst for the next promotion that caused his unbalance, but the mounting fear he felt inside himself following his act of treason in Geneva.

According to Leonid I. Yefremov, an officer of the Second Chief Directorate who worked under Nosenko, "Everyone in the Directorate knew that Idol had a patron. His father was a favorite of Stalin's, and Maxim Zacharovich Saburov, Deputy Prime Minister, gave his word to the father to watch out for him. After his betrayal, there was talk among his co-workers that Idol left not only armed with knowledge of our affairs but also the affairs of the 'higher-ups.' Everyone was convinced the Americans would welcome him with open arms."

As to what information about the ruling class Idol had at his disposal can be glimpsed from the following episode, also related by Yefremov:

"In autumn of 1963 a group of twenty-two Americans arrived in Moscow. They represented some of the biggest U.S. companies: U.S. Steel Corporation, General Motors, American Airlines, and others. Khrushchev invited them to the Kremlin for a reception to mark the anniversary of the October Revolution. The heads of the Seventh Department and several operatives, including myself, were also handed invitations.

"During the reception, Nikita had a bit too much to drink and began threatening the 'American parasites.' The bodyguards from the Ninth Department tried to sober him up with milk. In spite of everything, the 'parasites' invited Khrushchev to the Hotel Sovietskaya. He accepted, and everyone started fussing to go. We also went downstairs to get our coats, and there we witnessed some interesting scenes involving Nosenko, who was in our group.

"First, a respectable-looking woman, who turned out to be the wife of Kosygin, head of the Soviet government, enthusiastically greeted him, calling him "Yurochka" and inviting him to visit. Then Konstantin Andreyevich, Marshal of Aviation, exchanged a few words with him, addressing him as 'Yurka.' He was addressed in the same friendly fashion by a young general, who, as it turns out, was Mikoyan's son Sergei, commander at the time of the air force of the Kiev Military Region.

"After observing how Idol mixed with such elites, we 'peasants' became a bit frightened when we realized the level of his support."

Now the face of the "candidate" is becoming more complete. But there is still one major problem to resolve. If a lengthy and risky assignment is planned, using the legend* of "defector" no less, then his family, by extension, becomes accomplice to the operation, for it has to verify such a legend and bear the onus of being "the family of a traitor to the motherland." Naturally, the greatest burden falls upon the wife. This is one side of the problem, but there is another.

In addition to upholding the legend, the family also serves, no matter how cynical and inhumane it may sound, as an "anchoring" factor. In other words, it keeps the "plant" from making rash or ill-considered moves. But as I have already said before, the activities of the special services, from their very origins many centuries before the birth of Christ, are not always a manifestation of humanity.

The "family aspect" is one of the basic elements in the scenario of an actual operation and demands a thorough analysis of the candidate's overall relationship to family life, his inclination toward extramarital ties, and the situation in his family at the given moment if, of course, he is married. Therefore, let us take a look at our hypothetical candidate from this vantage point in order to make the final assessment of his suitability for the role of plant. Again we turn to Nosenko's biography and the testimony of his mother:

"We had to give our consent to Yuri's first marriage in 1946 to a girl he had impregnated. Our decision grew out of our desire to try to save the girl's honor. But Yuri announced that he did not like her and was not going to live with her. He left her."

That same year Nosenko met another girl, whose parents were on good terms with his. In January 1948 he married for the second time. But it was not destined to be a long union. For all practical purposes, it ended in December of that year but was not formally annulled until June 1953. As the former wife of a criminal, this

*A false story created around operatives to support a phony I.D.

woman submitted the following testimony in 1964:

"After a short life together I learned that he [Nosenko] was a total alcoholic.

"In October 1948 our daughter was born with serious physical defects. She had a cleft palate, a harelip, and she was cross-eyed. The physician who examined her said that her defects could have been the result of her body being poisoned by her father's alcoholism. My daughter could not breast-feed normally, so I had to express my milk and feed her from a spoon. This bothered Nosenko, and he couldn't bear to look at it. He tore my daughter away from me and beat me, ripped the clothing from my body, mocked me, and threw me out of the apartment."

According to this testimony, Nosenko was forced to sell his watch and suit as the result of his drinking. His parents responded by buying him a gold watch and a better suit. I won't describe the orgies he threw in the apartment.

Having comfortably settled into the KGB, Nosenko started a third family and turned into a loving husband and caring father. This is where he demonstrated his outstanding acting skills. He played the role to the hilt in accordance with his own scenario, performing before various audiences—co-workers, CIA officers, and his new family.

He told one of his colleagues during the first trip to Geneva in 1962 about how he loved his wife and daughter. At the same time he cursed his second wife for cheating on him with a relative.

By then he had already made contact with American intelligence. He told its representatives of his daughter's asthma, and how the medicine she needed could not be found in his country. The officers did everything possible to obtain the medicine, which did not even exist in the United States. They were only able to get it from a third country, and with the help of a special courier. He would later tell the American officers that the medicine had saved his daughter's life.

In expressing his readiness to continue working with the CIA, he declared at the same time that he did not intend to stay in the West, for he did not want to leave his family behind. Nosenko's roommate in the Geneva hotel in 1964 testified that "Nosenko always tried to emphasize that he really loved his daughters. It actually became unpleasant to hear. He was always telling me what he had bought for his daughters and what presents he had sent them. He said that he was married for the second time."

It is interesting to note that all this happened when the "caring" father announced to the amazed Americans his intention to flee to the West. This is how David Weiss, in his book *The Mole Hunter*, describes Nosenko's meeting with the American agents in Geneva in which he played his "family card":

> "Guk [his coworker] brought a letter," continued Kisel-vater. "Nosenko came to me early and read it to me alone. He was upset. It was an intimate and sentimental letter with news from his family. He said, "They [the KGB] may not send me abroad anymore. Maybe I have to stay.' Then he said, 'Maybe I'll never see her [my wife] again.' In George Kiselvater's opinion, Nosenko was fighting with his emotions and the pull of his family.

It was a brilliant move. At his first meeting with the American operatives he sounded them out and observed their reactions. Now he was throwing down the "family card" and introducing "emotions" into the game to put pressure on their feelings. And then came the knockout blow, as described in the same book:

> . . . The agents were flabbergasted, "numb" was how Bagley put it, when on February 4, Nosenko dropped the "bomb." He said that he had decided to stay because he had received a telegram from Moscow. He asked for protection from the CIA.*

The "family man" had not spent his eleven years in the KGB in vain. As mentioned earlier, the whole story about a telegram was fabricated.

No doubt aware that he was not going back home, Nosenko nonetheless continued to play the role of the loving husband and caring father. Consider this letter to his wife that was submitted by his family as evidence during the investigation into his case:

*David Wise, *Molehunt* (New York: Random House, 1992), p.136.

January 27, 1964

Greetings, my dear Milusinka!*

Tomorrow I am taking the opportunity to send you a letter with someone who is returning to Moscow. Today marks the ninth day since I left home. Of course I miss you and the kids very much. Although it has not been that long, I feel like a whole month has passed. I am always with you in my thoughts, thinking of you and remembering you. But don't worry, *tomorrow will be even more joyous* [author's emphasis].

Milusya! How do you feel? You have to take care of yourself and not forget about your health and eat proper meals. Of course, *the main thing is not to worry* [author's emphasis]. Okay?

How are the girls? Do they miss me? Do they remember me? Tell them I send them a big kiss and that they have to take care of their mommy.

Dear one! Big, big hugs and kisses,
                                    Yuri

Even after having realized, in his own words, his "longtime plan" of becoming a "political" refugee in the United States, he told representatives at the Soviet embassy in Washington, who asked him what his family would think about their father, that it was the "most painful questions, but I cannot say anything about it now. . . ."

He later returned to this theme on his own in his next epistolary work, posted this time from the United States:

Milusenka,
My decision to live and work in the United States is not accidental, it was developed over the years [author's emphasis]. I do not want to prove I am right, because you can't say everything in a letter.
The only thing that disturbs and tortures me is the absence of you and your daughters [author's emphasis]. Tell my mother

*A diminutive and endearing form of the name of Nosenko's wife, Mila (trans. note)

that, in spite of my deep love for father, I would have done the same thing even if he were alive, and my decision is one of the most correct decisions I have made in my life.

Yuri

If one can believe Nosenko's persistent statements that his decision to defect had been developing over the years, then it follows that the first people he deceived were his third wife and daughters. It can be assumed that he used this last family as a "cover" and saw them as a stepping-stone toward his move to a new life in another country.

Naturally, according to Bagley's logic, this all smacks of a story concocted by the "nefarious KGB" for their plant. Here I agree with him that it is a made-up tale, but it is a story which Idol elaborated upon and realized on his own and which he used to dupe everyone, including the KGB and the CIA, to attain his goals.

Thus, in my opinion, an analysis of the candidate's purported love for his family simultaneously demonstrates the profound dissolution of his personality and his advanced skills for fiction. On the basis of the latter skill, I have to rack up a point in his favor for assuming the role of a hypothetical plant.

Now that the main personality traits of the candidate have been examined, it is time to touch upon the political aspect of his suitability as a KGB plant. Earlier in this chapter the reminiscences of the former chairman of the KGB, Vladimir Semichastny, were cited in connection with Idol, who had become no less "a bone in the throat" for him, as he had been for Richard Helms,who eventually became Director of Central Intelligence. I asked him once again to share his thoughts with me about Idol and what he thought about his suitability for the role of a plant.

Q. American intelligence, especially the CIA, spent a long time thinking that Nosenko was our plant, sent to the United States to provide disinformation on Oswald and to protect our mole in the CIA. What is your evaluation of this view?

A. If someone had told me, during those days, that our enemies would assume that the traitor Nosenko was a plant, I would have laughed until I cried. I mean, to fabricate a traitor who was not only a minister's son but a highly respected and well-known minister at that. Who would have suggested such a thing to the Central Committee and come up with the arguments to justify it? At the very least, during my time at the KGB, we excluded the possibility of sending a very skilled person at this level under the guise that he was a traitor. Looking at Nosenko as a possible plant, his worthlessness was apparent, since he was a confirmed alcoholic. Even in 1955, we wanted to get rid of him, but his high-level patrons would not allow it.

I was told that the first person who told the Americans that Nosenko was a plant was his predecessor, another traitor, Anatoly Golitsyn. I think Golitsyn viewed Nosenko as a rival and invented the "plant story" to "unmask" Nosenko and to make the Americans suspicious. I do not exclude the possibility that one of our operatives, at home or abroad, suggested the "special mission" story to an American officer. When this information was added to Golitsyn's "plant story," it just strengthened that possibility. I still believe that our enemy was not really aware of what we were doing at this time, even though they had a traitor to explain it to them.

Having completed the evaluation of Idol's suitability as a KGB plant, I decided not to formulate or state my own conclusion. I leave that to the individual reader. I have only one comment to make: Idol had a better chance of being the future Chairman of the KGB than to be a defenseless "plant" in enemy territory.

Whatever the evaluation of Nosenko's personality and actions, the information he had passed on to the CIA on "KGB and Oswald" is basically true, though his presentation of these facts was contradictory. That was probably why the CIA did not dare to present Nosenko or his information to the Warren Commission as official evidence of the KGB's position toward the suspected assassin of the president. On the other hand, maybe the CIA had another agenda for its newly acquired KGB defector.

In my opinion, such an action by the CIA at that time would have put the Soviet leadership into a rather sensitive position. On one hand, they would be forced to admit publicly that Nosenko was a traitor and sentenced to death in absentia by the Military Board of the Supreme Court of the USSR. On the other hand, if they confirmed the trustworthiness of his evidence, it would make him a "defender" of the USSR's interests in the eyes of the world. Obviously, the CIA failed to calculate this opportunity in their gambit.

However, there is every reason to suppose that the CIA made use of AEFOXTROT's information in its own estimate of Oswald's stay in the Soviet Union. These estimates were passed on to the Warren Commission. This consideration is based on conclusions concerning Oswald's Soviet period, contained in the Commission's reports and presented in chapter 1. It is probable that the CIA estimates are still classified Warren Commission documents.

12

How a Fish Became a Dog

On one of the fall weekends of 1963, soon after the delegation of cosmonauts had left Mexico for New York, Pavel Yatskov, a fellow counterintelligence officer, and I went on a fishing trip. At that time the favorite place among the embassy fishermen was a man-made reservoir, called Presa Endo, situated in the Mexican foothills, approximately eighty kilometers outside Mexico City. We were attracted to the place because very few people went there. There were only two villages on the opposite shores of the reservoir, and it was filled with fish, primarily perch, black bass, and rather large carp. This time the rezident allowed us to go for only one day.

We departed early in the morning, while it was still dark, to get to the fish while they were still biting. As we approached the place where we always left our cars and pitched tents, we saw an old red Fiat nearby and a fisherman with a spinning rod. We walked up the water's edge and exchanged greetings with him. Even though he answered us in Spanish, he was clearly not Mexican. He looked to be somewhat older than thirty. He was six feet tall, thin, light-haired, with an elongated face and gray or blue eyes. Pavel, then forty-three, asked him how the fishing was going, and the stranger answered amicably. The two then struck up a lively conversation. I quickly clambered up on one of the large stone ledges and began casting somewhat off to the side from Pavel and our new friend.

Our team of fishermen from the embassy had discovered the reservoir a year and a half ago, and we visited it rather often, which was a well-known fact, but this was the very first time that I had ever met a fisherman here who was not from the local population and obviously not a Mexican. Soon after, jumping from one stone to another, Pavel joined me.

On the way home, Pavel said that our new fishing partner was a gringo named John. He lived in Mexico City and taught English at Mexico City College, the graduates of which went on to careers in the Mexican diplomatic service. John was married to a Mexican woman, had children, and lived near Pavel's apartment. Since the gringo called himself an inveterate fisherman, he and Pavel agreed to continue their friendship and to go on fishing trips together. I expressed my surprise to Pavel that we should meet a gringo after we had been coming here for a year and a half, and then I asked him, "Why do you think he came here? Was it to catch fish or to become acquainted with us?"

Pavel and John's friendship continued in Mexico City. John behaved naturally, didn't pry into details about Pavel's life, and at the same time talked openly about himself.

During one of their meetings after the tragedy in Dallas, when Oswald's visit to our embassy in Mexico and his meetings with the consular officers were already an established fact, John began to ask Pavel very specific questions, such as: "Whom precisely did Oswald talk to when he visited the consulate?" "How did he act?" "What kind of impression did he make upon those who spoke with him?" "What was the evaluation of his ability to carry out a terrorist act?" And other questions. We concluded that there was a professional "need to know" behind these series of questions. From then on, Pavel's future relations with John were based on the fact that the two of them were under CIA surveillance.

On June 12, 1964, Pavel informed Moscow Center about this new contact and signed the report using his code name—"R."

R became acquainted with John (hereafter referred to by his codename "Pez"—Spanish for "fish"). He was born in 1931, an American citizen, a resident of Arizona, of German background, married to a Mexican woman, with three children. Teaches English language. Pez was born into the family of a civil servant. After the death of his father he was forced to go to work at age sixteen to help support the family. At the same time he did not curtail his studies. He served in the army, in aviation units based in Alaska.

After military service, he enrolled at Syracuse University in the Department of Foreign Languages, where he studied Russian. Because of material shortcomings, he transferred to Mexico City College in Mexico City, where he studied in the Department of International Law, that is, he was preparing for the diplomatic service. While a student, he married a Mexican. Because of financial difficulties and a desire not to leave Mexico, he quit his studies in 1958. For some time, in order to save money, he worked in the United States as a bus driver. Up until last year [1963] he was a teacher at Mexico City College. At the present time he has left that position and taken on a new job as teacher of English in the newly opened Catholic Institute, where the salary is twice as much.

His wife, who is a teacher by training, works as a director in one of Mexico's state schools. Judging by their conversations, she has some influential relatives in the Mexican government. She apparently is also a friend of the wife of the present Mexican president.

Based on preliminary data, Pez has wide-ranging contacts among the Americans living in Mexico. Pez has an American friend who is head of the Customs Control Group on the Mexican-American border. Through him Pez sometimes received duty-free goods from the United States.

His mother and an older brother, a farmer, live in the United States. Pez is a great fishing enthusiast. R became acquainted with him on one of his Sunday trips outside the city. R developed friendly relations with Pez and with his family and visited him at his home. Pez and his family also visit R at his home. [He is the agent from the Mexican embassy who sent this report to Moscow Central.]

From the initial data, the conclusion can be made that Pez shows no interest in politics. However, he seems to be rather well oriented in international life and is abreast of events taking place in the United States and in Mexico. Although he criticizes the local bureaucratic apparatus, its corruption and bribe taking, so far he refrains from criticizing the politics of the government and the ruling circles of the United States.

P's main desire at the present time, as far as can be determined, is to earn enough money to open his own business.

R will continue to solidify his friendly relations with him and to study both him and his connections. Moreover, through the rezidentura, we will try to gather information on both him and his wife. We request the Center to check on him in their data banks.

The Center quickly answered the Mexico rezidentura by saying that it had no records on Pez. The question of whether it was worthwhile to study Pez for recruiting possibilities or other purposes of intelligence use could only be decided after receiving additional information on his situation, political views, and intelligence possibilities.

The subsequent study of Pez did not give any reason to think that he had such serious possibilities, however, we in the rezidentura believed that his approaching us was not accidental, and we surmised that American intelligence was most likely behind it. In the meantime, relations were maintained with him as a "neutral" connection, but sometime after the first meeting with Pez, Pavel told me about an invitation Pez had extended him to go on a fishing trip together to a lake near Cuernavaca. Pavel asked if I was ready to join them and, at the same time, to observe how Pez behaved. I had no objections, and on the following Saturday morning we set off for Cuernavaca, where we were to meet up with Pez, who had gone there the day before and would be waiting for us either at his home or at a home belonging to a relative of his wife's.

Once we met, we quickly made our way through the local villages to the lake. We put Pez's boat into the water and headed toward the nearest fishing spot. To my and Pavel's misfortune, it turned out that the fishing here was not nearly as great as Pez had promised. All in all we only spent a few hours at the lake. During the course of the day Pez turned out to be a very good companion. He was generally sorry for not explaining to us beforehand what kind of fish were in the lake and then seemed rather upset that we were disappointed with the fishing. By dusk we bade farewell to Pez and drove out of Cuernavaca. This is my last personal meeting with him, but as it would turn out later, it was not my last in a professional sense.

Pavel's friendship with Pez continued. They visited each other's families and went in search of new fishing places together. Since Pez was listed in the category of neutral contacts, no correspondence with the Center regarding him was carried out, but Pavel kept the resident informed about their meetings. In the summer, the term of my stay in Mexico had come to a close. Four years had flown by in a flash, but we had added a son to our family. In August 1965 we returned to Moscow, where I went to work at the branch of Service Z of the First Chief Directorate, which guided the counterintelligence activities of our rezidenturas in Latin America.

In the beginning of May 1967, by which time I had become director of the aforementioned branch, an employee brought me a telegram from our Mexico rezidentura. The rezident reported that Pavel's friend Pez had handed Pavel a letter in Russian during a fishing trip in a place far away from the capital.

It was a recruiting letter, and John, that is, Pez, told Pavel that two representatives from the CIA wanted to meet with him. Two excerpts from the letter and the circumstances regarding the approach followed. It was also mentioned in the telegram that the rezidentura, which had analyzed the events, decided that this letter should be viewed in a calm fashion and that for the time being no attempt should be made to gather information on the CIA employees in Mexico who were party to this provocation. During a meeting among the operatives of the rezidentura, Pavel was rebuked for having insufficiently studied his contacts and for not displaying the necessary caution in regard to Pez. As a result, measures were taken so that another employee of the rezidentura would be prepared at any moment to continue working with Pavel's contact. The ambassador was informed about the matter.

While reading the telegram I had a good laugh when I saw that the rezidentura had written John's former nickname Pez, which is Spanish for fish, as "Pyos," Russian for male dog. Thus, *the fish had become a dog.* Notes were made in the margin of the telegram about informing heads of the KGB of its contents.

It was clear that this incident had reached the highest levels of the KGB leadership. At the same time, the contents of the telegram did not cause any alarm at the top. This meant a calm but quick answer had to be prepared.

The rezidentura called a special meeting and informed the operative personnel about the incident. The bland reaction of Moscow Center implied that it approved of Pavel's behavior. Such a low-key response also meant some kind of support for other officers in case there were new recruiting attempts at the top.

I was already aware from my own experience regarding the events in Dallas how important it was to know in time the Center's position on a sticky problem. This information removes the uncertainty and the nervousness among the employees of the rezidentura.

It fell upon me to answer the telegram. I was there when Pavel struck up a friendship with Pez. I had a good understanding of the operative situations in Mexico. Moreover, I was Pavel's KGB curator, or case officer, whose operative file was kept in my safe. First, though, I had to ask one of our employees to carry out an immediate check in our card file for the two recruiting Americans, but the information on them was scanty and undoubtedly fabricated by the CIA for deception.

In order to be fully armed in the event of possible questions from my superiors, I decided to use everything known to me by listing the reasons for Pez making our acquaintance.

- Pavel had recently arrived in Mexico (1963). Therefore, his meeting with the American and then the development of their friendship on fishing expeditions allows the CIA to have an access agent around him, that is, someone who could establish a personal relationship with a Soviet officer and with whose help American intelligence could gather information on Pavel and observe his behavior and psychological state. By connecting Pavel to Pez, the enemy clearly wanted to limit Pavel's ability to establish new contacts. Proof of this variation, in my opinion, was the length of their friendship, which, up until the moment of recruitment, had lasted more than three years.

- The object of the contact could have been me. Up until the time of Pez's appearance at the reservoir, more than two years of my stay abroad had passed. I was a captain in counterintelligence then and rather well known to our opponents, as was my interest in American citizens. My age and predilection for fishing coincided with the same "parameters" as those describing Pez.

- It is possible that Pez's mission in visiting the reservoir at Presa

Endo was to attract the attention of anyone from among the Soviet embassy fishermen (in general it was the agents from the KGB and the GRU, military intelligence, who went there), become acquainted, and then to take additional steps based upon the opportunities he saw.

These were only my hypotheses explaining the reasoning of Pez or his CIA superiors. But since I could not confirm whether my theories were correct, all I could do was guess. The second question that I mulled over was the purpose of the approach. I had known Pavel for several years, including our work together in Mexico and, as his curator or case officer, was well acquainted with his background.

Pavel was born in the Voronezh region in 1920. Soon after, he moved with his parents to Siberia, where he spent his youth and adolescence. At the end of the 1930s the family moved to Khinki, outside Moscow, where he finished high school. He dreamed of becoming a forest ranger and then a geologist. He was a great sports enthusiast and took up boxing, sambo (a Russian type of martial art), skiing, soccer, volleyball, tennis, and sharpshooting. Later, his main hobbies turned to hunting and fishing, but in general he was devoted to sports throughout his life. His attempt to enroll in the forestry institute did not meet with success. Before World War II he was mobilized into the Red Army, where he became a communications expert. He spent almost the whole time on the front. He was commander of a detachment who would advance beyond the front line to capture German personnel as sources of military intelligence. He was twice wounded, and when the war ended he found himself in Prague. He had been awarded medals for Honorable Service, Liberation of Cities, Bravery, Valor.

In 1945 he was sent to the SMERSH (Death to Spies) School. After graduating, he attended intelligence school, where he studied Spanish. While Pavel was in school in Russia, one of his older brothers, Anatoly, an employee of the rezidentura in New York in the early forties, was primarily responsible for supervising the stealing of the atom-bomb secrets from Los Alamos.

Pavel's first experience in foreign intelligence work was spent at an exhibition of Soviet progress in Argentina, where he resided for six months at the beginning of the 1950s. This posting was followed by his first lengthy trip to Mexico, from 1956 through 1960. By April 1967, that is, up to the moment of the attempt to recruit him, he had devoted almost nine years to expatriate foreign intelligence work, of which nearly eight were spent in Mexico. It is clear that during this time American intelligence, primarily the CIA, had put together a solid data bank on him. I find it hard to believe those who approached him with a letter asking him to become a traitor had seriously hoped to succeed. The shock came with money offered for his defection, the huge sum of $500,000. However, the very idea of "buying Pavel," that is, asking him to commit treason for money seemed ludicrous to me, knowing him as I did.

This was not the first attempt by the other side to attract Pavel's attention. During his first tour of duty in Mexico, the local Ministry of Foreign Affairs summoned Russian ambassador Bazykin to its offices and announced that the third secretary of the embassy, Yatskov, was occupied with matters incompatible with his status as a diplomat. This was in 1958. The ministry cited the fact that he had recently spoken out at a trade-union meeting, trying to incite the workers to strike. The ambassador answered that this incident simply could not have occurred, because the diplomat in question had already been on vacation in Moscow for a month. The episode ended with great embarrassment for the Mexican officials.

So what, then, did our opponents want? In those years the predominant reaction of the KGB leadership to recruiting offers made to our officers abroad was to quickly call them back to the Soviet Union "to avoid possible future provocations by the enemy." The enemy, knowing this, carried out such approaches in virtually a no-lose situation. Either the officer consented to cooperate or he was recalled. In either case, it was a blow to our service. Therefore, the CIA made active use of this method. Without a doubt, this approach made the employees of our rezidenturas nervous and heightened their psychological defenses.

Sometime at the end of the 1960s and beginning of the 1970s, our leadership began to adopt a different position by soberly evaluating the situation while adopting alternative responses. Later, however, when our opponents began to feel the shift in our position, they, too, took up a new tactic without completely abandoning the old one. This was the use of natural or artificially created situations for mass expulsion of employees from Soviet official offices, with the aim of paralyzing the activities of our rezidenturas.

As I continued to muse over what the CIA hoped to accomplish by recruiting Pavel, I arrived at two conclusions:

1. Based on Pavel's imminent departure from Mexico, the CIA had approached him, but without hoping for his recruitment and not doubting that he would report it. Rather, they were trying to get him discredited and possibly recalled immediately from Mexico, thereby creating difficulties in replacing him. After the approach it was axiomatic that his cover would be "deciphered" or blown. Therefore, we would have to choose not only an operative but a new cover position for him as well, and this required a great deal of time and effort. Thus, for a certain period, the counterintelligence activities of the rezidentura would be weakened

2. It cannot be excluded that the action against Pavel was part of a much wider operation. The news of the attempt to recruit such an "iron" KGB operative and his possible immediate recall from the country could create in the rezidentura a nervous situation and psychological stress among its employees.

Similar mental exercises constitute most intelligence activity, and that is the reason it is called a "war of the minds." Unfortunately, an operative is usually in charge of several cases and participates in various operations at the same time, resulting in inevitable conflicts in both time and space. The principle of intelligence activity are in many ways analogous to that of chess. An operative in a specific situation reacts to his opponent's last move, considers all his possible new moves, and tries to determine the interim moves and the final goal while developing his own strategy. He is always acting within "a definite indefiniteness and time limit."

My thoughts were interrupted by an employee who came into my office and reported that there was no information in the card files on the CIA operatives who had approached Pavel. In fact, I hadn't expected otherwise, because we were talking about an intelligence service which takes the safety of its employees very seriously. After sending a draft of the coded telegram to the rezidentura in Mexico, I submitted my report. Viewing the telegram was an interim move until a detailed report came from the rezidentura, I made it extremely short. It said that the action of the rezidentura for localizing the CIA provocation was correct. It was also recommended that Pavel's meetings with agents should be temporarily halted and that the future situation should be carefully observed.

I have to say that neither then nor during the discussion of this operation in the future did it ever occur to me that the attempt by the CIA to obtain details on Oswald's visits to our embassy and the Cuban embassy in September 1963 lay at the basis of Pavel's seduction—even though it was precisely Pez's interest in those visits and the content of his conversations with Pavel that had confirmed our opinions that his relationship with us was being developed under the control of American clandestine services.

The director of the First Chief Directorate of Service 2, simply called "D," to whom I reported the draft of the telegram, signed it without making any corrections. Afterward I explained to him my analytic conclusions about the situation, which he listened to attentively, but when my eloquence had been exhausted, he said, "Well, what the hell, Oleg Maximovich? In autumn Pavel's four years are up, and if the situation around him is normal, let him ride it out. We're not going to make any moves ahead of time. Since you drew up the plan of preparation, you can replace him. There's really nothing for you to do to get ready. Just continue working. We only need to confirm that we have begun to fill out the forms for a business trip. If you don't have any questions, get to it."

While I was going to make my report, I had prepared myself to answer various questions posed by my superiors, but I hadn't anticipated such an unexpected directive. I grabbed the signed telegram to take it for coding and left. The thought entered my mind that the "fish" that had been transformed into a "dog" had now turned me into a candidate for a new mission to Mexico. If the CIA had not carried out this operation, it is possible that I would have met them again in a completely different country. And then I thought to myself: Is it even possible for an operative to predict his fate even just a few days in the future?

About three weeks later, materials arrived in the diplomatic pouch from Mexico concerning the April recruitment attempt. Among them was the original CIA letter, which read as follows:

Dear PA [Pavel Antonovich]

As John already told you, I would like to meet with you in order to discuss a serious business proposition. I think that it will interest you.

I hope that you will not feel offended by the way I am approaching you. Do not think that this is a sloppy approach calculated on a false estimation of the situation. On the contrary, it is precisely because we have complete reason to respect you as a very strong and capable adversary that I have the authority to make such a unique offer to you.

I know that you are an experienced operative and do not need someone else telling you how to act. I want to assure you that you have nothing to fear from a personal meeting with me. First of all, I have no materials whatsoever or any other cause for blackmail, threats, etc. None. In any case, I already know that this would be useless. Second, and more important, *no one* in Mexico knows that I am writing to you, with the exception of John, my colleague (who came with me), and myself. Our station in Mexico considers you to be an iron-willed person to whom any approach would be hopeless. As far as this operation is concerned, there were no coded messages, no correspondence, no conversations, nothing. Everything is clean.

As far as the offer itself is concerned, I will only write in brief. If the matter interests you, then we need to speak in greater detail. I am proposing that you come to us in the literal sense of the word. If you agree, but prefer to remain in place until the expiration of your term in Mexico, I have no objections, but I do not want you to return to the Soviet Union. I am not asking from you any risks but simply that you come to us with that knowledge which you already possess and that you completely and in good conscience share that knowledge with us. From our side I am authorized to offer you $500,000 and citizenship in the United States (or wherever you prefer).*

In a word, the means which will allow you to live the way you

*The CIA considered Pavel the KGB's station chief, or rezident, in Mexico.

like and the freedom in the full sense of the word to make use of these means as you wish.

I don't know how you will decide, but I hope that you will think over my offer and that you will not be afraid to discuss the matter with me before making your final decision.

N.

Excuse me for the grammatical errors, but I thought it worthwhile to write in Russian. I think that when we meet we'll find a common language.

I liked this letter, with its respectful and gentle tone. It was obvious that more than one person had worked on it for more than a day. It could even be assumed that the document was first drawn up in English and then rewritten in Russian. It was also obvious that whoever wrote the Russian version had a good command of the language but was not a native. Proof of this view were several unusual turns of phrase and spelling and grammatical errors characteristic of foreigners who know Russian but not as a native Russian, even one who's not very well educated. Of course, one could allow that the author was of Russian origin, but in that case he would have had to have lived and studied abroad starting at an early age.

What I didn't like about this letter was the attempt by its authors to convince the addressee, an operative—indeed, a professional counterintelligence officer—that *"no one* in Mexico knows that I am writing to you, with the exception of John. . . ." But John is Pyos. Later, it says, "As far as this operation is concerned, there were no coded messages, no correspondence, no conversations, nothing. Everything is clean." This is complete nonsense. All intelligence services in the world always, and I emphasize *always,* try to convince the person to be recruited that all measures of caution have been carried out in order to keep the fact of his future, or already realized collaboration, a secret. That the "circle of individuals who know about this is extremely limited" or, as a variation, "have been kept to a minimum" is usually not mentioned in such letters. Such statements are a canon of recruiting work, but to say so in this letter to an "experienced operative" asking him to "share his knowledge" in good conscience is not serious.

Having an idea of the technological chain of preparation and execution of the operation, and they are virtually the same in all intelligence services, one can figure out the minimal number of people who must have known about it. In the American intelligence station at least four to five employees: the Chief of Station, his deputy for operative work, the leader of the Soviet Bloc Group, a case officer who is carrying out the "operation," that is, working on Pavel, and someone working in the code department. At Langley headquarters the case officer of the Mexican station, his boss in the Western Hemisphere Division, and a certain group of people in the Soviet Division, the leaders of the Directorate of Plans and the highest command chain of the CIA—someone had to have sanctioned the offer of $500,000 and residency in the United States—representatives of counterintelligence, and possibly a psychologist acting as a consultant. Thus, by even the most modest standards, one comes up with no less than twenty people in addition to the direct participants who approach our man. Whether it is the KGB, the CIA, the FBI, or any other comparable organization, the nature of bureaucracy in intelligence services is universal.

Eight years later, only after Philip Agee, a former employee of the CIA's Western Hemisphere Division and the case officer in 1968 of the CIA's Mexican station came out with a book called *Inside the Company,* were we able to look behind the scenes of the operation against Pavel. In the list of operations which took place against us in Mexico there is a description of its preparation by Philip Agee under the CIA code name "LIOVAL-1."* Thus, we learned the

---

*LIOVAL-1 is not as interesting a case but is more important. The agent is an American who teaches English in Mexico City and is an ardent fisherman. Through fishing he became acquainted with Pavel Yatskov, the Soviet consul and a known senior KGB officer—possibly the Mexico City *Rezident*/KGB chief. Yatskov and the agent spend one or two weekends per month off in the mountains and have developed a very close friendship. When Yatskov is transferred back to Moscow—he has already been in Mexico for some years—we shall decide whether to try to defect him through LIOVAL-1. There is some talk of offering him $500,000 to defect. The company is also willing to set him up with elaborate cover as the owner of an income-producing fishing lodge in Canada. Recently, Peter Deriabin, the well-known KGB defector from the 1950s who is now a U.S. citizen and full-time CIA employee, went to Mexico City to study the voluminous reports on Yatskov written by LIOVAL-1. He concluded that there is a strong possibility that LIOVAL-1 has been recruited by Yatskov and is reporting on Paul Dillon, the station officer in charge of this case. Nevertheless, the

American nickname for Pez. Our doubts were dispelled and our suspicions confirmed.

In Agee's book there is no description of the final stage of the operation with the participation of LIOVAL-1. Therefore, I think the reader will find it interesting to learn all the details about it firsthand from the hero and participant for whose sake the whole operation was carried out. Thus, what follows is Pavel Yatskov's own story:

"At one of our meetings in the beginning or middle of April 1967, John told me that he had learned from one of his friends about an interesting place situated on the Pacific coast south of Acapulco. He was effusive in his praise and described it as a wonderful site for fishing and suggested that we go there for a few days.

"Up to this time we had known each other for a little more than three years. Together we had scoured all the well-known fishing places and discovered many new ones outside Mexico City. Moreover, in most cases John was the instigator of the trips to these unknown corners. In general, he always tried to emphasize—I would even say demonstrate—his longtime affection for fishing, although from my observations his fishing equipment bore witness to the fact that he had taken up this hobby relatively recently. An experienced fisherman can be determined by the way he approaches his tackle, his method of fishing, and his choice of lures, depending on the place and weather. I never observed any of this knowledge on John's part. However, such observations did not affect my good relationship with him, although I was certain he was an informant of the CIA.

"For a certain time now there was something in John's character that had begun to bother me. In my experience at the front during the war, in operative work, or in hunting and fishing trips, I have often found myself in dangerous situations, and I know full well the value of relying upon others who are with you at the time. That is why I always divide people into two categories—brave and cowardly—and only after that do I evaluate them by other categories.

operation continues while the counterintelligence aspects are studied further." Philip Agee, *Inside the Company: CIA Diary* (New York: Stonehill, 1975), pp. 529–30.

Such has life, and in many ways my profession, taught me.

"On one occasion John said he had found another mountain lake on the outskirts of Cuernavaca which, according to him, was filled with trout. We soon set out in search of it. Somehow we reached by car a village in the foothills where the road ended. We left our car there, asked the natives about the lake, and one of the local lads, who supposedly knew how to get there, offered to be our guide. For a rather long time, under a blazing sun, we climbed up the mountain paths. Finally, we came to a small lake. After having a bite to eat, we set out to fish. Dusk soon appeared, and as happens in these parts, it began to get dark quickly. As soon as the sun went down, it immediately became cold. We quickly gathered our things and set out on the return path. In complete darkness we guided ourselves by little fires in the valley and practically made our way by touch alone. The boy who during the day had led us up the trail now was in back of us, and then he disappeared altogether. We stopped and began to call his name, but without any results. We could really feel the cold and were shivering in our light clothing.

"After waiting for a while, we decided to go down the mountain to get help and go back and look for him with flashlights or torches. When we returned to the village and approached our car, there was a crowd around it. When they saw only the two of us, they began to ask us where the lad was. We explained that during the most difficult portion of the road he had been with us but then had fallen behind. We waited and called for him, but he did not answer, and we decided to get help in the village. The voices in the crowd were agitated, and someone loudly expressed the opinion that these gringos had probably killed Panchito.

"John attempted to explain something else to them in a quivering voice. I tried to make my way to the car, but we stood surrounded by a ring of angry people, some of whom had clearly been drinking. Suddenly, someone yelled that Panchito was found, and then the crowd unwillingly broke up, and we immediately got inside the car and drove off. For a long time John could not settle down, and even at quite a distance from the village he kept fearing that we could be shot.

"After this and other incidents I realized that John was a bit of a coward and that I could not rely on him in a difficult situation. Nevertheless, his suggestion that we go to Puerto Escondido, which he heard was a very good place, was very alluring. The seduction was calculated on my love for fishing. On this occasion, John correctly chose the right trap. I reported the trip to the rezident and agreed with him that I would make use of the upcoming holidays in May for the trip.

"We left at night in John's vehicle, something like a Land Rover. It was a very long journey, most of it on mountain roads. To keep from getting tired, we periodically took turns driving. I was in a good mood, thinking of the fishing we were about to enjoy and the relaxation on the banks of the ocean, away from the bustle and smog of the capital and the daily consular and espionage worries. Besides the surprises which every fisherman dreams about before going out, I did not expect any others. I could not assume that the surprise was traveling with me in the pocket of my fellow traveler, my 'fishing friend' and agent of the CIA. John kept the conversation going and seemed relaxed. We somehow managed to make the long trip pass quickly.

"It was daytime when we arrived in Puerto Escondido, and then we drove to a very small village. We took two rooms in a tiny hotel, quickly unpacked our things, and hurried off to the shore. After renting a boat, we went out a certain distance from the shore and made our first casts. We did not have to wait long for results. We began to pull out one big fish after another. The fishing really was fantastic. But soon the sleepless night and the fatigue from the long road began to have their effect. In spite of the light ocean breeze, we melted under the tropical sun and became sleepy. When we finished with our fishing for the day, we returned to our rooms and wished each other good night. As soon as my head hit the pillow, I fell dead asleep.

"The following morning there was a knock at my door and then John somewhat sheepishly squeezed himself in. He handed me an envelope and left without saying another word. I turned the envelope in my hands and then opened it and pulled out a folded piece of paper on which something had been typewritten in Russian. It was clear that it was addressed to me. I quickly glanced over the contents one time and then read it and reread it. There could be no doubt—I was holding in my hands a direct recruiting offer from American intelligence.

"I'd be lying if I said I had been expecting this. I had to admit that such a turn of events dumbfounded me. One of my first thoughts was that my enemy had put a pretty good price on my head for those times. The sums that were offered in other recruiting approaches to our agents had been significantly lower. So at least I could be proud of that.

"But then my thoughts were interrupted by growing anger toward my so-called friend. Just as we had suspected, he had been a Pyos* from the very beginning. Seducing me with excellent fishing, he had lured me into his trap. He had brought me to a remote area and deprived me of any possibility of contacting my people, and he had created a favorable situation for the scriptwriters of this real-life scenario. But since we had suspected him, I should have known that sooner or later he would spring a trap. I had no one else to blame but myself. Now I had to control my anger and weigh the situation.

"The written and unwritten instructions had determined the course of behavior to take in such situations: to take a hard position, not to enter into lengthy conversations, to categorically deny affiliation with the KGB, and to protest the provocation. If an offer of collaboration was made while being caught red-handed, for example, while receiving materials or documents from a plant or an agent, then the instructions were not to sign any protocols or any other papers and to demand immediate contact with official Soviet representatives. Obviously, not everything in life goes according to instructions.

"Fortunately, at this time, the Center had begun a review of agents' actions during recruitment approaches. Now it was recommended not to shy away from conversation but try to learn as much as possible about the kind of information the other side had. The reasoning behind a specific recruitment, is to secure as much as possible information about the recruiters. An operative was allowed, depending on the circumstances, to make a counteroffer to

Pyos is the Russian for "male dog"—in this sense, a son of a bitch.

the recruiters seeking collaboration with Soviet intelligence.

"The situation in which I found myself, or to be more precise, was put in, was not an easy one. I was very far away and completely isolated from the embassy. I had neither telephone nor my own transportation. The day before we left, I found out that there was no telephone connection from our 'hotel' to the capital. Obviously, the planners of the operation had given serious attention to these details, choosing the 'battlefield' for the future conflict. It was still unclear which forces and where the enemy had concentrated and who was opposing me besides the cowardly Pyos. Naturally, this tactic was conceived in order to cause psychological stress before the possible meeting and conversation with the recruiter. Therefore, it could have been expected that in spite of the 'elegance' of the letter, with its aim to 'soften me up,' my American colleagues would have another surprise for me from their arsenal, which I knew was quite rich and varied.

"Taking all this into account, I thought that under such circumstances I should not give the other side reason to believe that I was shocked or distressed or uncertain of my own powers. I decided not to sit in my room but go straight to the little restaurant next to the hotel, where I could have breakfast and look around. Later, I would respond to the possible actions of these "fishermen." Now I myself had been turned into a little fish, although my CIA nickname was probably something quite different.

"From an old army habit I had, I usually brought with me some kind of weapon, usually a knife, before going out into the field. This time I had grabbed a small 22-caliber revolver, and naturally, like any good fisherman, I had a good working knife with me. When I opened my case, which was standing at the head of the bed, I discovered that the chamber of the revolver, which I had loaded before leaving, was now empty. That son-of-a-bitch buddy of mine had managed to empty it.

"The restaurant was just as tiny as our hotel. It contained only a few small tables on a veranda under a canopy. At one of them I spotted Pyos in the company of two strangers who struck me as being Americans. Two more visitors, clearly not locals, stood at the side at another table. When I walked under the canopy, all three from the first table turned to me.

" 'Good day, Pavel Antonovich, have a seat," said one of them in Russian with a slight accent. He offered me a chair. I accepted the invitation. The speaker was of medium height, normal build, with a pale, round face and incredibly blond hair. The feature noticeable about him was his crooked lower front teeth. The second was tall, with an athletic build, dark complexion, and regular features.

"I began the conversation by asking them to tell me whom I was dealing with. The blond, apparently the chief of the team, became animated and quickly answered, 'My name is Nick Benz. I am from the CIA. This is my colleague John Kelly.' He pointed to the tall American, who nodded his head. 'We came especially from Washington to meet with you.'

"I interrupted him and noted, 'If you're the author of this letter, it means you don't know me very well if you decided to make such an offer.'

" 'Yes, I wrote the letter,' Benz replied. 'But I don't see anything in it that should offend you. I am authorized to talk to you about the issues discussed in the letter, and I ask you to begin 'the conversation.' "

" 'I am afraid that we have nothing to speak about,' I responded rather sharply.

"The head of the CIA team said, 'I'm not surprised by your answer, Pavel Antonovich, but did you know that the CIA has never offered such a large sum to anyone else? You will be able to do what you wish this money. Moreover, haven't you ever thought about owning a hunting lodge on some beautiful lake in the United States or maybe Canada? Such a possibility can also be offered to you if you agree to our proposal. (Nick Benz clearly was adhering to the recruiting scenario concocted at Langley or the CIA station.) I no longer felt tense and even allowed myself to smile.

" 'But all this is not something I wish to negotiate,' I said, 'Therefore, Mr. Benz, such conversations will not take place.'

"Suddenly, the chief, either as part of the plan or improvising, asked, 'And what is your attitude toward Svetlana Alliluyeva [meaning Stalin's daughter] and her decision to remain in the West?'

"I didn't even want to talk about this whore who abandoned her children. Then, interrupting Benz, I turned to the CIA chief and said, 'You know I had a better opinion of my American colleagues, who should understand that such serious matters as recruitment are discussed tête-à-tête, and not in the presence of a group of witnesses, especially someone like Pyos [Pez]. Are you afraid to meet with me alone?'

" 'If there were just the two of us, the conversation might go differently.' The CIA chief stopped my tirade, turned to his team, and said something to them in English. I understood that he asked them to leave us alone, and then I took up the conversation again. 'You're sending your people away in vain. What do you think of my offer to you to work for Soviet intelligence? Perhaps you're ready? The rewards will be no less than what you promised me.'

"Perhaps I was wrong, but it seemed to me, judging by the chief's reactions, that he had not anticipated such a move on my part. At first, he stiffened, then, after a short pause, said, 'Your offer has no merit. Now I'm asking you to think once again about my proposal.'

"Rising from my chair I told him that I hoped to get his collaboration agreement at our next meeting and left the veranda. The chief could not contain himself and called out, 'Why didn't you try to recruit John?' Clearly this question had occupied my opponents.

"Turning around, I said loudly and derisively, 'What do we need a piece of shit like that for? Why did you bring him here?' And with that I walked back to the hotel without looking back. Once again I tried to find a way to contact the embassy back in Mexico City. It turned out that the nearest telephone was located a few kilometers down the road. Maintaining my composure, I grabbed my flippers and mask and headed toward the ocean as if nothing had happened.

"After a few hours of diving and fishing, I returned to the hotel, where I ran into Pyos. He did not look nearly as cheerful as he had been which we drove to this godforsaken hole. Without giving him a chance to speak, I called him Judas and added a few other choice expressions in Spanish and Russian.

"Pyos stood there with a guilty look and began to apologize and justify his actions, saying that he was made to do it. He added that about a month ago John Kelly visited him with a letter of reference from his brother. Kelly had introduced himself as an employee of the CIA and was interested in Pyos's relationship with me. He had asked 'Pyos' to think up a situation where we all could meet. But he supposedly warned Pyos of serious consequences for him if the fact of our meeting became known.

"Along with the threats, Kelly spoke about the need to fulfill his patriotic duty and to help the American government. According to Pyos, Kelly told him that I was KGB and that a conversation with me would be of mutual interest. Later, demonstrating his 'candor,' he shared with me that before our meeting the recruiters felt uneasy and asked a couple of times if I had a weapon. So that's why you disarmed me, my friend, I thought to myself, but kept quiet.

" 'Pack your things and take them out. We'll meet by the car,' I said.

" 'Pablo, forget what happened. Let's stay; the fishing here is so good. We'll swim around and dive a bit.'

" 'Yeah, you prepared an excellent fishing trip. Get a move on.' Giving him a withering look, I marched back to my room. He didn't wait long. After we had loaded our belongings into the car, I took the keys from him. I made him sit in the backseat, where I could observe him through the rear-view mirror. This cozy little corner on Mexico's Pacific coast, which had become such a memorable place for me, was soon far behind.

"I drove through the night. For most of the ride, Pyos slept or pretended to be asleep on the backseat. It was clear that the poor guy was very upset and was glad to have a chance to relax. Not a single word passed between us the whole trip back. Generally speaking, the return trip went off without a hitch except for one hairy moment when I was practically creamed by a bus and managed by a miracle to pull into a ditch. Fortunately, it wasn't too deep, and we got out without any help. When we arrived in Mexico City, we drove to my home. I silently took out my things and left without saying good-bye. Pyos tried to say something about continuing our 'friendship,' but all he got in answer were a few more strongly worded 'wishes.'

"On that same day I gave a detailed report to the rezident. So as not to show the enemy that we were reacting nervously to their attempt to recruit me, we decided to wait it out and send a message to Moscow Center a few days later. Our embassy was closed for the holidays, so any urgently coded telegram sent over the enemy-controlled teletype to Moscow would give the CIA reason to believe that we had contacted the Center about the attempt to recruit Pavel."

Thus, one of the duels between the CIA and KGB during the height of the Cold War had ended. One side had prepared for it in advance according to a carefully worked out scenario. The reaction from the other was practically impromptu. So who won this duel?

I have not read the draft of the CIA's Operation LIOVAL-1, code name Pyos, and only added my own conclusions concerning its possible purpose. I also have not had the opportunity to become acquainted with the report of the Americans who carried it out or directed it. Therefore, I can only judge it unilaterally, looking out from our trench. The recruitment, or treason, that is, Pavel's going over to the side of the enemy or his immediate recall from the country, did not occur. After a short interruption, he was able to resume his operative activities. The rhythm of activity inside the rezidentura was not disrupted, and the internal atmosphere remained calm after the news of the incident became known.

Pavel worked another seven months in Mexico without any problems, until the end of 1967, when I came to replace him. The only difference was that my cover had to be changed. I returned to Mexico as the second secretary of the embassy, and only afterward was I able to work under the same cover as Pavel, deputy head of the consular division.

No one questioned him when he returned to Moscow. Afterwards Pavel worked for a while at headquarters, then moved on to Italy, Cuba, Nicaragua, and Mozambique. Although he was psychologically shaken in Puerto Escondido, he was not "wounded" in his duel and remained in the ranks of the active warriors who fought with cloak and dagger.

While working on this chapter, I asked Paul if he still felt anger toward John B, a.k.a. "Pez," a.k.a. "Pyos," a.k.a. LIOVAL-1.

Pavel laughed and waved his hand. "What anger? A quarter century has passed. Back then we fought. As an agent he did a pretty
good job. He 'befriended' me, got me used to taking trips with him,
and then skillfully led me into a recruiting situation. Perhaps he
played his role better than his handlers played theirs. Besides, this
is a weak person who could easily be frightened or seduced by
material means. May he lead a blessed life."

In addition to not knowing why John B. served as an agent of the
CIA, we also have no idea what became of him after we had flushed
him out. But I have to think that if he were to read this book, John,
his case officers, and we could sit down at the same table and knock
out a pretty good screenplay for a suspense film. If I had dreamed
of such a thing twenty-five years ago, I would have woken up in a
cold sweat or laughed hysterically.

In early November of 1992, Valery Kostikov and I visited Pavel
at home. Pavel at the time was seventy-two, Valery was fifty-nine,
and I was sixty. "So Pavel," I said, "if you had taken up that offer,
you could have been the owner of a hunting lodge on a Canadian
lake, and Valery and I would be visiting you there for some real R
and R."

Pavel replied, "If I had accepted that offer then, I don't think that
you two would now be honored veterans of the KGB."

I said, "You're probably right, my friend, you're probably
right."

In the winter of 1993 I was visited in Moscow by Anthony
Summers, a respected journalist and writer who was the author of
a well-known book in the West entitled *Conspiracy: Who Killed
JFK?* Summers also wrote the recently published *Official and Confidential: The Secret Life of J. Edgar Hoover.* Obviously, our meeting centered mostly on the events in Dallas in 1963. Summers
showed me several documents from the CIA which he had obtained
through the Freedom of Information Act. Some of them concerned
the activities of our embassy in Mexico and its employees, including
people who worked within the KGB rezidentura and were involved
in Lee Harvey Oswald's September visits.

One of the documents especially captured my attention. With
Summers permission, I copied the text, which I offer to the reader:

Central Intelligence Agency

Commission No. 1216
2 July 1964

Memo for: J. Lee Rankin
General Counsel
Presidential Commission
on the Assassination of
President Kennedy

Subject: Lee Harvey Oswald

1. The following remarks have been recently attributed to
Soviet Consul Pavel Antonovich Yatskov in Mexico City
regarding the subject.

"I met Oswald here. He stormed into my office and wanted
me to introduce him to the Cubans. He told me that he had
lived in the USSR. I told him that I would have to check
before I could recommend him. He was nervous and his
hands trembled, and he stormed out of my office. I don't
believe that a person as nervous as Oswald, whose hands
trembled, could have accurately fired a rifle."

2. . . . has checked its records for the period Oswald was in
Mexico City and has advised it is quite possible that Oswald
thought he had talked with Valery Kostikov when he actually
had spoken to Yatskov; or that he first spoke to Kostikov who
turned him over to his superior Yatskov.

3. The source of the above information is a confidential
contact . . . who is believed to be reliable. In view of this
relationship an appropriate sensitivity indicator has been
affixed to this memorandum.

Stamped July 3, 1964

The contents of the CIA document, along with the coincidence in
dates of its preparation and the period of Pavel's friendship with
Pyos lead me to assume that the latter is the "source of . . . informa-

tion" and "confidential contact . . . who is believed to be reliable."
Pavel, when he saw the document, had to agree and suggested that
the ellipsis in the third paragraph of the document be filled in with
LIOVAL-1.

13

The Making of a Conspirator

In hostem omnia licita. (All's fair in war.)
—Latin saying,

Catch as catch can.

The interoffice line rang, and I picked it up.

"Oleg Maksimovich, you have a letter marked 'personal' from New York. Can I bring it in?"

"Please do."

A young officer from the American section of our foreign counterintelligence directorate came into my office and handed me a medium-sized yellow envelope sealed with scotch tape. It was marked *personal* in black fountain pen. I thanked the officer and put it in plain sight on the corner of my desk.

During this period, at the end of the 1970s, my title was deputy chief of information and analysis division, in the foreign counterintelligence directorate of the First Chief Directorate. Officially we were known as directorate "K"; and in correspondence with the rezidenturas, as the "KR line." The division's responsibilities can be inferred from its title. We received counterintelligence information from all the KGB rezidenturas and used this "product" to concoct "tasty dishes."

One of our main functions consisted of writing informational summaries and analytic bulletins discussing operational conditions throughout the world's regions. We also wrote reports describing subversive activities of enemy clandestine services aimed at Soviet businesses and citizens. These summaries had to be prepared on a daily to quarterly basis, depending on the subject. For instance, we wrote our prognosis for the enemy's activities against our intelligence agencies during the New Year. All this material was distributed through various channels, ranging from the chairman of the KGB to different department heads. Division heads who received this material, could thus familiarize themselves with operational conditions abroad, taking them into account when they organized the operative work within their divisions. Having this information made it possible to improve security.

On the same day I received the envelope from New York, I was checking the reports prepared for the daily summary. Normally this task belonged to the division chief, but since he was on vacation, it was added to my daily concerns. The draft of the summaries had to be on the chief directorate's desk no later than 1:00 P.M. After obtaining his approval and comments, I would then have the reports copied and prepared for distribution. That is why I did not open my letter when I got it; I decided to wait until I had finished with current business. After presenting the summaries and eating lunch, I returned to my office and opened the envelope. It consisted of a note and a paperback in English. The note said:

> Oleg,
>   We couldn't find the book that you wanted. I'm sending you this one, hope you'll find it useful for your library.
>   Regards,
>   Aleksei

I looked at the book, written by two authors, whose names meant nothing to me, the title *L.B.J. and the J.F.K. Conspiracy,* and the short blurb "A documentary account of Johnson's advance knowledge about the 'Meeting in Dallas.' "* Such intriguing phrases compelled me to open the book and start to flip through the pages. Right after the title page was a blurb that promised so much more: "The documentary account of Vice President Johnson's advance

*Hugh McDonald and Robin Moore, *L.B.J. and the J.F.K. Conspiracy*

knowledge of the 'meeting in Dallas'—the assasination of Kennedy."

In the prologue, I noticed names very familiar to me; Lee Harvey Oswald, George DeMohrenschildt, Lyndon Johnson, Vladimir Semichastny, KGB chairman from 1961 to 1967, Mikhail Tsimbal, Deputy Chief of First Directorate, KGB foreign intelligence, and Grigorii Visko commercial representative of the Soviet Embassy in Mexico City in the early 1960's and places like: Moscow, Dallas, New Orleans, New Laredo, and Mexico.

I started to skim, and soon everything became clear. The "documentary account" narrated a Soviet "conspiracy," originated by Khrushchev himself, to kill Kennedy because he had offended the Soviet premiere and hurt his pride. Naturally, the KGB was chosen for this task under the leadership of Semichastny.

When I reached chapter 20, I came across a name familiar to me since early childhood: Oleg Maksimovich Nechiporenko. I had always been used to having my name misspelled even in Russian, and here it was, in the Roman alphabet, spelled absolutely correctly. It seems as if someone used official documents to check the spelling, to make sure there was no confusion caused by the name.

Now I was no longer content just to skim. I holed up in the office and decided not to answer the telephone unless it was the Chief calling on his private line. I started to read in earnest. I paid special attention to the descriptions of our embassy and rezidentura in Mexico and to the mention of my biography and intelligence activities. Then I put the book down and thought, I've already seen this, maybe even word for word. Of course, it was all taken from our "coffee table" book, John Barron's *KGB: The Secret Work of Soviet Agents,* which was published four years earlier in America and translated into many languages. I kept this title in my library. It was among the reference books I used at work. Just to confirm my suspicions, I opened Barron's book to chapter 11, "The Plot to Destroy Mexico." I put the two books side by side and started comparing them. Their texts were amazingly similar.

According to McDonald and Moore, for example, the "Russian Embassy in Mexico City is considered the most important post in the vast Russian system of embassies. It is the heart of Communist subversive activities for all of the Americas." Barron says essentially the same but takes it one step further by declaring that the KGB "had completely taken over the Soviet Embassy in Mexico and developed it into one of the world's great sanctuaries of subversion."

Then I switched over the sections describing me and compared them. McDonald/Moore flatteringly called me "without question the best KGB field operative in the Americas." Barron echoed their compliment with "Nechiporenko simply was the best KGB field operative in Latin America."

I was so engrossed in my comparisons that I didn't notice that it was already evening. I returned home late, ate, watched television, and went to sleep.

The next day, I continued to think about these books. John Barron, in discussing my "merits" in 1971 and 1974, presented me as a dangerous opponent who directed all my energies toward toppling the Mexican government and undermining democracy in that country. First I was the main inspiration for the student demonstrations; then I selected candidates for an underground terrorist group. But what did the authors of the "documentary account," written in 1978, cook up for me? Evidently quite a bit, if you consider the following: "This man was a perfect selection to direct, at the regional level, those preliminary events that would lead to the assassination of President John F. Kennedy."

My activities extended from involvement in one country to a region and eventually went intercontinental. There is a Russian saying "If you're making cabbage soup, don't make it thin, make it thick." Well, it seems that this "cabbage soup" was cooked and then reheated in the same "kitchen." Where and how it got so "thick" could take up plenty of time, but there was another book that had the key to the puzzle. It was published in the United States in 1976, in between the other two books, and was called *Portrait of a Cold Warrior,* written by a high-ranking CIA officer, Joseph B. Smith. This veteran of American intelligence, who had just retired, described his career in various regions, including Latin America.

It just so happened that the Cold War placed us in Mexico, as enemy soldiers on opposite sides of the trenches of the "invisible front." Smith, or "little Joe," as he was known to his colleagues, was one of the people in charge of the Soviet operations of the CIA, meaning any activity directed against us.

My main interest at that time as deputy chief of counterintelligence at our Mexico rezidentura was the CIA station, which was under the cover of the American embassy. I do not remember if I was personally acquainted with Smith, but his name was well known to me.

His memoirs indicate that he had an immediate connection to my work and consequently knew about me. It's even possible that he was the "godfather" responsible for ending my "extended" intelligence mission in Mexico. Still, I respect his many-sided operational skills and especially his firm, principled position, that despite its blunders the CIA was a necessity in the real world of competing clandestine services, which would not have been easy to maintain as a CIA veteran during those complicated times in the mid-1970s. I'm sure he needed a great deal of personal fortitude to maintain his stance. Therefore, when I use "esteemed" in conjunction with his name, it is sincerely meant, without any irony intended.

I turned to his book and called it the key to the puzzle, since it describes the "kitchen" authentically, the kitchen that served up active measures to compromise the other side's intelligence, in this case, the KGB. In my opinion, Smith's work can act as a special-services textbook teaching intelligence tradecraft.

I hope the author forgives me, but I need to quote from his work for purposes of further clarification:

> One night in February, 1970, we received a tip that Raya Kiselnikova had walked into a police station asking for political asylum. Mexico's policy toward granting an alien this privilege assured approval of her request. The Mexican authorities were happy to turn her over to us and forget about what happened to her. . . . Raya was a secretary in the Soviet Trade Mission whose members were all KGB. . . .
>
> Raya defected for very personal reasons . . . on her own, found a boyfriend and decided she liked the boutiques and discotheques in the Pink zone enough to walk out of the embassy."*

*Joseph B. Smith, *Portrait of a Cold Warrior* (New York: G. P. Putnam's Sons, 1976), pp. 413, 416, 417.

It was an interesting situation, and someone viewing it from the sidelines might have found it funny. If the CIA station, doing all it could to penetrate our establishment in Mexico, was not ready for the "arrival" of Kiselnikova, then the Soviet rezidentura, responsible for the security of Soviet citizens, slept through her "departure." As a result, our opponents received an unexpected find, and we suffered an unpleasant loss.

Kiselnikova worked as a secretary in the trade delegation of the USSR. Her working hours were spent within the confines of the Trade Delegation Building, where several of our, and the military's, "foreign traders" were placed among the "clean" employees. On work-related trips into town she was always accompanied by one of these "reliable" employees. She had a small room in the housing wing of the building. It was located on Soviet territory, which excluded the possibility of visits by foreigners. Her leisure time was spent within the framework of "planned" cultural activities of the Soviet colony. Therefore, we could monitor her activities practically twenty-four hours a day; therefore, she was not considered a "security risk."

We attached no special meaning to her increased attention to her appearance and clothing, even though the women noticed this change. Regarding the "friend" that Smith mentioned, it was later determined that she did not "find" him and that he "came" to her. He was a local representative of a small business who dealt with the delegation and visited regularly. This is how the Kiselnikova affair began.

A worrisome incident occurred either at the end of 1969 or the beginning of 1970. One weekend she left the building on a Saturday morning and did not return until the following evening. When we discussed her absence with her, she said that she was with one of the male members of the Soviet colony but did not want to compromise him by revealing his name. Obviously her fabrication was checked, and since she had broken the rules, the question of punitive actions arose.

After discussing her situation, it was decided not to recall her immediately to Moscow but to wait for favorable circumstances. We informed Moscow Center of our recommendation. After a while, there was a directive issued to the trade delegation stating that Kiselnikova be transferred to East Germany. Since she spoke German, this made sense, and she was told that she had a week to complete her work and leave for the Soviet Union. She was surrounded with the "proper" help, who assisted in making last-minute purchases and generally diverted her attention from the transfer.

We believed that she accepted the transfer story and that everything would proceed smoothly. But, completely unexpectedly, a telegram, sent on the unsecured line, fell into her hands, and it discussed a "recall" and not a "transfer." Then her "friend" took her to the police department. I'll continue the story using Joseph Smith's words:

> After that, however, her information and insights dropped to our customary level of personal information and gossip about KGB people in the embassy. . . . One important thing we did identify was the location and layout of the Referentura—the KGB equivalent of a CIA station.*

Kiselnikova could, at least partially, describe the "Referentura," but only because it was not located in the rezidentura. She was asked how she, without having anything to do with us, ended up in the holy of holiest sancta, the foreign referentura. Interestingly enough, Joseph Smith called her a "KGB secretary." Anyway, she found her way into the referentura, where the secret coding was done, shortly before her departure, even though she did not have clearance for this area. A trusted representative of the ambassador included her in the typing of a report detailing trade relations with Mexico. He did this without our agreement and on his own authority. Since the document was considered secret, it had to be typed in a guarded location. This is how Kiselnikova, despite our instructions, ended up in the rezidentura that wasn't the rezidentura of the KGB.

We assessed the level of her knowledge and how much damage it could cause. Since she didn't work on secret documents except for this one instance, her informational baggage would consist of the

*Ibid., p. 418.

internal workings of the Soviet colony. That is, who's who among the diplomats and officers of the delegation. Certainly we understood that the enemy could utilize this information to create compromising material and thereby recruit our people. We could not say on whom and when this material might be used.

Here, in Smith's words, is how our opponents used her information within the CIA:

> The principle use we were able to make of Raya's information was to make it public in order to embarrass and harass the KGB officers in Mexico. In the intelligence trade this is called "burning." The KGB officer we decided to burn with the hottest fire was Oleg Nechiporenko. Nechiporenko had arrived in Mexico City in 1961 and, hence, had been there nine years by the time Raya defected. We decided to pay special attention to him because he had been a recruitment target for all these years and a hopeless one. Since we couldn't recruit him, we took advantage of Raya's defection to give wide publicity to the fact that he was a KGB security officer and, with the help of Raya's press conference, *we invented the story* [author's emphasis] that he had been the major instigator of the Mexico City student riots of 1968, which culminated in a shoot-out in which a number of protesters were killed.*

I have to give our opponents their due for their organization and staging of this press conference. As a result of her prepared speech, Kiselnikova seemed to be an active participant in the residentura's secret operations. The blow to me was well calculated. The CIA was personally displeased with my behavior and knew that the Mexican authorities were already tired of my various activities. They managed to infer that I was meddling in internal affairs, which strongly provoked the nationalistic feelings of the Mexicans.

But this sharp blow did not obtain its desired effect. It did not knock us out, and it couldn't even be counted as a knockdown. The local press squawked about it for a few days, and then it blew over. There was no negative reaction from official Mexican sources. I

*Ibid., pp. 418–19.

continued to work to strengthen Soviet-Mexican relations, through my cover of head of the consular section of the Soviet Embassy and the second secretary of the embassy, while simultaneously continuing my counterintelligence work aimed at our main adversary, Mexico's neighbor to the north.

Our opponents also made headway in their intelligence work and waited patiently to strike the next blow. The opportunity presented itself in the beginning of 1971.

On the morning of March 16, a colleague from the KR line and I left for the resort town of Cuernavaca, sixty miles from Mexico City. During the second half of the 1970s, while reading Joseph Smith's book, I felt that I was in Cuernavaca again and reliving the events of those days. In chapter 21, with the multilayered title "We Don't Spy on Fellow Americans Unless They Disagree With Us," the author describes in great detail the cultivation of Americans who were victims of McCarthyism and who lived in Cuernavaca as well as the social organizations and their participants who worked on befriending them.

Again our paths crossed, but on opposite sides. My interests in these same people and organizations were based on the following. U.S. citizens living in Cuernavaca on a permanent basis had opened boarding schools for American students. These students came on their vacations to begin or to continue their study of Spanish and to acquaint themselves with Mexico's rich culture and history while relaxing in this heavenly place. There were different "academies," or research centers, which specialized in the humanities and operated as summer schools. It was understood that potential agents could be found in these schools, and "recruiting contingencies" were established for this purpose. The goal was to recruit a young, prospective agent who, while working for us, would also join the FBI or CIA.

By March 1971 I had "labored" for several months in Cuernavaca and strengthened relations with a contact, who made it possible to for me to penetrate one of the summer schools and obtain the background of, and biographical information on, its American students. This information could be useful later to rezidenturas in the United States. I was acquainted with, and well received at, the school for American students of Lini De Vries. She left America as a result of persecution during McCarthyism. Joseph Smith details the CIA's interest in her in chapter 21 of his book.

When we arrived in Cuernavaca on that March day, we saw the huge headlines in all the local newspapers. The newsboys screamed "Guerrilas arrested." Having purchased several newspapers, we found out that the Mexican police had discovered and crushed a pro-Communist, extremist group. Its stated goal was the overthrow of the Mexican government, and its members had already participated in violent diversionary actions. There were pictures of the suspects and their confiscated arms. The news story stressed that the group's leaders attended the Patrice Lumumba University in Moscow and received special training in camps in North Korea.

As the result of these arrests, we expected trouble for our embassy. Fully aware of the fact that I was considered dangerous by many of the Mexican authorities and realizing the possibility of repressive measures from their quarter, I decided to insure my project and introduced my co-worker to my contact at lunch. We returned to the capital that evening. The nightly news featured the same headlines as in the morning.

On March 18, 1971, Soviet envoy Dmitri Diakonov, temporarily in charge at the embassy, was called to the Mexican Ministry of Foreign Affairs. We were already aware of the sanctions that would be imposed against the workers of our embassy and the names of those who would be involved, but we waited for the official announcement. The evening edition featured the following statement:

> The Minister of Foreign Affairs, Emilio Rabasa, today called Dmitri A. Diakonov, adviser-envoy and temporary head of the Soviet Embassy to the Foreign Ministry. The Minister of Foreign Affairs informed the envoy that he, as well as Boris P. Kolomiakov, first secretary; Boris N. Voskoboynikov, second secretary; Oleg M. Nechiporenko, second secretary; and Aleksandr Bolshakov, serving the Soviet embassy, are *persona non grata* in the Mexican Republic, and, in this regard, the government of Mexico demands that they leave the sovereign state of Mexico as soon as possible.*

Tiempo. March 29, 1971, p. 10.

On March 21, four of us, all officers of the rezidentura, headed by Boris Kolomiakov, left on Sabena Airlines for Brussels, en route to Moscow. Diakonov, who was also "labeled" KGB, deliberately waited an extra day to stress his nonparticipation in our activities. My family and I were driven to the airport by Valery Nikolaenko, also a second secretary at the embassy. He worked strictly for the Ministry of Foreign Affairs. We decided to include a number of "clean" diplomats in our sendoff to "confuse" the enemy.

I remembered our doing this when I saw in Smith's book that he named Nikolaenko as an object of his personal recruitment activity. Smith called him, to my great surprise, a potential CIA agent. Was it possible that our "brilliant" plan of mixing KGB personnel with "clean" workers actually worked? Nickolaenko subsequently became an ambassador and during the perestroika years served as deputy minister of foreign affairs for the Soviet Union.

This is my quick summary of our country's reaction to those March events. Here is the view of Joseph Smith, also a direct participant from the other side:

> As a result of our identifying him [Oleg M. Nechiporenko] as a dangerous KGB officer and someone who had intervened in Mexican affairs, when the Mexican government uncovered a small band of guerrillas and found that they had gone via Russia for training in North Korea, Mexican authorities blamed him for this even worse intervention in their country's political concerns and threw him out of Mexico. Getting KGB officers publicly identified as such, and whenever possible, declared *persona non grata* was something we tried to do whenever we failed to recruit them.*

On this occasion our opponents could celebrate victory. Their efforts had not been in vain. Their spark started a flame. This flame was so hot that a significant part of our rezidentura "burned." Those remaining within the rezidentura felt threatened and anxious, which had to hamper their intelligence work.

We were well received at Moscow Center. They understood that

*Ibid., p. 419.

our recall was the result of political acts from the other side and not due to any failure on our part. We were "scattered" among our divisions within the KGB. I returned to foreign counterintelligence and went to work, but with a new status, as an officer who had been "decoded" or discovered.

Shortly thereafter, our friends sent local newspapers with photographs and a detailed description of our departure. One of the articles caught my eye:

> The plane's departure was delayed, probably due to the fact that airline representatives did not permit several dogs belonging to the diplomats deported from Mexico, to depart.*

I asked my fellow passengers how they managed to transport the canine "contraband," and while not one of them admitted to it, we had a wonderful laugh. Another newspaper said that the two-hour delay was due to defects in the airplane's engine.

The description of our parting was exaggerated.

> Approximately twenty Russians sent off the evicted diplomats on their flight to Moscow. Judging by their behavior, the crowd treated these diplomats like heroes. The departure was announced and each person, before climbing into the airplane, was hugged and kissed by members of the crowd.
>
> One tall mustached Russian warmly hugged and kissed Oleg M. Nechiporenko right on the lips in accordance with the Russian custom.†

In September 1971, the sensational March story of the eviction of five Soviet diplomats from Mexico was surpassed by the English expulsion of 105 people working in Soviet businesses in London. My brother Gleb Maximovich also worked for the First Chief Directorate and had returned from London the year before, where he served in the rezidentura. In those days we worked in the same building, on Dzerzhinsky Square, but in different subdivisions. The

---

*El Heraldo, March 22, 1971.
†Ibid.

office was on the sixth floor in Directorate "S" or "illegal S" unit. This unit was responsible for placing Soviets with false identities into host countries under deep cover. I worked on the seventh floor in foreign counterintelligence. Having heard of the expulsion of our "Englishmen," I went down to visit my brother. There were several colleagues in his office discussing the event. After I greeted everyone, I turned to my brother: "Listen, Gleb, we almost made it into the *Guinness Book of World Records.*"

Everyone turned to look at me. "How?" asked my brother.

"First answer this question: What kind of brothers are there?"

"Well, there's blood brothers, like you and me."

"Stepbrothers."

"Brothers-in-law."

"Brothers-in-arms."

"Well," I continued, "if you had stayed in London, you would have definitely ended up as one of the 105, and for the first time in history, we would became the Brothers Non Grata."

Everyone around nodded and expressed their "condolences" for this missed opportunity at being record holders.

At the beginning of November, I was given a special assignment in my favorite region, Latin America. While I was there, the enemy came up with its next surprise. In the November and December issues of *Reader's Digest,* fragments of the "Soviet Conspiracy to Undermine Mexico" appeared. This was from John Barron's book, essentially much of chapter 11, scheduled for publication in 1972. The contents of the article left little doubt as to its source, the CIA, which was only too happy to be a "nice guy" and help Barron add fuel to the fire. In defiance of the "don't knock a man when he's down" rule, they pounded me with both fists. By my count this was the third hit. Now I was presented as the number-one enemy of Mexico. This view was reinforced by Kiselnikova's "confessions" and "proof." Statements attributed to her claimed that I participated in the organization of the "Movement of Revolutionary Activities." Simultaneously, I was presented as a "superman" and a Soviet James Bond.

Wherever James Bond goes there are women. Through the author's endeavors, Kiselnikova had been transformed into my lover, with whom I "found everything that was lacking" in my wife. She was also allegedly "my only real friend in Mexico," with whom I "shared" insidious, subversive plans during many "moments of candor spent together." According to the article, other agents worshiped Kiselnikova to the point where she accompanied them and "witnessed meetings between the KGB and Mexican agents." My official conversation with her in the police station, during which, in reality, her boss had been present, appeared like some pastoral scene of two lovers separating and was concluded with "kisses and tears" on both sides.

I must admit that while reading my praises, I experienced two feelings: on the one hand, the pleasant stroking of ego, and also a definite uneasiness, wondering how my bosses would react to this description of my sojourn in Mexico. After all, it was one of our ideologues, Lenin himself, who said that praises from the other side should be treated cautiously, for if the other side praises you, it means you're likely to be doing something wrong on your side.

There was no need to be uneasy. After I returned from Latin America, at the end of December, I learned that I had been promoted up to the position of director of the branch in the American Division, of the just restructured foreign counterintelligence Service 2 into directorate while I was away. Eventually, I was transferred to the position of director of the American Division.

There was another "thunderbolt" in 1974: John Barron's *KGB. The Secret Work of Soviet Agents* was released in the United States, and subsequently all over the world.

For the first time in the entire postwar period our activities were presented with great clarity. Intelligence and counterintelligence operations were detailed. There were descriptions of recruiting methods and intelligence work. The departments of the KGB and their responsibilities were delineated in graphic form. There was a section describing the work of the First Chief Directorate. But perhaps the most injurious element of the work was "Appendix D, Soviet Citizens Engaged in Clandestine Work Abroad." This appendix contained a list of several hundred names, mainly KGB operatives, and also members of GRU-military intelligence and personnel whose only function was purely diplomacy. The last group was included in this list in order to frighten them and to cause animosity between "clean" personnel and the intelligence community.

Serious effort went into the preparation of Barron's book, and the information was well documented. It was skillfully presented, with the goal of influencing various groups in different countries. My personal opinion is that Barron's work can be called the most successful active measure taken by the CIA against our service in many years. As a result, the KGB suffered a significant loss of morale. All the operatives mentioned in the book had their files marked "Mentioned in the KGB book." This meant that several hundred experienced operatives' usefulness abroad was curtailed. Some of them could no longer function beyond our own borders. I remember how even retired colleagues would call me and ask me to check if their names were included on the "blacklist."

Colleagues also came from other divisions and glanced through the book, searching for their names. Those whose names were not disclosed breathed a sigh of relief, and the "mentioned" left scratching their heads. So the influence of this work was not only felt at the rezidenturas but also at Moscow Center. By the time this book was published, I had already developed an immunity to enemy attacks, and I responded calmly to the "advertising" of my activities. More so in this case, since the chapter in which I was one of the "villains" did not add anything to the *Reader's Digest* revelations. But I did count this as the fourth hit.

My wife, however, felt she had been seriously insulted by the author, who unfairly defamed her in front of the entire world: First of all, he acted in an ungentlemanly fashion and showed a lack of tact in describing her physical characteristics. Second, Barron attributed "commissar-like" functions to her among the women in the Soviet colony in Mexico. Well, why don't you sue him for defamation of character and moral damage, I suggested more than once. She refused.

But I had one question for John Barron: Where did my "Spanish" roots come from in 1974 when they weren't mentioned in the 1971 article? In his book, Barron states that with my

debonair mustache, and wavy black hair and olive complexion [Nechiporenko] looked utterly Latin. Indeed, Mexican au-

thorities theorized that he was either the child of Spanish
communists who had fled to Russia after the Spanish Civil
War or perhaps the son of a Spanish father and a Spanish
mother.

Again, I found the answer with Joseph Smith. He wrote, "He
evidently had some Spanish blood, possibly one parent was a Spanish Communist—one of the thousands who fled to Russia after the
Spanish Civil War."*

But how could an experienced colleague make such a suggestion
and allow for negligence by not checking the facts? In my file at the
CIA it clearly states date of birth: July 4, 1932. The Spanish Civil
War began in 1936 and ended in 1939. That means that "the Spanish Communist—one of the thousands who fled to Russia" after
this war could not "possibly" be one of my parents. He could have
met me going to school and heard me say, *"No pasarán!,"* a popular
revolutionary greeting in those days. There was obviously some
discrepancy in my "Spanish" conception. John Barron probably
received a "worked-up" thesis of my origin and decided to give the
Mexicans full responsibility.

Messrs. Hugh and Moore evidently found the second version
more to their liking and without checking simply wrote that I was
"born in 1921 [?!] of a Russian father and a Spanish mother."†

It is, after all, a delicate operation, working in the kitchen of
active measures—if you don't include enough or include too much,
the dish is ruined.

To set the record straight about my origins and maybe make the
necessary corrections to my file in the CIA archives, I can say that
I truly am a Slavic half-breed. My mother was Russian, born in
Central Russia, and my father was Ukrainian, born in Kiev. There
is some Cossack blood; my father's mother was a Cossack from the
Don. But there's no smoke without fire: my grandmother on my
mother's side told me when I was a child that her grandfather had
Gypsy blood. Anyway, that makes my genealogy a stone's throw
from Spanish. It cannot be excluded that the CIA was somehow

---

*Smith, *Portrait of a Cold Warrior,* p. 419.
†Hugh McDonald and Robin Moore, *L.B.J. and the J.F.K. Conspiracy,* p. 126.

aware of this and that its specialists "nurtured" my "Spanish" origins.

In discussing me, Joseph Smith mentions my "nonrecruitability" and another incident which demanded "satisfaction."

> Once he had even gotten into the U.S. Embassy posing as a visa applicant and was not discovered for several hours. How much he learned about the way embassy offices were arranged and what other information he gleaned, we don't know. So he was somebody we were particularly happy to harass.*

Barron compared me to a chameleon and presented the same incident as follows:

> With the same ease, he could affect the manners of a bright young Mexican business or professional man. He once assumed just such a pose and strode into the United States embassy. For more than an hour he wandered about, gleaning what information he could, until a security officer recognized him as a KGB officer."†

I agree that this kind of insolence should not be tolerated. But it was nothing special. How will my former opponents react when I tell them that, in fact, I sat in the American ambassador's chair, in his office on the fifth floor. In addition, Valery Kostikov and I walked down the corridor that led to their CIA station. It may sound fantastic, like a sequence in an adventure movie, but life is always richer than fantasy. It happened a long time ago, and I don't think anyone on either side will suffer if I tell this story.

Even during the tensest periods of the Cold War, we had good relations with our American embassy colleagues in Mexico. We stayed in touch, since one of the flight routes for departing diplomats to the Soviet Union went through New York. So each time someone went on vacation or finished an assignment and was scheduled to return, we had to get transit visas from the American

*Smith, *Portrait of a Cold Warrior,* p. 419.
†John Barron, *KGB: The Secret Work of Soviet Agents* (New York: Reader's Digest Press, 1974), p. 231.

embassy. In addition, both sides were active members of the Foreign Consular Association, which consisted of accredited diplomats in Mexico. We met in conjunction with this group's functions.

The episode brought up in Smith's book, and subsequently "put into" Barron's work, which so perturbed the Americans happened sometime in 1970. For whatever reason, it was necessary to get transit visas immediately. I grabbed the necessary passports and went over to the U.S. embassy. At this time, a security system for admitting people was already in place. It was occasioned by an increase in anti-American activities. I presented my diplomatic identification to the girl at the information desk, received permission to enter, and showed my pass to the marine guard. I went downstairs to where the consul's offices were located. Only diplomatic and service visas were handled here, so there was limited access to this section. Regular visas were issued on the same floor, but on a different side of the building. In the office, I met a woman with whom I was friendly, primarily because Spanish was her native language, and explained my situation. She promised that she would start processing the visas and I could pick them up in about an hour. I thanked her in advance and left the office.

Since I had time and a good "cover," I decided to utilize it for other things and headed in the direction of the buffet bar for American embassy personnel. I can't remember exactly where it was located, but the entrance was on the same side as the gallery. The purpose of my visit was to determine how accessible the buffet bar was to those who were not employed by the embassy. This information could be potentially useful under the right circumstances.

I entered a small hall and sat at a table near the entrance. I casually observed my surroundings and the people in them. A waiter came fairly quickly and asked for my order. I asked for orange juice. He asked if I was an embassy employee. He didn't mention which embassy, and neither did I when I affirmed that I was an embassy employee. Considering the question, I gave the right answer.

Shortly thereafter, the waiter reappeared, this time accompanied by a man in civilian clothes. Approaching my table and studying me carefully, he asked if I was an employee of this embassy. I had to answer that I was an embassy employee, but not at this embassy, and was here on official business. I came to the buffet bar to wait until my visas were ready and to have something to drink.

The man in civilian clothes explained that this area was for American embassy employees only and that no one else could be served here. I pointed to the waiter and explained that I had already ordered and as soon as I finished my juice, I would leave. But I was politely and firmly told that I would not be served here. I shrugged my shoulders and left. I found out everything I needed to know.

Returning to the visa division, I picked up my visa to the United States, thanked my acquaintance, and left my hospitable surroundings. It would not be difficult for the security officers to identify me, since there were only a few people who dealt with visas. Obviously this story reached the fifth floor of the American embassy, where the CIA station was located.

And now for how I became "the person temporarily in charge" in the U.S. ambassador's office and managed to spin around in his chair for a bit. This happened, if my memory is correct, in 1964. Our embassy received three invitations, from the Foreign Consular Association, to a reception for the official opening of the new American embassy, located on one the most beautiful streets in Mexico City, Avenida Paseo de la Reforma. The invitations were specifically for Pavel Yatskov, consul, Valery Kostikov, and me, as vice consuls. It was clearly understood that as intelligence operatives this was an "occasion" we could not miss.

Valery and I dressed up and went to the reception. Amid all the high-level foreign diplomats and Mexican officials, we met our ambassador. He was surprised to see us, since the lowly rank of third secretary was not commensurate with the rest of the guests. A group of American congressmen visiting Mexico also took part in the ceremonies.

When enough of the invited guests had arrived, an excursion of the premises began. Naturally, Valery and I were in the front line of this group. We were shown the lower floors, their conference room, movie theater, library, and dining room. Then the group was invited to walk along the esplanade, located above the main entrance, where the main ceremonies were scheduled to take place. Lagging behind now, we found ourselves surrounded by congressmen, accompanied by the embassy's security personnel. This group was invited to see the upper floors. Valery and I looked at each other and couldn't resist. We had to join them.

I started to ask a distinguished-looking gentleman what he thought of the view when the elevator came and we were on it. The elevator operators were dressed in civilian clothes but had the bearing and haircuts of marines. When we got off on the fifth floor, all my interest in my distinguished friend's story vanished, and I became a movie camera, recording and remembering everything. Our "chosen" company was led through the ambassador's quarters. Several rooms were windowless, and the last one had windows facing la Reforma. These rooms had people working in them who cheerfully nodded at the passersby. Our guide opened a door and invited everyone to take a look at the ambassador's office. Valery and I entered with the rest of the crowd.

It was a corner office, and one window faced the façade; the other, a side street, directly northeast. The office did not strike us as overly large. In the center was a desk; behind it, the American ambassador's chair.

The guests, who by now filled up the room, started to ask questions, and the guide began to answer them. I approached the desk, walked around it, but could not deny myself the pleasure of sitting in the ambassador's chair, and began spinning in it. I thought, When will I ever get this chance again. Valery, standing nearby, smirked as he witnessed this scene—a KGB officer sitting at the desk of the American ambassador in Mexico.

Looking the table over, I saw the internal telephone directory for the embassy and used my eyes to point it out to Valery. He nodded in understanding.

All the KGB rezidenturas constantly searched for this document, since it was an invaluable resource in organizing operational measures against our main opposition. With the help of this kind of directory and other embassy publications, it was possible to create an almost 100 percent accurate structure of the CIA station operating in Mexico or any other country.

After the publication, in the 1970s, of John Marks' famous key to the codes of American intelligence, the CIA instigated countermeasures that limited the effectiveness of this type of publication. But by this time we had a massive accumulation of data that enabled us to track U.S. intelligence operatives as they switched countries and regions. The man at Moscow Center responsible for working out and maintaining this information was known as our "walking computer." Hearing the name of a CIA operative, he could tell you the country the person was working in and the cover he used.

This is why our hands started to itch when we saw the internal telephone directory on the ambassador's desk. It would not have been difficult to "remove" it, but we wavered. What a souvenir it would have made, possibly filled with the ambassador's personal notes. But it struck us as unethical to steal while we were guests. We also knew that our rezidentura already had a copy.

While I was engaged in this battle with my conscience, someone jokingly asked me if the seat was comfortable. I got up and in a friendly manner offered him the chair. Valery and I had already had a new interest. Near the desk was a rectangular column extending from the floor to the ceiling. Valery appraised the column from all sides. Looking at it more closely, we suggested that it might be a personal elevator. One of the embassy personnel, who spoke Spanish, confirmed that it was. Valery and I spoke Spanish to each other, and our "guide" must have assumed that we were Mexican guests. The other details in the ambassador's office escape me now, but I remember that we were impressed by the vertical venetian blinds.

After visiting the ambassador's quarters, members of the excursion scattered about the corridor and started looking at other offices. We were told that this was the political affairs division, and we knew that this was the principal cover employed by the CIA. I ended up in an office adjoining the ambassador's belonging to an embassy adviser. There was a safe with a combination lock in the windowless section to the left. I became interested in the plate attached to the safe's door, and I went for a closer look. At this moment, someone behind me started to explain that the plate lists the names of those people with access to the safe and all who know the combination and what order they should be called in case of an emergency. I carefully listened to this helpful information and thanked the person providing it while thinking, If you only knew to whom you were so diligently giving this information.

Valery strolled through another section, and I joined him. We concentrated on memorizing all that we could, including the number of offices, the construction of the walls, the soundproofing system, the characteristics of the furniture, number of places for people, and the type of telephone equipment. All of this could come in very handy in the future for our operative activities.

As I just noted, we knew that the political affairs division was the CIA's cover. But based on the office telephone numbers, it was impossible to determine how the section was divided into "clean" government agency personnel and intelligence personnel. It was also unclear if the CIA agents mixed their cover functions with their intelligence functions and if they conducted intelligence work in this section or somewhere else. Since we were in their offices, we could now clarify this question.

The "clean" personnel occupied half of the fifth floor, in the section near the ambassador's quarters, facing the building's façade. The CIA station was on the other side; entry into this section was restricted by a partition made of semitransparent material, possibly optical glass. Based on our reconnaissance, it was possible to determine which offices housed the station and who worked there.

Having completed the excursion, Valery and I and the distinguished congressmen descended to the first floor. Drinks were being passed out. Valery and I grabbed a highball and drank to the hospitality of our hosts and to time well spent. Then we found the president of the Foreign Consular Association, Dr. Paz, the honorable consul of Haiti, and thanked him profusely for the invitations. It was time to go home.

The next mailing to Moscow Center included a detailed account of our observations in Object No. 1, with diagrams, and included booklets of wonderful photographs in color of various parts of the embassy, supplied by the embassy.

The contents of the mailing were much more accurate than my sketchy description. Those who are familiar with the embassy's structure will most certainly be able to point out discrepancies in my account. But please remember that I am writing from the movie reel of memory, which has faded over the course of thirty years, although certain frames have retained their vividness.

I address my embassy stories to the esteemed Joseph Smith to assure him that what I "learned about the way embassy offices were arranged" and "other information" occurred five years before his arrival in Mexico City and I simply used this information for operational measures. For example, in 1970, during the soccer championship series, life demanded that I again experience an "operational" visit to the U.S. embassy. We received a tip that a person calling himself a Soviet tourist attempted to enter the American embassy and speak to the consul. I rushed over with some pretext and asked one of my contacts if this incident had actually occurred. I looked through as many offices as I could, including the section dealing with foreigners wishing entry to the United States. I did not find anyone who resembled a Soviet citizen. My contact reiterated that someone had been to the bureau for admitting foreigners and had uttered the words "Soviet tourist" and "consul," but due to the language barrier he was not able to speak to the consul and subsequently left. We found the "visitor," deduced the reason for his visit to the American embassy, and the next day put him on a plane headed for the Soviet Union via Havana.

After this detour, I would like to return to the problem of active measures. In this chapter, using myself as an example, I tried to show how, on the basis of gathered information, the opposition can utilize "personal" measures to compromise and neutralize the other side's intelligence operatives. How an active measure prepared in another country (the United States) can cook up "conspiratorial" implications on an international scale and "burn" an uncomfortable opponent in his country (Mexico). If, in the words of Joseph Smith, "The CIA then assisted John Barron with material for his book *KGB: The Secret Work of the Soviet Secret Agents. . . .* He also used our story about Nechiporenko among the many examples he gave of Soviet spying,"* then the authors of the "documentary" creation *L.B.J. and the J.F.K. Conspiracy* copied, almost verbatim, many sections from chapter 11 of John Barron's book and on this basis turned me into a participant in a "conspiracy" to kill an American president. With the help of some mythical agent, the authors asserted that I was "managing" Oswald. It is significant to

*Smith, *Portrait of a Cold Warrior,* p. 419.

note that Barron openly admits to using material provided by
Western intelligence agencies. Messrs. McDonald and Moore do
not even bother to acknowledge Barron as a source of their material. It can somehow be presumed that they never read this book
and utilized firsthand sources, since one of them was a former
contract agent for the CIA.

I had some difficulty writing this chapter. I quoted three identical
portions from three different books, by different authors, published
in different years. Each book states that "any reproduction in any
form" demands the authors' or publishers' permission. Briefly the
question arose as to whom I should ask for permission. Then I
thought the three previous authors would not be offended if I was
the fourth who utilized the long-worked-on creations developed by
active-measure specialists in the CIA. And I doubt if my CIA
colleagues would be offended, since I'm quoting from available
publications and not from their secret files.

Although I consider the "documentary account" the fifth blow
against me, I do not consider it a serious act and do not intend to
sort it out in detail. I do have to state that McDonald and Moore
were first to bring up a point. That I was the third person involved
in meeting Oswald in Mexico City was only known in very limited
KGB circles and was never previously discussed publicly. So fifteen
years ago, in *L.B.J. and the J.F.K. Conspiracy,* my name was mentioned in conjunction with Oswald for the first time, albeit in completely nonsensical fashion. I publicly announced my meeting with
Oswald for the first time at a press conference in Moscow on
January 9, 1992.

What happened to my career as a result of the enemy "hail"?
After 1971 I no longer worked on long-term assignments in foreign
rezidenturas for the KGB. But between 1971 and 1985, short-term
foreign assignments, lasting anywhere from several days to several
months, felt like one long assignment. It may seem strange, but the
range of my activities did not narrow; instead, it widened geograph-
ically. I had to travel to many countries, ranging from the Near
East to Latin America, from Europe to Southeast Asia. It seems
that I only missed the African continent. I was also engaged in
intelligence operations with our colleagues, or "friends," as they
were then called, in other socialist countries. In May 1991, I retired.

I feel the urge to conclude with that emotional phrase so beloved by writers and journalists: "Thus ended the professional career of one of the warriors on the invisible front or a Cold War soldier." Only those who are not on it can speak of the "invisible front." Intelligence adversaries clearly see and feel each other through constant interaction. The front becomes "invisible" only when there is no battle, and this does not occur in the world of intelligence.

Epilogue

Words fly away, what is written remains.
                                        —Latin saying

On May 29, 1993, I completed the manuscript that was to become this book. A few hours later, while reading a Moscow newspaper, I learned that John F. Kennedy was born on this same date, May 29, 1917, to be exact.

This is one of those mysterious coincidences which sneak up on us in life and which, when strung together, could have led to the November 1963 tragedy in Dallas.

This news item set me to thinking that were it not for Dallas, John Kennedy might still be alive to write his own memoirs instead of being on the receiving end of posthumous gifts in the form of books devoted to investigating the still obscure circumstances behind his death.

Looking back on my career of more than thirty years as an officer in the former Soviet intelligence organization, I see that almost all of it was spent under the sign of this earth-shattering event and the ripples it produced for many years after. Fate, the arbiter of the world, led me and two of my closest colleagues directly into the path of one of its participants, the president's alleged assassin, turning us all into "accomplices."

It should, therefore, be self-evident as to why my heightened interest in the Dallas "enigma" has not waned with the years and

311

why I have tried to indulge myself as much as possible in the materials that have been published about it both in my own country and abroad. When the historic events at home made it possible for former employees of the state security apparatus to step out from behind the looking glass and even to make public their thoughts, I also resolved to share information at my disposal about Lee Harvey Oswald.

At first this was only a modest desire to say something about the details of his visits to our embassy in Mexico in September 1963. But gradually I came to the realization that it is impossible to speak of an episode involving the alleged murderer of the American president and three KGB officers without a broader outline of the relationship between the KGB and Oswald during the latter's stay in the USSR and after his return to the United States. The result of my research into the subject is this book.

In the thirty years between now and 1963 the theme of "the KGB and Oswald" has given rise to a variety of theories, many of which are rather speculative. The goal which I set for myself was to remove the uncertainties which exist and, at the same time, to answer the questions concerning Oswald's two and one-half years in the USSR. I leave it to my readers' judgment to decide how well I have succeeded.

I believe that after the publication of this information, only one bare spot will remain, and that is the relationship between all the American intelligence services—the CIA, FBI, and Office of Naval Intelligence—and Lee Harvey Oswald.

Exercising my investigative rights, I have laid out my own views concerning three fundamental aspects of the Dallas question, which could be briefly formulated as follows:

1. Analysis of the available information makes it possible to say, with a great degree of certainty, that the intention of certain forces in the United States in 1963 to liquidate the president acquired certain organizational tendencies of a specific conspiratorial structure.

It is difficult, however, to judge by the same information the degree to which this conspiracy had "ripened" by November 1963, but it is clear that John F. Kennedy did not die at the hands of an assassin or assassins hired by a conspiracy structure.

2. The sum total of all the facts indicate that within the framework of a certain group or structure united in its common goal of the president's assassination, Lee Harvey Oswald was viewed as a future scapegoat. Efforts were consequently made to create the public image of him as an evil antipresidential, sharpshooting, gung-ho terrorist.

However, there is no evidence to believe that Lee Harvey Oswald subordinating himself to someone else's will, was "led out" by someone onto the sixth floor of the Texas book depository as a scapegoat, or as a member of the conspiratorial structure to make an attempt on the life of the American president.

3. The complex combination of personal and political motives, which reached critical mass on the morning of November 22, 1963, forced Oswald to assume an assault position at the sixth-floor window and take several well-aimed shots from his rifle at the figure of the president.

Oswald, in an affected state following the realization of what he had done at Dealey Plaza, probably committed the murder of Officer Tippit.

The probability of Oswald having had contact with the elements of a conspiratorial structure, but without his knowledge of their involvement in it, is great, especially in the New Orleans period of his life (1963) which apparently also served to cause his own death.

All three deductions reflect the author's own point of view and do not claim to be axiomatic. I shall leave it to the reader to agree or disagree with them. The notion cannot be excluded that somewhere there still exists some factual information which could totally shatter my conclusions.

Having finished the final chapter, and with it the book, I played its contents before my eyes once again, and suddenly I had a revelation. It seemed to me that the main character of this book and the author were subjected to certain active measures which were identical in intended effect.

The first, while still alive, was fashioned into the image of a political terrorist and a player in a conspiracy; following his death, the tag of foreign agent for special assignments was added to his reputation.

The author was consecutively transformed from the initiator of student uprisings in Mexico to the organizer of terrorist organizations to the "manager" of a large-scale Soviet plot with the aim of murdering the president of the United States and, finally, to none other than Oswald's instructor.

It should be pointed out to younger readers that all this was "standard operating procedure" during the Cold War.

Both the death of John F. Kennedy and the skillfully created aura surrounding the "enigma" of this sad event, which has existed for so many years, may be considered another consequence of the Cold War.

If the information on Oswald, kept by the intelligence services on both sides of the front lines, could have been combined for joint analysis, it is highly unlikely that he would have assumed his position in the "sniper's nest" on November 22, 1963.

If this "unification" had taken place after Dallas, there would likely have been no need for the litany of subsequent investigations or the construction of enigmatic theories, and different fodder would have found its way into movies and books.

Alas, all this is now just musing after the fact. As far as solving the "enigma" is concerned, I have a feeling that our former American intelligence adversaries still have a good deal to offer on this matter.

In conclusion, I want to express my gratitude once again to everyone who helped me conduct my investigation and to all who spent the time to become acquainted with its results.

Appendix I: Memorandum to the Central Committee of the Communist Party

Copy

Copy No. 4

Central Committee of the Communist Party of the Soviet Union

American citizen Lee Harvey OSWALD, in the USSR in the capacity of tourist, has appealed to the Presidium of the Supreme Soviet for Soviet citizenship and permanent residency in the USSR.

Lee Harvey OSWALD, born in 1939, a graduate of a radio electronics school, arrived in the USSR on October 15 of this year. Upon his arrival in Moscow, OSWALD submitted a petition for Soviet citizenship. Insofar as at the time of his visa's expiration the question of granting OSWALD's wish had not been resolved and he should have left the USSR, OSWALD attempted to commit suicide by slashing his wrist. At the present time, following his treatment, he continues to insist on being given Soviet citizenship and refuses to leave the USSR. On October 31 of this year he visited the American embassy in Moscow and renounced his American citizenship.

Considering that other foreigners who were formerly given Soviet citizenship (SITRINELL, AFSHAR) left our country after having lived here awhile and also keeping in mind that OSWALD has not

315

been sufficiently studied, it is advisable to give him the right to temporary residency in the USSR for one year, with a guarantee of employment and housing. In this event the question of OSWALD's permanent residency and granting of Soviet citizenship can be decided during the course of this term.

The draft of the Resolution is appended. We ask you to examine it.

Minister of Foreign Affairs   Chairman of Committee
USSR   For State Security
(A. Gromyko)   (A. Shelepin)
27 November 1959

Appendix II: Ballistics

Report

Ministry of Internal Affairs, Russian Federation
Central Administration Internal Affairs of the City of Moscow

Moscow, Petrovka 38   Telephone 200-82-41
Ballistics Laboratory
Expert Criminology Department
SKM GUVD Moscow
No. 671A   June 28, 1993

Conclusions of the Examination

I, N. V. Martynnikov, senior expert in the Expert Criminology Laboratory Department of Moscow, with a law degree and eight years' experience, certify that I conducted ballistic experiments on material concerning the death of President John F. Kennedy. My sources were a copy of the Zapruder amateur documentary film, videotaped material of the surroundings of the event, and documentary accounts consisting mainly of the following publications:

1. David S. Lifton, *Best Evidence* (New York: 1980).
2. Jim Marrs, *Crossfire: The Conspiracy That Killed Kennedy* (New York: 1989).
3. *The Warren Commission Report* (New York: 1965).
4. The conclusion of medicolegal experts and also experts specializing in the field of ballistic investigation: R. A. Freiling, from the

317

FBI, length of service twenty-three years; C. Cunningham, also of the FBI, length of service five years; D. D. Nichols, superintendent of the Illinois Criminal Investigation and Identification Division, firearms expert since 1941. Photographs were also available, including the rifle, bullets, cartridge cases, bullet wounds on the person and clothing of John F. Kennedy, and Governor John Connally's, as well as Kennedy's remains.

As a result of the comprehensive analysis of the aforementioned material it is possible to conclude that John F. Kennedy's and John Connally's bullet wounds were probably caused by two bullets fired from behind and to the right and from a slightly elevated position in relation to the victims. There is no evidence in this material which contradicts the conclusion reached by the Warren Commission that the shots could have come from the rifle identified as Mannlicher-Carcano, model 91/38, 6.5 caliber, serial number 2766, fired from the sixth story of the building known as the Texas School Book Depository. The conclusions of this investigation cannot claim to be complete or objective, since there was no accessible physical evidence, and all information is based on the conclusions of the Warren Commission.

In addition, within this material there is no concrete proof of two facts:

1. That President Kennedy and Governor Connally were wounded by the bullets found in the limousine, since there were no bullets actually removed from the bodies of Kennedy and Connally.

2. That if the president and governor were wounded by bullets fired from the Mannlicher-Carcano rifle, serial number 2766, it was fired by Lee Harvey Oswald and no one else. This is based on the short time frame and the high degree of shooting accuracy required. Also, the fact that the bolt action was manual and not automatic calls into question the gun of origination of this highly professional shooting.

These possibilities are highly unlikely, but it must be noted that they are impossible to fully exclude them.

In the presented material there are definite omissions, which attest to either the incompleteness of the investigation or to a lack of sources. To retain objectivity, these will be mentioned at the point that they are presented.

Factors Supporting the Stated Conclusion

The main indications that a wound is caused by a bullet, accepted in Russian criminology practice, are the presence of a *wiping path** and *minus tissue.*† Along with other indications, these two factors enable an exact determination of the injuries being caused by arms fire and not by any other manner, such as being struck by a sharpened file, awl, etc. The wiping path presents itself as a dark rim around the wound and consists of material from burned powder, particles of soot, oil, and so on, carried out by the bullet as it traveled through the barrel. It also includes particles of the bullet's metal casing.

The appearance of minus tissue is connected to the mechanics of a bullet passing through barrier material and is fundamentally different from the mechanics of a knife, file, etc., passing through the same material. Sharp instruments tear or cut the tissue (barrier material), while a bullet cuts out part of the tissue and its flight through it slightly spreads the walls of the wound. How does this appear on the barrier material? In comparing the wound's edges, in the event of a bullet passing through, part of the material will be missing (fibers of the jacket, skin on the body, bone tissue, etc.). Simultaneously, this missing material will indicate the point of entry.

The point of exit will not exhibit the presence of minus tissue; the edges of the wound can be placed back or folded into their original position. From the size of the entry wound, it is possible to determine with relative accuracy the bullet's *caliber.* It will coincide with the external diameter of the wiping path.

In examining *The Warren Commission Report,* there is practically no mention of the above-cited material. The following statement is made regarding the damage done to the president's jacket: "Traces of copper were found in the margins of the hole and the cloth fibers

---

*Poiasok obtiraniia in Russian. Each bullet, after it is fired, retains on its surface some quantity of grease and other residue. When it penetrates some object, the residue remains on the surface of the penetrated (entrance) channel, leaving less and less residue as it travels.
†*"Minus tkan"* in Russian. What this means is that after a bullet impacts against any object (cloth, wood, metal, etc.), a part of the material is destroyed and disappears upon the entrance of the bullet. On exit a bullet separates and pulls apart the material. This is how the difference between a bullet's entrance and exit points can be determined.

around the margins were pushed inward."* This classification of the wound as a caused by a bullet is based on the presence of metal and the direction of the fiber! But this evidence would have been found if the wound was caused by a copper metal rod of suitable diameter. At the Naval Hospital in Bethesda, Colonel Finck used similar information to conclude that the president's back wound ". . . is a wound of entrance. The basis for the conclusion is that this wound was *relatively small, with clean edges.* "†

Notwithstanding this information, from the available photographs it is clearly seen that the damage to the clothing fibers and the wounds on the two bodies have *residue* and minus tissue. This is partially proven by the description of the wounds found in the sources for this inquiry. In other words, this description will not create any doubt that the shots came from behind the president and the governor. The front of the bodies and the clothing exhibit signs of tearing and cutting, but no *negative tissue* is observed and this is characteristic of an exit wound caused by a bullet.

Criminology methods enable the diameter of the bullet to be determined by the diameter of the minus tissue. Also, by utilizing the deposits of various metals found, it is possible to determine the distance of the shot to within a few meters. In the material we analyzed, the question of identifying the bullet's caliber from the size of the wound is not introduced. However, the description of the wounds' diameters verify that they were approximately 6.5 mm. There is no mention of utilizing the bullet to ascertain the distance of the shot.

It is necessary to examine the bullet wound President Kennedy's head sustained separately, since there are aspects of this question that are still debated even among experts. Ballistic analysis shows the shot fired at the president's head produced the expected results. Let us examine the mechanics of a bullet hitting the head. The head is essentially liquid (composed predominantly of brain matter), enclosed in a hard cover (the skull). It is known that liquid is incompressible, and this principle is utilized, for instance, in the hydraulic brakes of a car. That is, acted on by a mechanical influ-

---

*Warren Commission Report, p. 92.
†Ibid., p. 88.

ence, liquid will adequately transfer this force to the opposite barrier material. Because of these conditions, when a bullet strikes the head, it first breaks through the bone tissue, forming the signs of an entry wound, as just described. The indications of the entry wound were present at the back of President Kennedy's head and not at the front. As the bullet continues, a large hydrodynamic force is created that spreads in a widening cone shape from one point (corresponding to the bullet's point). This cone shape expands and spreads to the opposite side of the skull, by which time it is already several square centimeters in size. As a result, the force can at times break away large pieces of the skull (as happened in this case), and on certain occasions it can blow the skull into pieces. Such a result depends on the power and caliber of the rifle and several other factors.

The round bullet wound on the back of the president's head corresponded to the size of the bullet, and the large, torn-out piece of the skull was in front. This proves that the shot had to occur from the rear and is verified by frames of the Zapruder film, where the shot to the head is captured. When the bullet hit, it caused brain matter to be blown out, naturally in the same direction as the bullet's flight. Assertions to the contrary are not logical and can only be based on a misunderstanding of the mechanisms of hydrodynamic impact. The exit wound cannot be a small, even opening because the liquid interior of the brain travels in all directions, much like the waves from a stone hitting water.

Regarding the moment that the president's head and body were jolted back when he was shot in the head, every effort to explain this aspect as due to a bullet striking from the front makes no sense because:

1. The characteristics of the head wound attest to the shot being fired from the back.

2. The backward jolt of the body is delayed; it occurred shortly after the bullet's impact, which blew out the brain matter. This means that the backward jolt was not caused by the bullet but was connected with its arrival. This is clearly seen in the Zapruder film.

3. During the first shot, when the bullet hit the president and governor's backs, this backward jolting did not occur in either man's body.

4. Believing that the shot came from the front contradicts ballistic calculation, which is based on an understanding of the results of masses colliding.

It appears that three basic factors contributed to the body jolting backward: the blowing out of the brain matter, the movement of the automobile, and the rapid weakening of the president's body with the loss of vestibular control. This loss was due to the paralysis of his central nervous system from the bullet striking his head.

A powerful hydrodynamic blow caused the brain matter to be blown out. During this event a recoil (similar to the recoil of a fired rifle) causes a small explosion in the temporal region of the skull. The opposite vector of force from the explosion jolted the head and torso backward.

Ballistic calculations also show that in principle the impact of a bullet fired from a Mannlicher-Carcano, 6.5-caliber rifle, regardless from which side the shot originated, could not cause the head and torso to be thrown for such a distance or with such speed as indicated in the Zapruder film. The bullet's mass is sufficiently small and incomparable to the body's mass, but the bullet's speed and specific kinetic energy is so great that even if we assume the weight of the head to be 5 kilograms, the speed of the body thrown cannot exceed 0.16 meters, that is, 16 centimeters per second. But these calculations work for an isolated body, for instance, a ball lying on a table. In reality, the head is connected to the body, and the total weight must be considered. Based on this factor, if the weight is 10 kilograms, then the speed of the throw is 0.08 meters per second; in other words, the human eye can barely detect it.

By calculating the strong piercing ability of the bullet (fired from a Mannlicher-Carcano rifle), it is more probable that the governor and the president were wounded by two bullets. It is also likely that the bullet that hit the president's neck also hit the governor. This deduction stems from the fact that if separate bullets had hit the president in the neck and the governor, they would have "passed through" and gotten stuck in part of the limousine and would not have been discovered simply lying on the floor. Along with this, the aggregate bulk of the president and governor's bodies served as enough barrier material to slow down one bullet. Further indirect proof of the wounds being caused by two bullets is indicated by the presence of two cracks in the window of the limousine and the frame of the windshield, which were most probably caused by the bullet exiting the president's head and from the body of Governor Connally. The cracks were on the inside of the window, and the frame and the bullet fragments were found in front of the two people they hit. This further attests to the shots coming from the back and above.

In conclusion, it should be noted that on the basis of existing evidence there is the possibility of extracting further data which can clarify several aspects of the events in Dallas.

1. By examining the *radial cracks in the limousine's windshield*, it can be ascertained where the shot that hit the windshield came from.

2. The traces left on the bullets by the rifle's barrel can determine *which of them was fired first*.

3. Conduct an experiment to *create a whole bullet* from the fragments with the purpose of answering the question Do these parts constitute a complete bullet? Reassemble the cartridge cases and fragments to see if they can be formed into a complete bullet.

4. Reconstruct the event using lasers to simulate the bullet wounds, from the sixth story of the Texas School Book Depository. This experiment would enable the direction of the shots to be more accurately determined and could ascertain their number and possibly their consequences.

N.V. Martynnikov   [Expert Criminology
Senior Expert of the ECD   Directorate of the
SKM GUVD Moscow   Ministry of Internal Affairs]

Bibliography

Agee, Philip. *Inside the Company: CIA Diary.* New York: Stonehill, 1975.

Andrew, Christopher, and Oleg Gordievsky. *KGB: The Inside Story of Its Foreign Operations from Lenin to Gorbachev.* New York: HarperCollins, 1991.

Barron, John. *KGB: The Secret Work of Soviet Agents.* New York: Reader's Digest Press, 1974.

———. "The Soviet Plot to Destroy Mexico." *Reader's Digest,* November 1971.

Beschloss, Michael R. *The Crisis Years. Kennedy and Khrushchev 1960–1963.* New York: Harper/Collins, 1991.

Blakey, Robert G., and Richard N. Billings. *Fatal Hour: The Assassination of President Kennedy by Organized Crime.* New York: Berkeley, 1992.

Crenshaw, Charles A., with Jens Hansen and Gary Shaw. *JFK Conspiracy of Silence.* New York: Signet, 1992.

Davison, Jean. *Oswald's Game.* New York: W. W. Norton, 1983.

Duffy, James P., and Vincent L. Ricci. *The Assassination of John F. Kennedy: A Complete Book of Facts.* New York: Thunder Mouth Press, 1992.

Eddowes, Michael. *The Oswald File.* New York: Clarkson N. Potter, 1977.

Epstein, Edward Jay. *Legend: The Secret World of Lee Harvey Oswald.* New York: Reader's Digest Press, 1978.

———. *The Assassination Chronicles: Inquest, Counterplot, and Legend.* New York: Carroll and Graf, 1992.

Garrison, Jim. *On The Trail Of the Assassins.* New York: Penguin Books 1992.

Halpern, Samuel, and Hayden Peake. "Did Angleton Jail Nosenko?" *International Journal of Intelligence* (Winter 1989): 451–64.

Hinckle, W., and W. Turner. *The Fish Is Red: The Story of the Secret War Against Castro.* New York: Harper & Row, 1981.

Hougan, Jim. *Secret Agenda: Watergate, Deep Throat and the CIA.* New York: Random House, 1984.

Kessler, Ronald. *Inside the CIA: Revealing the Secrets of the World's Most Powerful Spy Agency.* New York: Pocket Books, 1992.

Klein, Ray. *The CIA: The Evolution of the Agency from Roosevelt to Reagan.* New York: Liberty Publishing House, 1989.

Knightley, Phillip. *The Life and Views of the KGB Masterspy Andre Deutsch.* Moscow: "Respublika," 1992.

Parkinson, C. Northcote. *Parkinson's Law.* Boston: Houghton Mifflin, 1957.

325

Peter, Laurence. *The Peter Principle.* New York: Morrow, 1971.

Report of the Warren Commission on the Assassination of President Kennedy. New York: Bantam Books, 1964.

Report of the Select Committee on Assassinations. U.S. House of Representatives, Ninety-fifth Congress Second Session. Washington, D.C.: U.S. Government Printing Office, 1979.

Russell, Dick. *The Man Who Knew Too Much.* New York: Carroll and Graf, 1992.

Sauvage, Leo. *The Oswald Affair. An Examination of the Contradictions and Omissions of the Warren Report.* New York: World Publishing Company, 1966.

Smith, Joseph Burkholder. *Portrait of a Cold Warrior.* New York: G. P. Putnam's Sons, 1976.

Stone, Oliver, and Zachary Sklar. *JFK. The Book of the Film: The Documented Screenplay.* New York: Applause Books, 1992.

Summers, Anthony. *Conspiracy,* New York: Paragon House, 1989.

———. *Official and Confidential: The Secret Life of J. Edgar Hoover.* London: Victor Gollancz, 1993.

U.S. Congress. Final Report of the Committee to Study Governmental Operations with Respect to Intelligence Activities. Senate. *The Investigation of the Assassination of President John F. Kennedy: Performance of the Intelligence Agencies.* Book V. Washington, D.C.: U.S. Government Printing Office, 1976.

Ungar, Sanford J. *FBI.* Boston: Atlantic Monthly Press, 1975.

Wise, David. *Molehunt: The Secret Search for Traitors That Shattered the CIA.* New York: Random House, 1992.

Woodward, Robert. *Veil: The Secret Wars of the CIA.* New York: Random House, 1988.

In Russian (and Other) Languages

Amerikanskii kharakter ocherki kul'tury SSHA. [The American character, essays on the culture of the USA]. Moscow: Nauka, 1991.

Bleik, Dzhordzh. *Inogo vybora net* [No other choice]. Moscow: Mezhdunarodyne otnosheniia, 1991.

Bloch, Jonathan, and Patrick Fitzgerald. *Tainye operatsii angliiskoi razvedki* [Secret operations of British intelligence]. Moscow: Politizdat, 1987.

Freling, N., *"Smert' kontrabandista"* [Death of a smuggler]. Vilnius: Polina, 1991.

Geevskii, Igor, A. i Chervonnaia, A. Svetlana. *Pod kodovym nazvaniem i bez . . . : Za kulisami amerikanskoi politiki* [Under code name and without . . . : behind the scenes of American politics]. Moscow: Izdatel'stvo Agenstva pechati Novosti, 1985.

Gromyko, A. A. *Pamiatnaia kniga: pervaia* [First volume of memoirs]. Moscow: Izdatel'stvo Politicheskoi Literatury, 1988.

Guerin, Alain, and Varin. *Jacques les gens de la CIA* Moscow: Editions Sociales, 1985.

Iakovlev, N. N. *Prestupivshie gran'* [Transgressing the border]. Moscow: Izdatel'stvo Mezhdunapodnye Otnosheniia, 1971.

Ivin, A. A. *Po zakonam logiki seria Evrika* [The laws of logic, Evrika series]. Moscow: Molodaia Gvardiia, 1983.

———. *Akademiia Nauk SSSR, Institut Philosofii. Logika [Logic].* Edited by D. P.

Gorskoy and P. V. Tavants. Moscow: Gosudarstvennoe Izdatel'stvo Politicheskoi Literatury, 1956.

Losev, Sergei, and Vitalii Petrusenko. *SSHA, operatsii po unichtozheniiu,* [USA, operations in liquidation]. Moscow: Sovetskaia Rossia, 1984.

Sagatelian, Mikhail. *Vashingtonskaia karusel'* [Washington merry-go-round]. Moscow: Sovetskii Pisatel', 1987.

———. *Formal'naia logika, uchenbnik dlia filosovskikh fakultetov Universitetov* [Formal logic: a textbook for university philosophy departments]. Leningrad, Izdatel'stvo Leningradskovo Universiteta, 1977.

Segeth, Wolfgang, *Elementare logik* [Elementary logic]. Berlin: VEB Deutscher Verlag der Wissenschaften, 1973.

Sergeev, Fedor M. *Esli Sorvat' masku . . . : TsRU kak ono est'* [If the mask is stripped away . . . : the CIA as it is]. Moscow: Politizdat, 1983.

Sluzhba Bezopasnosti. *Novosti razvedki i kontrrazvedki* [Security Service. Intelligence and counterintelligence news]. Moscow: 1993.

Tarasov, Dmitrii. *Zharkoe leto polkovnika Abelia* [Colonel Abel's hot summer].

Valle R., *"Proshchai Politseiskii"* [Goodbye Policeman]. Vilnius: Polina, 1991.

Yefimov, Igor. *Kto ubil Presidentia Kennedii?* [Who killed President Kennedy?]. Moscow: Terra, 1991.

Zhukov, Iurii. *SSSR-SSHA. Doroga dlinoiu v sem'desiat let ili rasskaz o tom, kak razvivalis' sovetsko-amerikanskie otnosheniia* [USSR-USA. A road seventy years long or a tale of how Soviet-American relations developed]. Moscow: Politizdat, 1988.

Index

ABOUT THE AUTHOR

OLEG MAXIMOVICH NECHIPORENKO was a colonel in the First Chief (Foreign Intelligence) Directorate of the KGB (Soviet Committee for State Security) and considered one of the KGB's most intrepid "Special Operations" officers. In 1961, Colonel Nechiporenko was posted to the KGB station in Mexico City under diplomatic cover of the Soviet embassy. Following his secret meeting with Oswald, Nechiporenko remained in Mexico until 1965 and returned again in 1967.

From 1971 until 1985 he was dispatched on numerous special missions for the KGB throughout South and Central America and North Vietnam. From 1985 he taught at the Soviet Intelligence officer's college, the Andropov Institute. He retired with distinction in 1991. In 1992 he provided assistance to Senator John F. Kerry's Senate Select Committee on POW/MIA Affairs. Colonel Nechiporenko resides in Moscow, where he writes about the world's "second oldest profession."